IMAGES
of America

EARLY SETTLERS OF THE PANHANDLE PLAINS

On the Cover: Clarendon was founded as a temperance colony in 1878 by a Methodist minister. Cowboys called it "Saint's Roost." Surrounded by ranches, the town became the center of Donley County until it was bypassed by the Fort Worth & Denver Railroad in the 1880s. As was typical at the time, residents moved the settlement six miles so that it would sit comfortably on the new railroad line. This May 1904 photograph shows cowboys at the end of a trail drive for the Llano Cattle Company, which was based at the Curry Comb Ranch in northeastern Garza County. Pictured here are, from left to right, Ben Wilkes, Samp Morrow, Tom Williams, John Doty, Andrew Coggins, Jim Weatherford, Ed Williams, Will Wilkes (on wagon), and brothers Hale and Sam Wilkes. (Courtesy of Norman Wayne Brown.)

IMAGES
of America

EARLY SETTLERS OF THE PANHANDLE PLAINS

Norman Wayne Brown and Sarah Bellian
with a foreword by Chuck Parsons

ARCADIA
PUBLISHING

ISBN 978-1-4671-3068-4

Published by Arcadia Publishing
Charleston, South Carolina

Printed in the United States of America

Library of Congress Control Number: 2013948428

For all general information, please contact Arcadia Publishing:
Telephone 843-853-2070
Fax 843-853-0044
E-mail sales@arcadiapublishing.com
For customer service and orders:
Toll-Free 1-888-313-2665

Visit us on the Internet at www.arcadiapublishing.com

To the memory of the brave pioneers who settled the west.

Contents

Foreword

If Spanish explorer Francisco Coronado or Comanche chieftain Quanah Parker or buffalo hunters such as Billy Dixon or William Barclay "Bat" Masterson could return to what is known today as the Panhandle Plains, they would not believe their eyes. In place of vast herds of shaggy buffalo would be such strange objects as windmills, turbines, derricks, and concrete strips crisscrossing the land, not to mention groups of buildings and houses, electric cars, and 18-wheelers. The current landscape is a drastic change from the way it appeared just over a century ago. It was formerly an endless range of grassland and of grazing buffalo. The vista contained no windmills, no irrigation ditches, no tall and bladed objects providing electricity. It remains a beautiful and wondrous land, now comprising 26 Texas counties north and west of modern Oklahoma and east of New Mexico. The Panhandle Plains is the northernmost portion of Texas. Some would say it is the most beautiful land in America.

Long before any white man trekked across the Plains, nomadic tribes lived on what became these 26 counties, wandering, hunting, and raising their families. They left no written record of their existence, but objects such as arrowheads and spear points provide evidence of their centuries-long place in the natural order of things. The people now known as the Apache ruled the land, but then Coronado appeared—a foreigner interested not in seeking harmony with nature but in instant wealth. He sought riches for his faraway king. His search for the Seven Cities of Gold in the middle of the 16th century proved to be in vain, but he left a paper trail detailing his exploits.

It was not long after Coronado's fruitless search that another invader appeared. This was no stranger on horseback, but an Indian people stronger than the Apache. The Comanche took control, pushing the Apache farther south and west. Conflict became more common on this land that had no lines drawn on a map to show where one township or county or state began and another ended. The land was the possession of whoever could control it. For centuries, the Comanche called this vast area their home. They lived in relative harmony with the buffalo and other forms of life. They had mastered the use of the horse, the bow and arrow, and the spear.

Early maps of the Southwest labeled this land and surrounding areas "Comancheria," the land of the Comanche, in recognition of the tribe's powerful hold on it. Some were brave enough to venture onto the land to trade, and a commercial way of life developed between the Comanche tribes and Mexicans and white men. From the Comanche's viewpoint, it was a beneficial situation, as trade brought them improved weapons and the vast buffalo herds provided the essentials of life. It was a perfect existence.

But the white man felt there was room for improvement in this way of life. After the Civil War, white settlers began to discover the importance of what the Comanche claimed. The two peoples signed a treaty at Medicine Lodge in 1867, which ostensibly protected the land south of the Arkansas River for Comanche hunting parties. If kept, it would have only been a minor inconvenience, but the buffalo were too attractive for white hunters. The animal, while not an object of wealth such as those Coronado sought, represented dollars on the hoof to these men. By the 1870s, the Medicine Lodge Treaty was ignored by white hunters; these men descended onto the Comanche lands with their wagons and Sharps rifles. The slaughter began in earnest. Buffalo were killed for their hides, and Indians were killed if they resisted. Millions of buffalo were killed, and the handful of white men who claimed the land of the Comanche began erecting buildings. Soon, the handful became a large wave of settlers.

The Comanche resisted as best they could. Quanah Parker became the most feared—and then the most respected—Comanche. In 1874, the Battle of Adobe Walls proved to the Comanche that their power was broken. The Red River War of 1874–1875 ended the superiority of the Comanche, and the land once exclusively theirs now belonged to the invaders. The buffalo guns wielded by men such as Billy Dixon and the blue-coated soldiers led by Ranald S. Mackenzie forced Parker and his followers to retreat to the reservation. A way of life had ended. The Comanche, as well as the vast buffalo herds, were nearly extinct.

Where the buffalo once roamed, sheep and cattle now grazed the land. Men such as Casimero Romero brought in flocks of sheep, but their numbers were insignificant compared to the numbers of cattle brought in by Charles Goodnight, James Adair, and Thomas S. Bugbee. What Quanah Parker had established in Palo Duro Canyon with his tents of buffalo hides, Goodnight replaced with the JA Ranch. Whereas the Indians' tents could be easily wrapped up and transported by travois, the white men established permanent towns such as Tascosa, Mobeetie, and Clarendon. The white man's map included lines to delineate Wheeler County, or Oldham County, or Donley County. Only a few of the Comanche names survived this division of the land. Ironically, Palo Duro Canyon and the site of Adobe Walls were preserved by the conquerors, perhaps as an admission of guilt for having destroyed a culture and a way of life.

The vast land was not without its problems. Overgrazing, absentee ownership, and the lack of a dependable water supply were only a few problems for the white men. Drought and severe winters decimated herds. Many farms and ranches did not survive.

The railroad crossing into the Panhandle Plains in the 1880s brought more change, and change seemed to be happening quicker than ever before. Amarillo became a cultural and social center of life. Lubbock became an important center as well. Countless smaller towns appeared. While the railroad brought change to the land, an even greater cause of change was oil—the "black gold" that Coronado could not have dreamed of but that proved to be of greater value. Taking oil out of the ground brought more businesses and new troubles to the Panhandle. Boomtowns attracted evil men and women, which in turn brought in Texas Rangers to establish order. The population increased, which led the state to improve the roads. The automobile and improved roads resulted in such institutions as Route 66 and, ultimately, the interstate highway system that now crosses the land where buffalo once roamed free.

With such vast changes from pre–Civil War days to the early 21st century—changes once scarcely dreamed of—who dares to predict what the Panhandle Plains will look like a century from now?

—Chuck Parsons

ACKNOWLEDGMENTS

We would like to thank all the libraries, museums, and individuals who readily provided images for this book. Special thanks are due to Don Jay; Linda Puckett of the Garza County Historical Museum; Roland Graham, a Texas cowboy; Billy Elkins; Tom Mann; Jane Adams; Ron Henderson; Paula Parks Fulford; Jerry Corkran; and a host of others.

Unless otherwise noted, all images are from the personal collection of Norman Wayne Brown. Several of the images used in this book are now held at the Scurry County Museum (SCM) in Snyder, Texas. We are most grateful to Don Jay, the family of Joe York, and the family of Aline Parks for having the foresight to donate these treasures of Texas history.

INTRODUCTION

We camped that night near the courthouse at Aspermont, Texas. The next day when our wagons crossed the Brazos into Kent County we experienced our first west Texas dust storm. The sky turned red and we couldn't see. The wind blew so hard we couldn't put up a canvas to block the wind. We started to turn around and go back to our old home, but the next day the dust was gone and it was a beautiful day. We followed dirt ruts with tall grass in the middle all the way across the plains.

—Nora Cox Drennan

For thousands of years, the only human inhabitants of the Panhandle Plains were nomadic tribes. In this region, most water supplies are seasonal. Rivers and creeks that run year-round are few and far between, and many are too brackish for human consumption. Paleo Indians and, later, the Apache, Kiowa, and Comanche tribes, followed the buffalo, camping at sites where natural springs occurred. Spanish and US Army expeditions noted these ancient watering holes on their maps.

After the Civil War, settlers began to move into West Texas. They immediately recognized the potential danger of drought in the arid region and were horrified by the dust storms and the threat of tornados. Still, the free range was a temptation few ranchers could ignore. The scarcity of water led to the establishment of "cow camps" about 20 miles apart from each other. When the herds depleted the grass, the ranchers moved the camps.

As barbed wire became popular and the era of fence-cutting wars began, ranchers erected dugouts and pens. Few sections of land were actually bought and paid for, except for those located near water. Those who controlled the water could easily control thousands of acres of adjacent dry land. Windmills tapped into the massive Ogallala aquifer, allowing ranchers—and, later, farmers—to remain on their land even when rain refused to fall. Without water, settlement was impossible. Where it occurred or could be accessed, towns and cities flourished.

The railheads were in Kansas during the late 1800s, and cattle drives took months. Still, the price of a steer in New York was 10 times what it was in Texas, which made the long trip worthwhile. By 1889, cowboys trailed herds to Estelline, Clarendon, Amarillo, Abilene, Sweetwater, and Colorado, Texas. With the railroads came merchants, ministers, skilled laborers, and all of the conveniences of modern life at the turn of the 20th century.

Early Settlers of the Panhandle Plains tells the story of the men and women who tamed Texas's last frontier.

They proceeded farther onto the plains,
and when they reached them found
So vast a sum of cattle [buffalo] grazing there
The mind reeled at the very thought of them . . .
And so extensive are the plains they roam
That for six hundred or eight hundred leagues
They stretch before you like a tranquil sea,
Without a trace of hill or fence.

—Gaspar Perez de Villagra, 1610

One

THE LAST FRONTIER

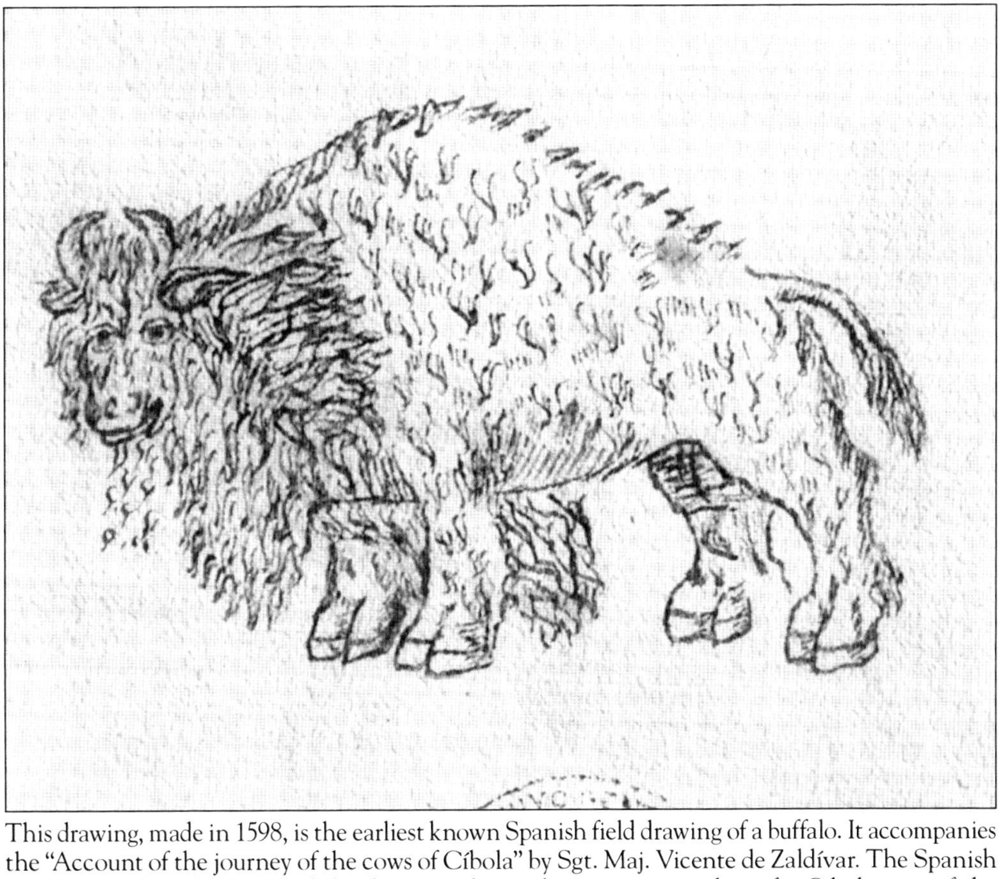

This drawing, made in 1598, is the earliest known Spanish field drawing of a buffalo. It accompanies the "Account of the journey of the cows of Cíbola" by Sgt. Maj. Vicente de Zaldívar. The Spanish gave the buffalo the name *cíbolos*, because the explorers were searching for Cibola, one of the legendary Seven Cities of Gold. (Courtesy of the Spanish Ministry of Education, Culture and Sport—General Archives of the Indies.)

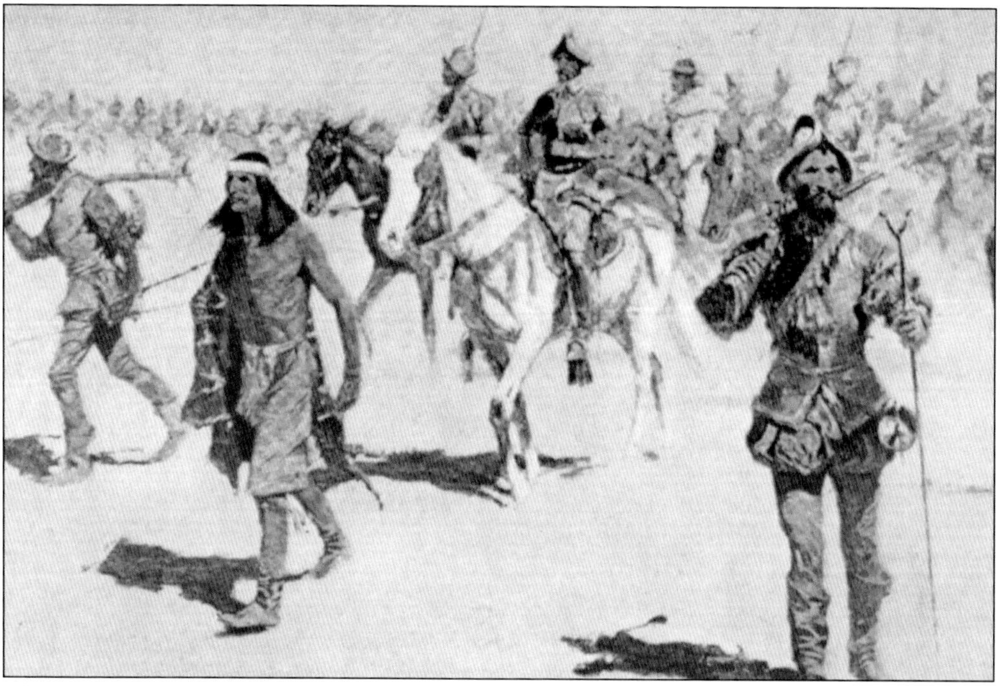

The painting *Coronado Sets Out to the North*, by Frederic Remington (1861–1909), is an artist's interpretation of what an early Spanish army expedition might have looked like. Between 1540 and 1542, conquistador Francisco Vasquez de Coronado explored New Mexico, West Texas, and as far north as Kansas. Like many of his peers, Coronado sought the Seven Cities of Gold. Although this might sound like a fool's errand, the conquests of the Aztec and Incan empires had proven to the Spanish that the Americas contained fabulously wealthy civilizations that Europeans had never before encountered. (Texas Council for the Humanities.)

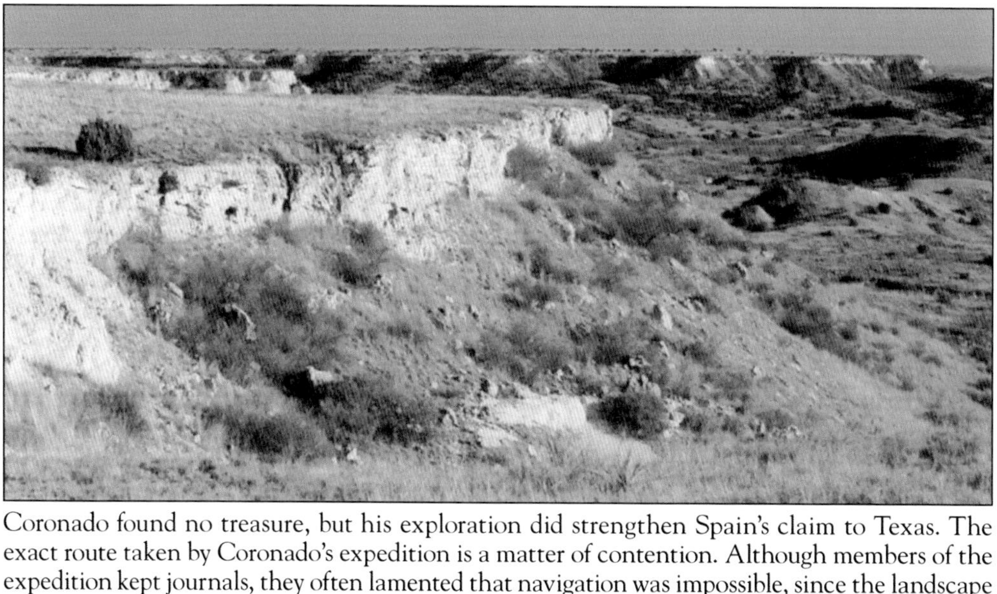

Coronado found no treasure, but his exploration did strengthen Spain's claim to Texas. The exact route taken by Coronado's expedition is a matter of contention. Although members of the expedition kept journals, they often lamented that navigation was impossible, since the landscape looked the same in all directions. In 1996, a campsite from Coronado's expedition was discovered at Blanco Canyon (shown here), not far from Floydada in Floyd County.

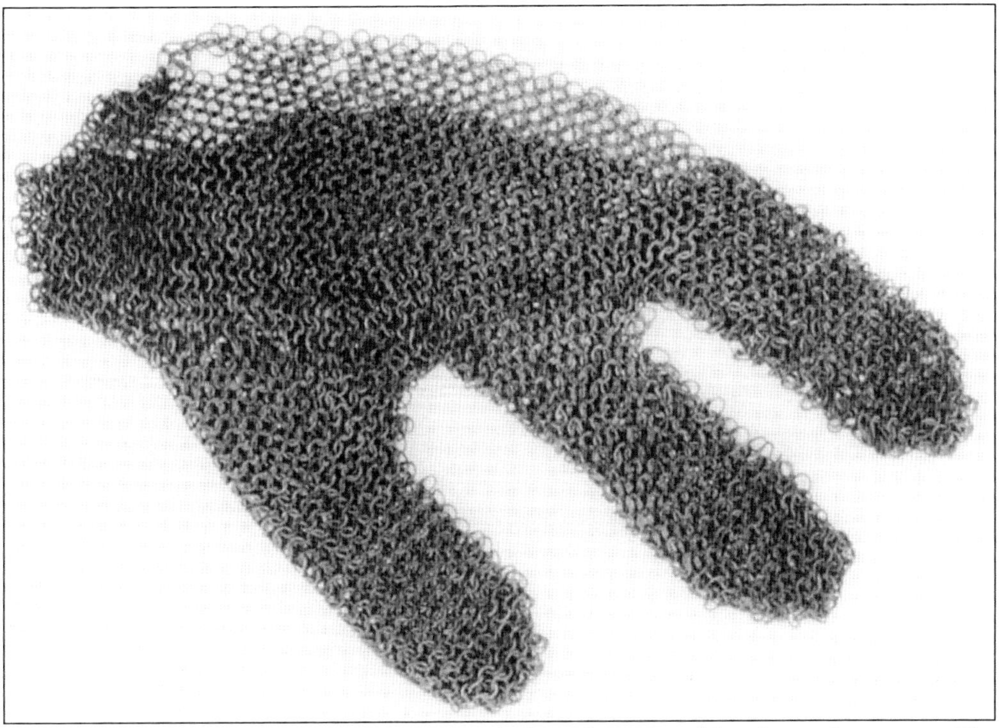

Evidence suggests that other Spanish sites might have been found by Native Americans. The Comanche chief Iron Jacket, grandfather of Quanah Parker, sometimes wore a Spanish coat of mail, from which his name was derived. This Spanish mailed gauntlet was found at the Blanco Canyon site. (Floyd County Museum.)

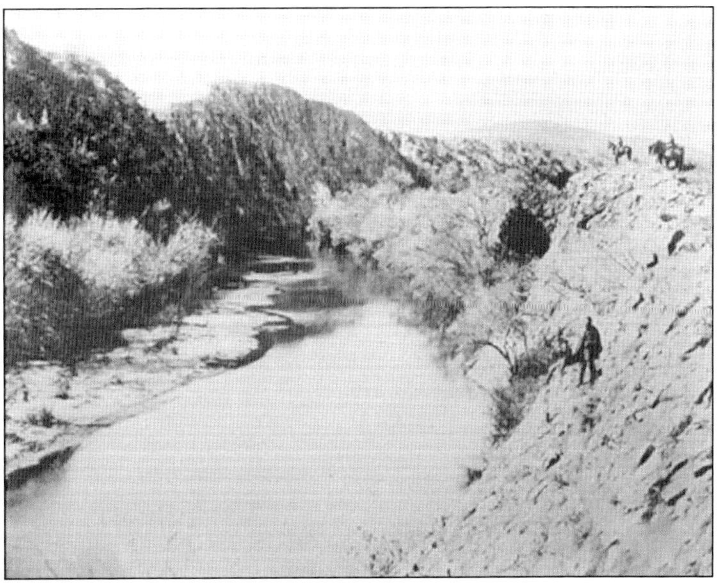

Though the Spanish were the first Europeans to explore the Panhandle Plains, the US Army also played an important role in mapping the region. An Army expedition is pictured here conducting reconnaissance near Medicine Bluffs in December 1868. Col. Benjamin H. Grierson led the expedition.

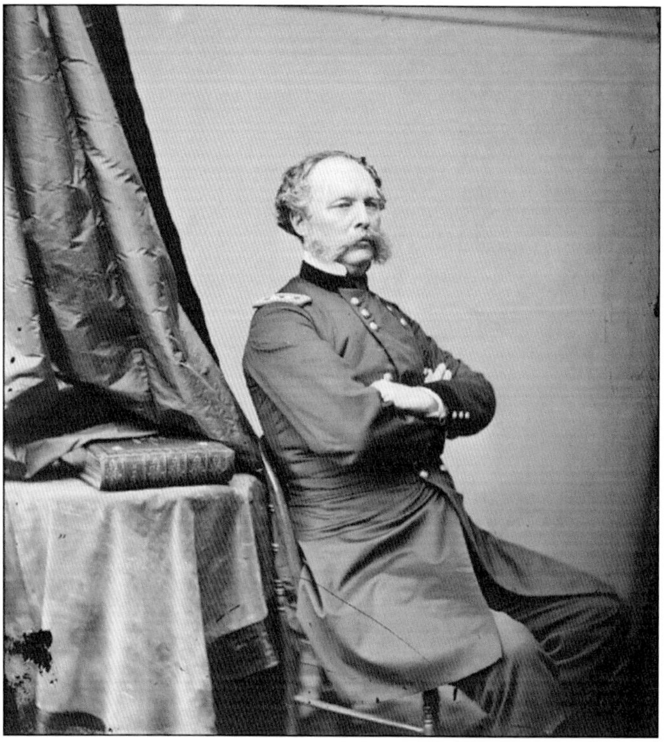

One of the foremost American explorers of West Texas, Gen. Randolph B. Marcy served with Gen. Zachary Taylor's army during the Mexican War. He came to Texas in 1847 and again in 1849, establishing the route called the Marcy Trail that extends from Fort Smith to Santa Fe. (Library of Congress.)

Some of Gen. Randolph Marcy's soldiers are pictured below at Camp Winfield Scott during the Civil War. This photograph was taken on May 2, 1862. (Library of Congress.)

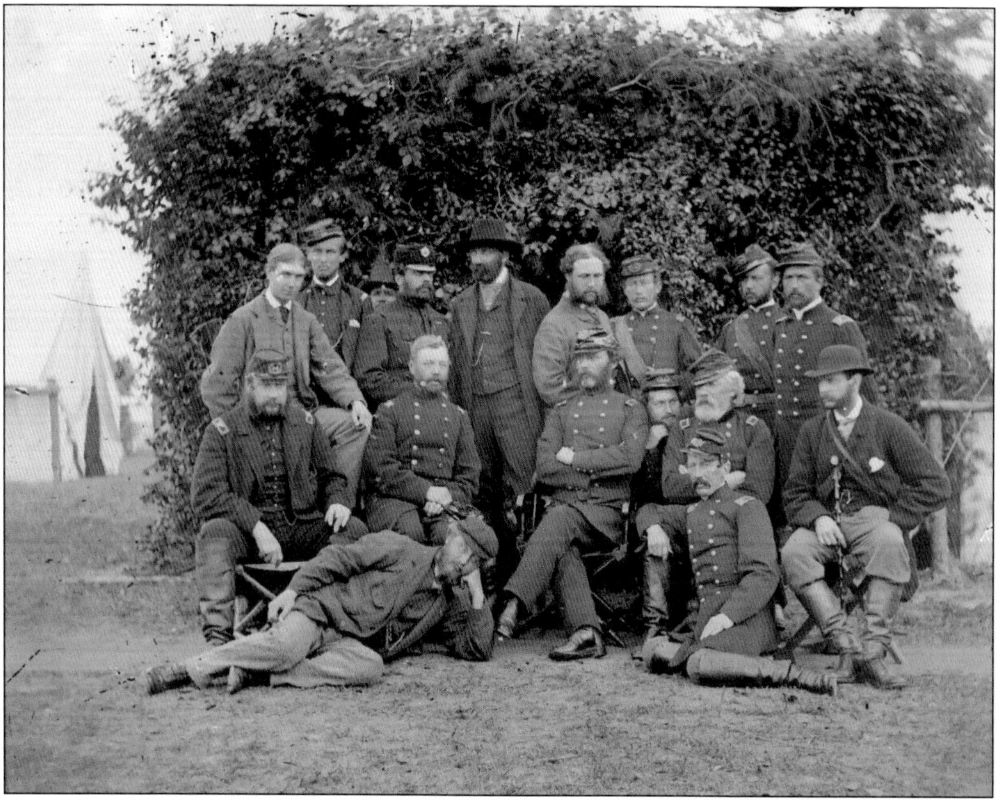

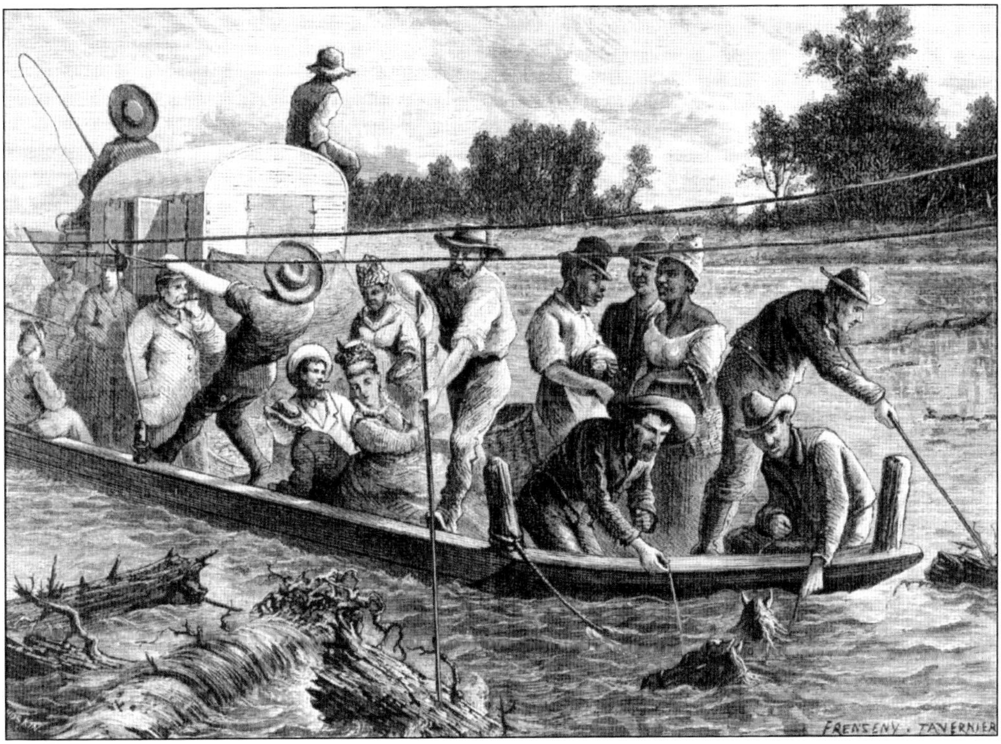

Rivers were especially important to early mapmakers. Most water supplies in the region are seasonal, and expeditions were often sent to determine the sources of important waterways. The Red River, a swift-moving river prone to developing spots of quicksand, flows from the Texas Panhandle to form the northeastern border of Texas and Arkansas. The river has historically been used for commerce and transportation, which led to the establishment of many trading posts in the 1800s. This *Harper's Weekly* illustration was published in 1874. (Library of Congress.)

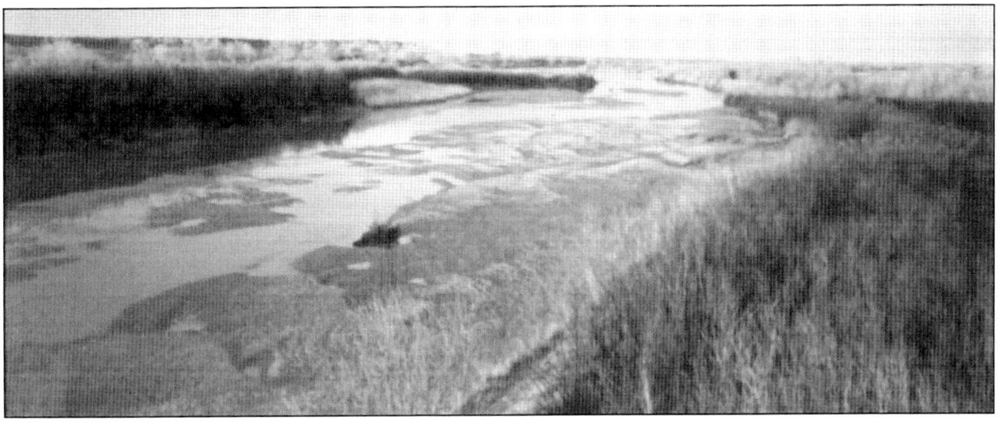

In 1852, Gen. Randolph B. Marcy commanded an expedition to search for the source of the Red River, crossing 1,000 miles of previously undocumented territory in Texas and Oklahoma. The expedition marked the locations of mineral deposits, collected information on plants and animals, and returned with information on Cynthia Ann Parker, a young white girl who was abducted by the Comanche. In December 1860, federal troops led by Sergeant Spangler, along with around 40 Texas Rangers led by Lawrence Sullivan "Sul" Ross, discovered a small band of Comanche camped along the Pease River. This photograph shows the Pease River as it looks today.

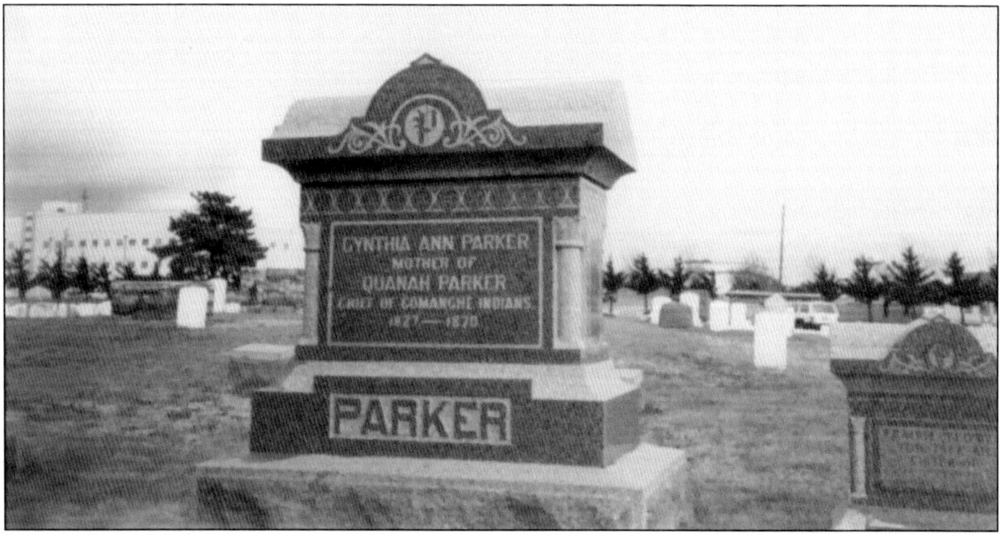

Cynthia Ann Parker was renamed Naduah by her Comanche family. They raised her from the age of nine. She became the wife of chief Peta Nocona and the mother of three children, including Quanah Parker, who would become the leader of the last Comanche resistance against the US Army. By all accounts, Cynthia Ann could not adjust to life with her white relatives. She repeatedly tried to return to the Comanche; in 1870, she died of influenza. Her grave was moved several times and is now located at Fort Sill.

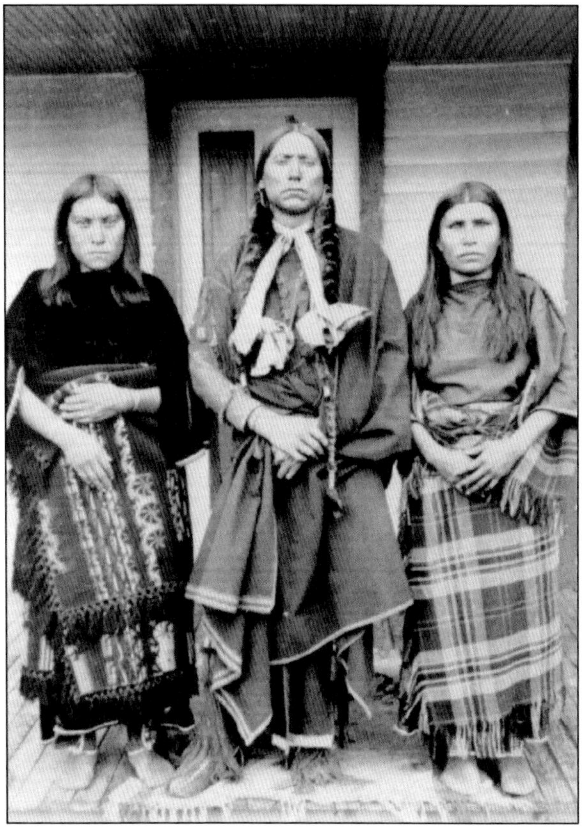

Quanah Parker (center), the last Comanche chief to be driven onto the reservation at Fort Sill, was a symbol of Native American resistance in Texas. Though he later became a successful rancher and investor, he continued to wear his hair in long braids and refused to divorce any of his multiple wives, two of whom are pictured with him in this c. 1890 photograph. He was also a leading figure in the Native American church movement, which combined elements of Christianity with native beliefs. (Clay County Historical Society, Henrietta, Texas; photograph by William E. Irwin.)

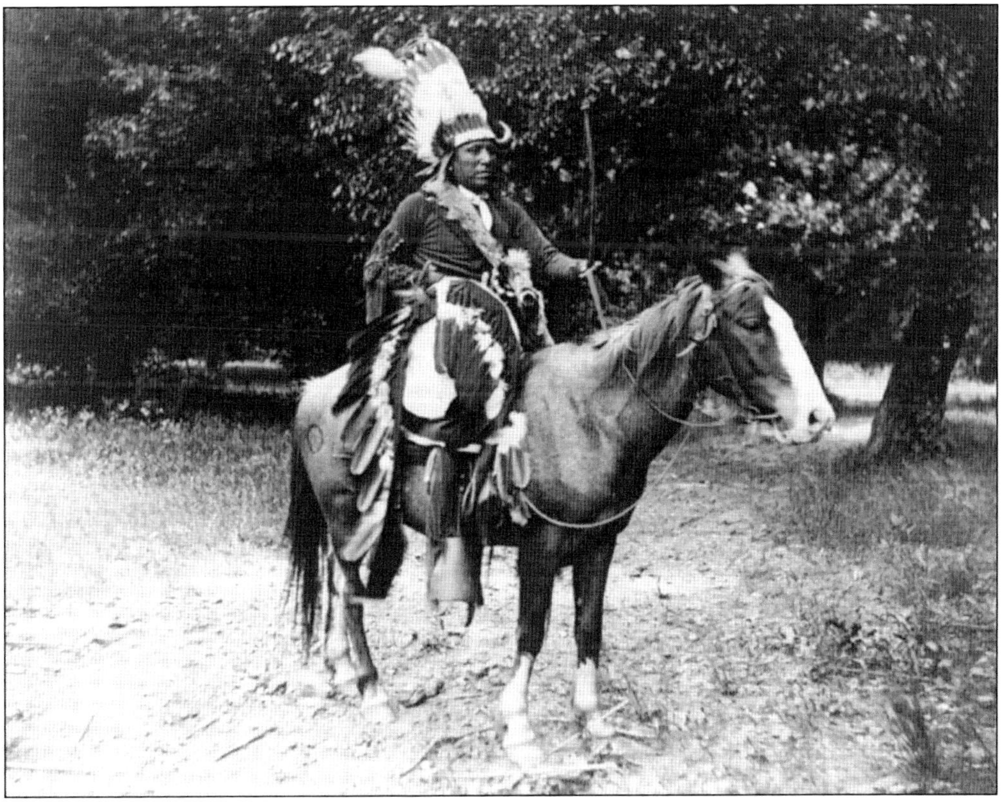

Though they are sometimes overshadowed by the powerful Comanche, the Kiowa tribe also hunted buffalo on the Panhandle Plains. Some Kiowa scouts, such as the famous Sergeant I-See-O, chose to assist the US army in fighting their traditional enemies (the Comanche). They also played an important role in negotiating peace settlements. This c. 1891 image shows Kiowa scout Elk Tongue wearing a war bonnet. (Library of Congress.)

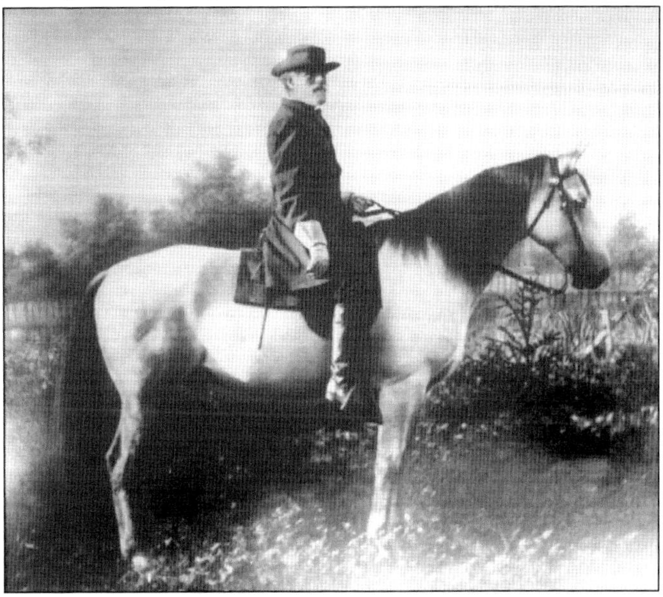

Before the Civil War made him famous, Robert E. Lee served in Texas from 1857 to 1861. He is believed to have camped at a site north of Green Mountain, near Rough Creek. In the years before permanent settlements were established, many of the famous characters of the Wild West, including Buffalo Bill and Doc Holliday, passed through the region, either hunting buffalo or on Army expeditions. This photograph of Lee on his horse, Traveler, was taken between 1861 and 1865. (Library of Congress).

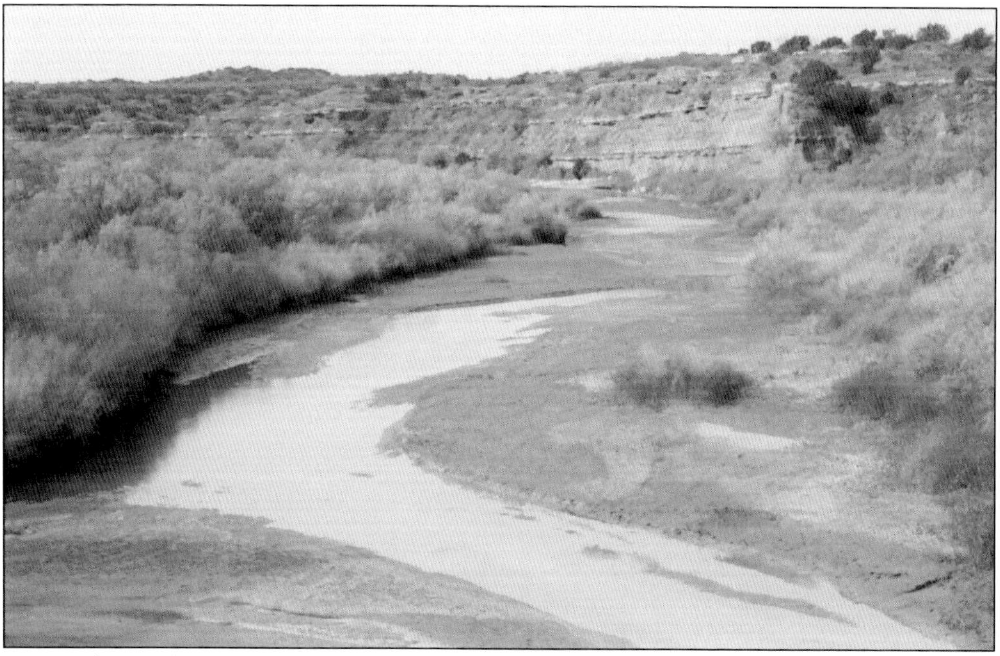

During the Civil War, salt was mined from the Salt Fork of the Brazos at the Double Mountain Salt Works in Kent County, the northernmost industrial site in Confederate Texas. The Confederate States of America could ill afford to expend manpower guarding frontier settlements and recommended that all people living on or beyond the line of settlement "fort up" for the duration of the war. The Comanche took advantage of this weakness and attempted to drive the settlers away with numerous raids.

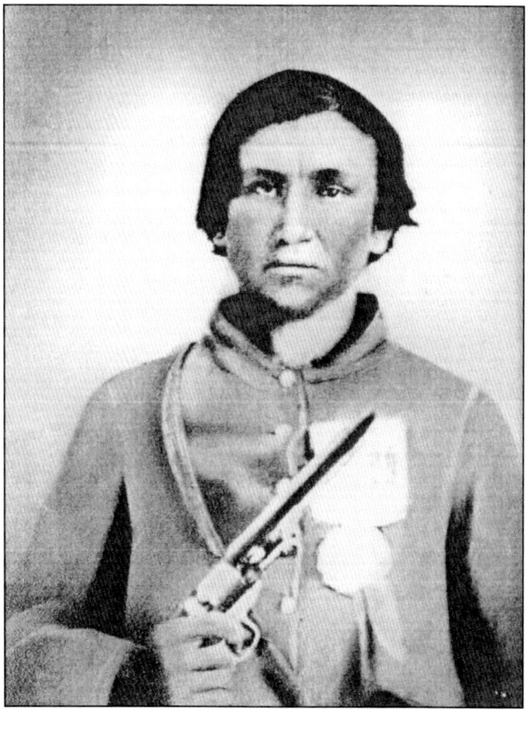

John M. Elkins (pictured) was a half-brother of George Kindred ("Kin" or "Uncle Kin") Elkins. When the Civil War broke out, John fought the Apache in Texas and in New Mexico territory. John evidently covered quite a lot of ground during the war years, because he was eventually captured by Union forces in Louisiana. Sent to Johnson's Island on Lake Erie, he remained a prisoner until the war ended. He was also a Texas Ranger and later became sheriff of Coleman County. (Randy Henson.)

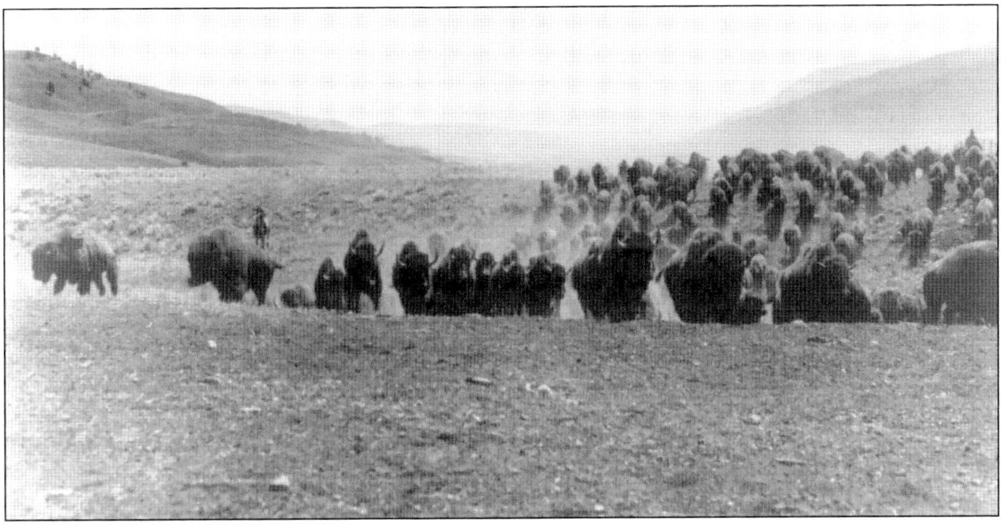

In the 1870s, regional military authorities Gens. William T. Sherman and Philip Sheridan believed that the only way to defeat the Comanche was to eradicate the buffalo. Buffalo hunting also provided jobs for disenfranchised Confederate veterans, who would scout ahead of railroad construction for hostile Native American tribes and would also hunt buffalo. In this 1917 photograph, hunters are purposely stampeding a buffalo herd. (Library of Congress.)

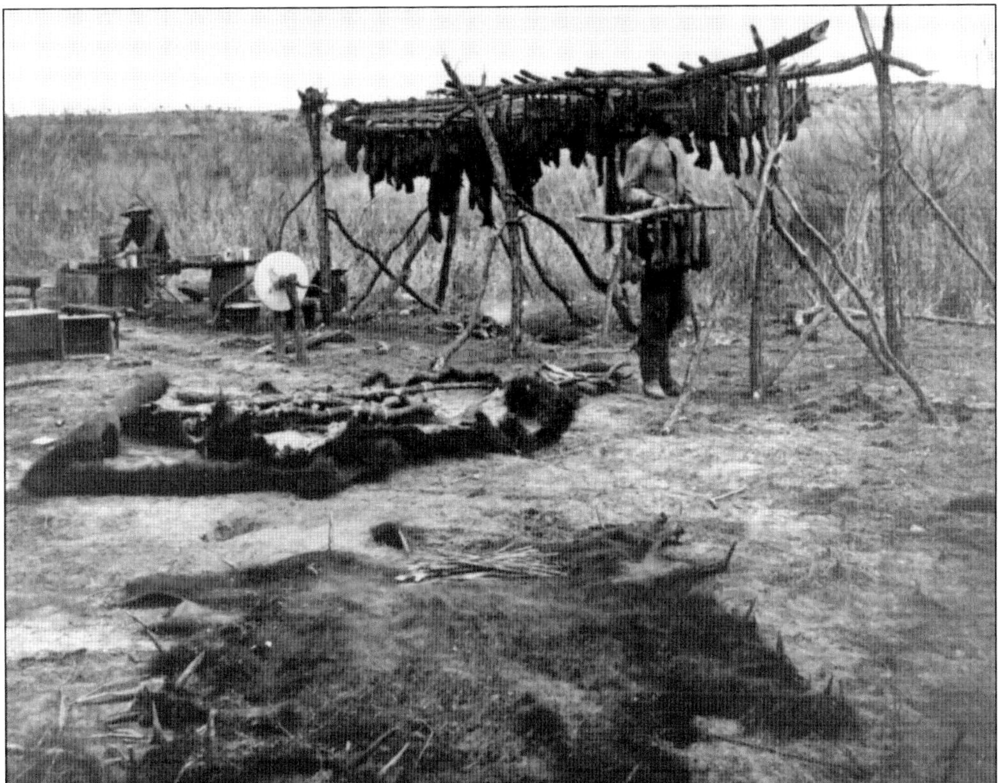

This photograph shows a typical buffalo camp around 1880. (SCM; photograph by Bill Malone.)

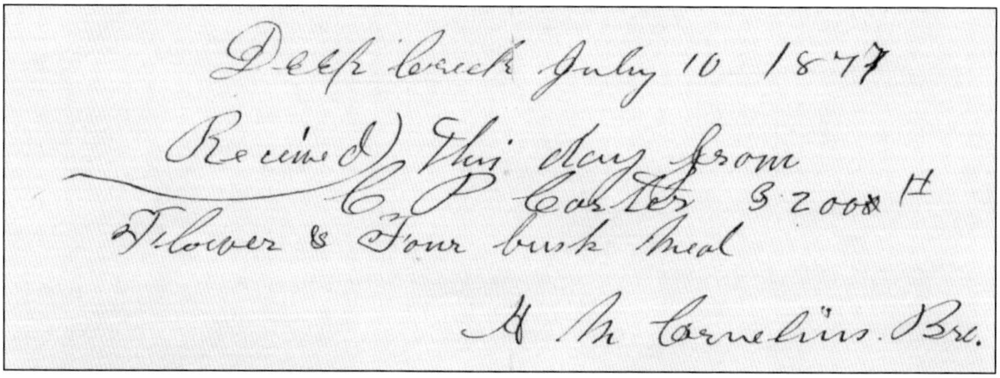

Deep Creek July 10 1877
Received This day from
C P Carter $ 2 00
Flower & Four bush Meal
D M Cornelius Bro.

Where buffalo hunters traveled, merchants followed. This receipt from a store on Deep Creek in Scurry County is dated July 10, 1877. The town of Snyder was established not far from where this merchant, D.M. Cornelius, and another merchant, Pete Snyder, originally set up their stores. Stores for buffalo hunters typically carried a limited inventory of necessities, including flour, baking soda, and salt (for preserving meat). Snyder had previously followed buffalo hunters working in Kansas. (SCM.)

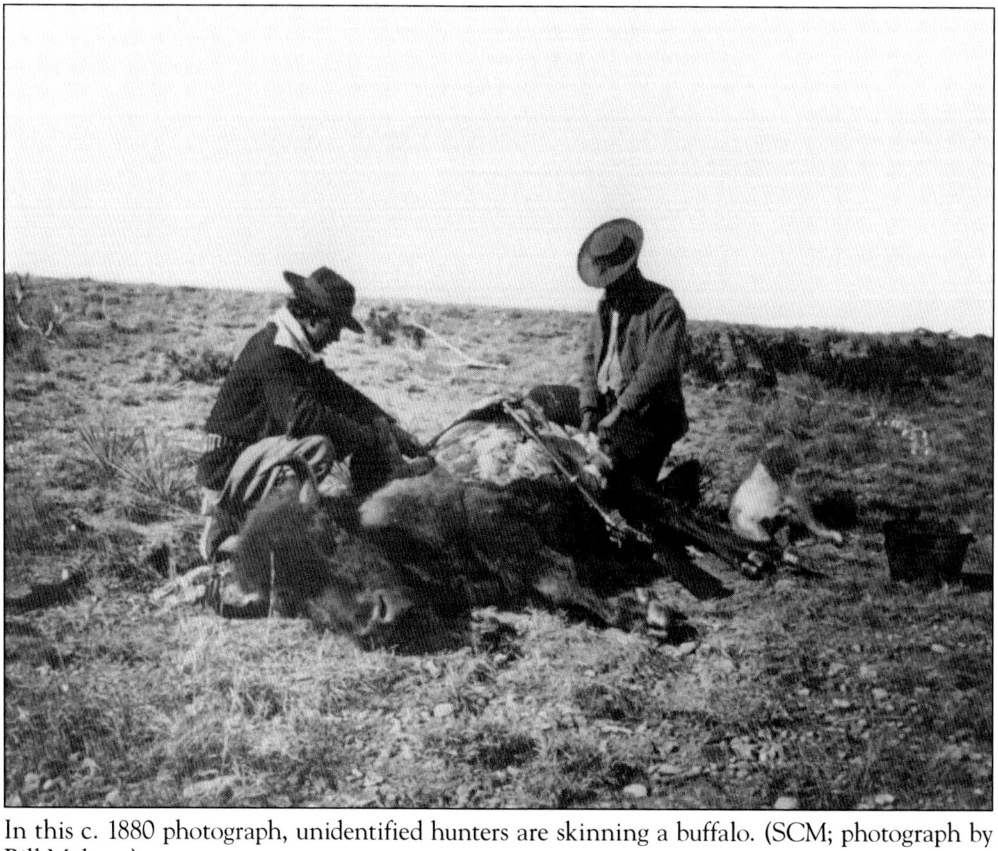

In this c. 1880 photograph, unidentified hunters are skinning a buffalo. (SCM; photograph by Bill Malone.)

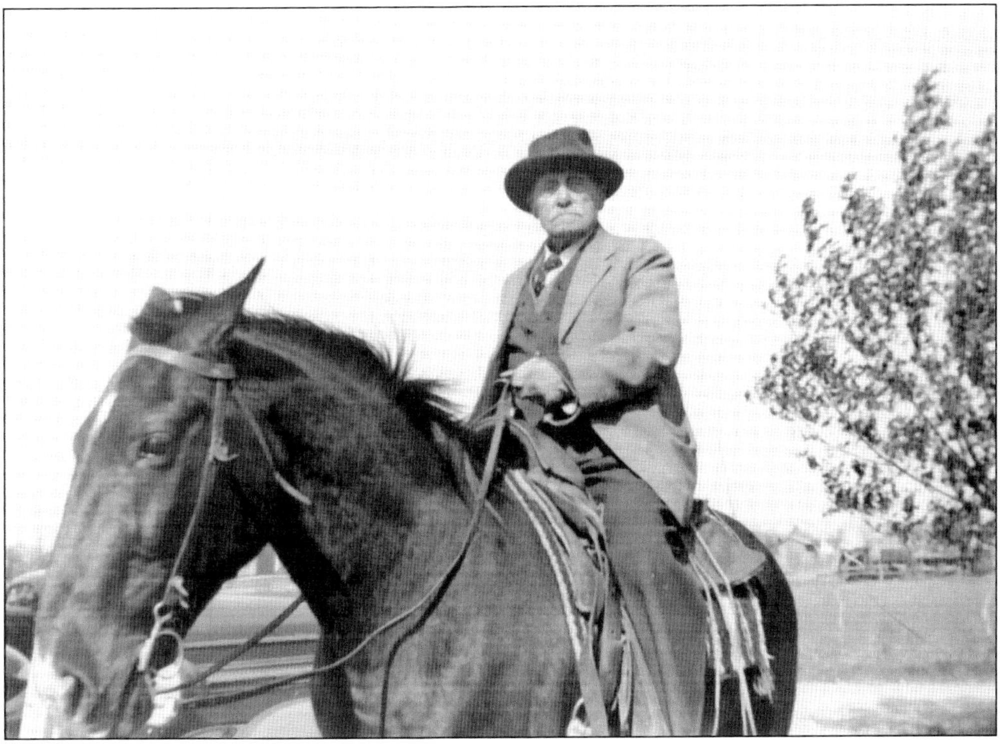

The buffalo were the lifeblood of the Plains tribes. The herds' destruction, more than any other factor, enabled the Army to defeat the last Native American resistance. According to buffalo hunter J. Wright Mooar, "The destruction of the buffalo did what all the millions spent by the United States and by Texas had not done—it settled the Indian question." This photograph of Mooar riding his horse was taken in Snyder, Texas, probably just a few years before Mooar's death in 1940. (SCM.)

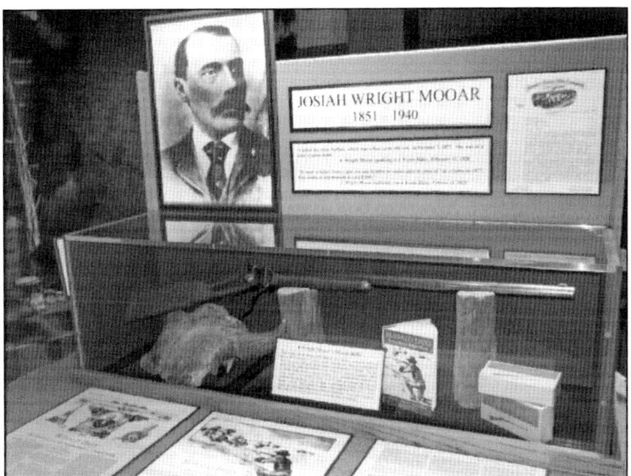

J. Wright Mooar achieved fame in 1876 when he killed a white buffalo on Deep Creek in Scurry County. Along with his brother, John Wesley Mooar, he killed an estimated 22,000 buffalo over the course of his career. He had his rifles modified so that he could easily shoot while wearing gloves in the winter. This image shows one of Mooar's .50-caliber Sharps rifles on display at the Scurry County Museum in Snyder, Texas. His other gun is displayed at Frontier Texas in Abilene.

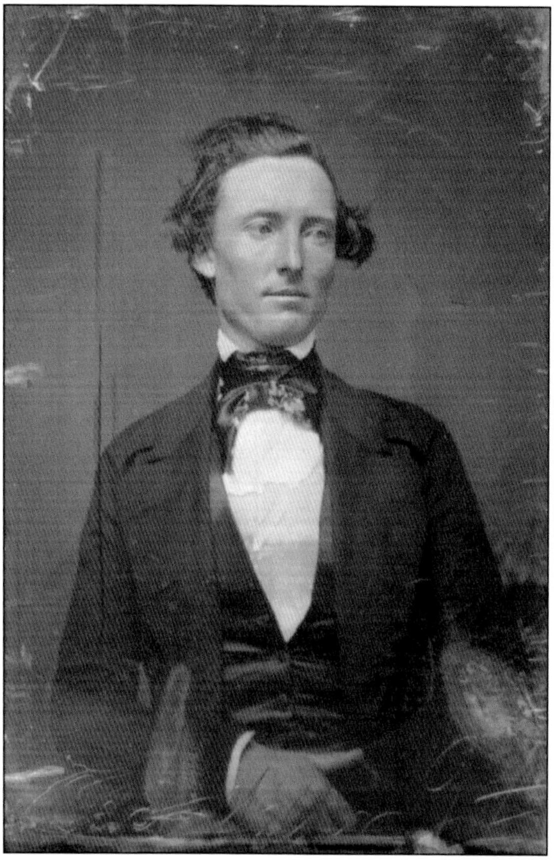

Texas Ranger Capt. Samuel Hamilton Walker, along with arms manufacturer Samuel Colt, was the inventor of the Colt Walker revolver, which became one of the most popular guns of its time. Along with the Winchester Model 1873 rifle, it was one of the guns that effectively "won" the West. (Library of Congress.)

The Army alone was not sufficient to handle the problems in the Panhandle. Early Texas Rangers had their work cut out for them. Desperate men who hoped to escape courts and jails headed west toward the sparsely populated plains. Frontier rangers were not well-paid and had to supply their own horses and weapons. Pictured here are, from left to right, Texas Rangers Charlie Price, John Caraway, Charlie Blackwell, and Will Erskin. There was no uniform for early Rangers, and most chose not to carry a badge; some believed that there was no reason to show a badge to a hostile Indian or outlaw, and others felt that a shiny silver star made for a tempting target. (Texas Cattle Raisers Museum.)

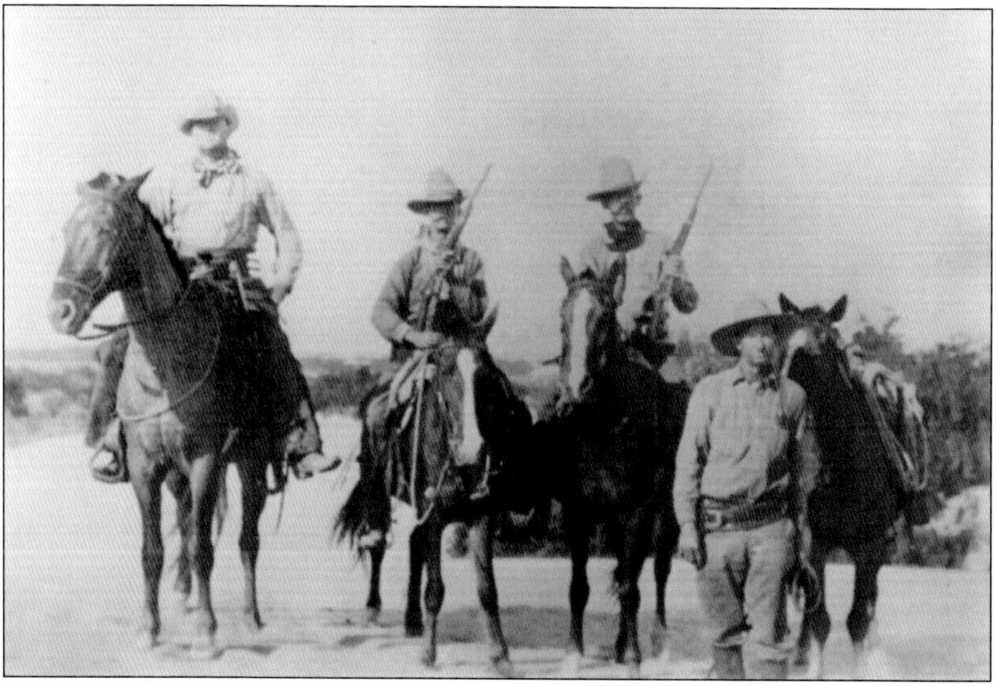

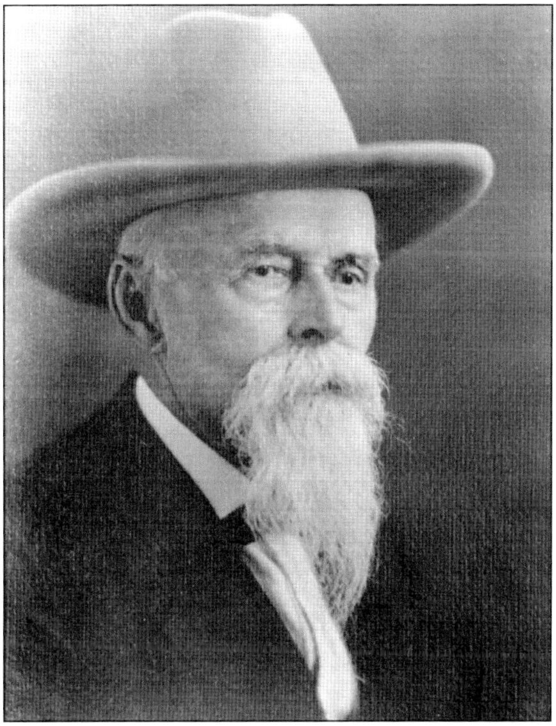

Texas Ranger George Washington Arrington was born John C. Orrick Jr. He changed his name to avoid prosecution for alleged acts he committed during Reconstruction. He was captain of Company C, Frontier Rangers. He later became sheriff of Wheeler County and Hemphill County. He is buried at Mobeetie. (SCM.)

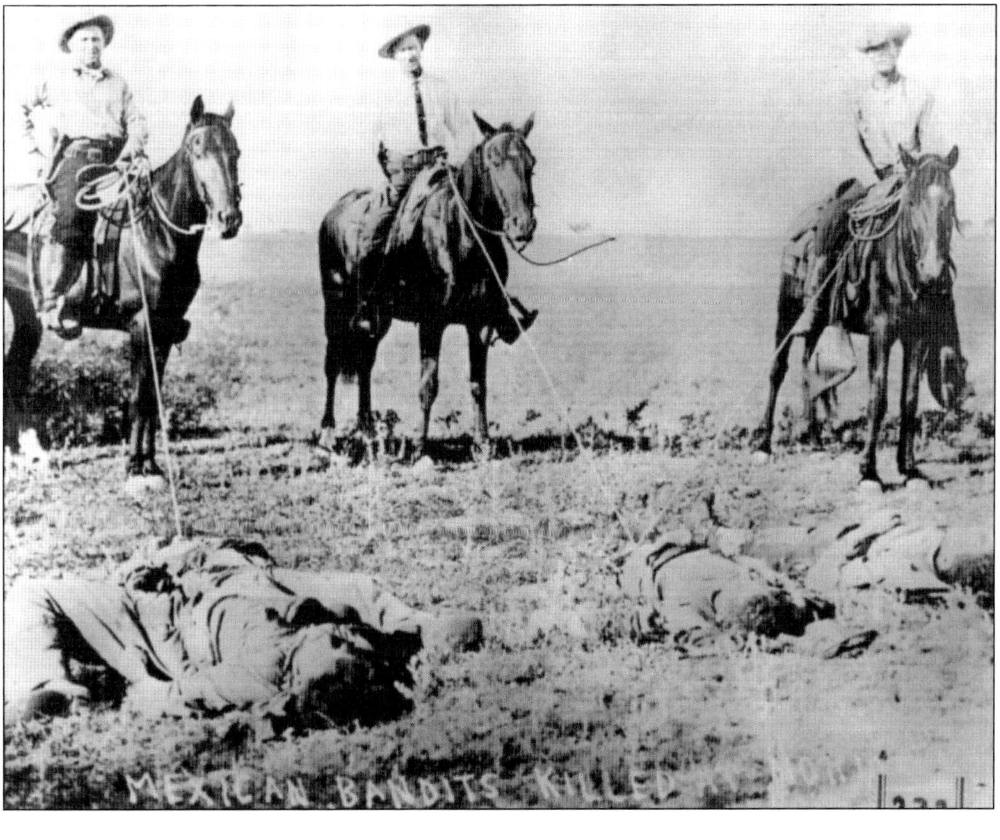

Trouble often came out of Mexico after the Mexican-American War of 1846–1848. Frontier justice prevailed, and problems were usually settled by the quickest gun, even into the early 1900s. These Texas Rangers have caught and killed a trio of Mexican bandits. (Texas Cattle Raisers Museum.)

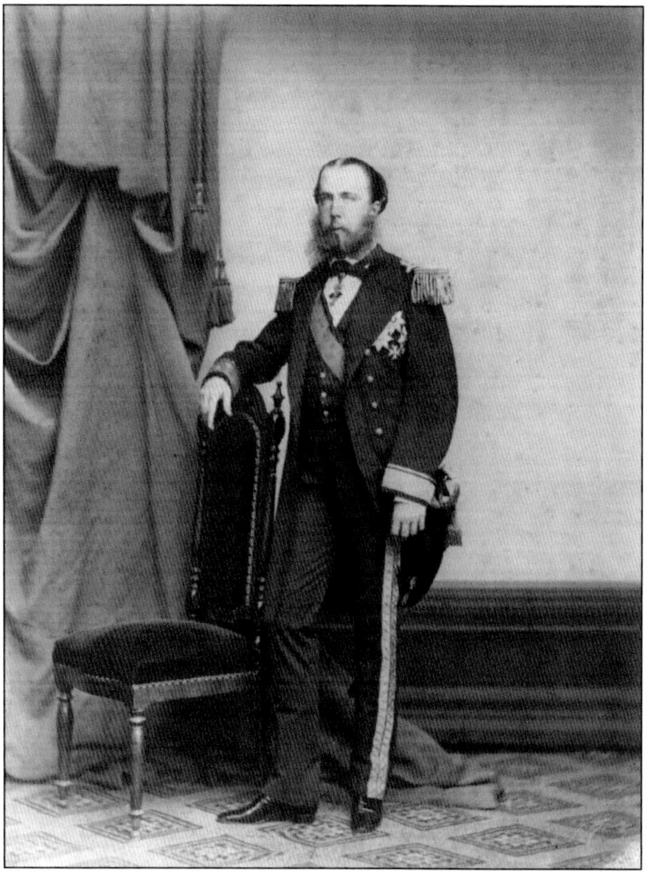

The folklore of the Panhandle Plains contains many stories about lost Spanish gold. One legend concerns the Emperor Maximilian I of Mexico, who decided to send most of his imperial treasury to Texas before revolution deposed him in 1866. Generations of treasure hunters have searched sites and found occasional coins, horseshoes, and nails, but nothing remotely close to the $10 million loot. In 1930, a 1845 Nicholas Boutet flintlock was discovered in a cave near Camp Springs in Scurry County. The weapon was decorated with mother-of-pearl, silver, and rubies. While some believe that it belonged to a member of Gen. Randolph Marcy's 1849 expedition, Boutet famously made guns for the family of Napoleon, and Maximilian I was a friend of Napoleon III. Maximilian I is pictured here around 1864. (Library of Congress).

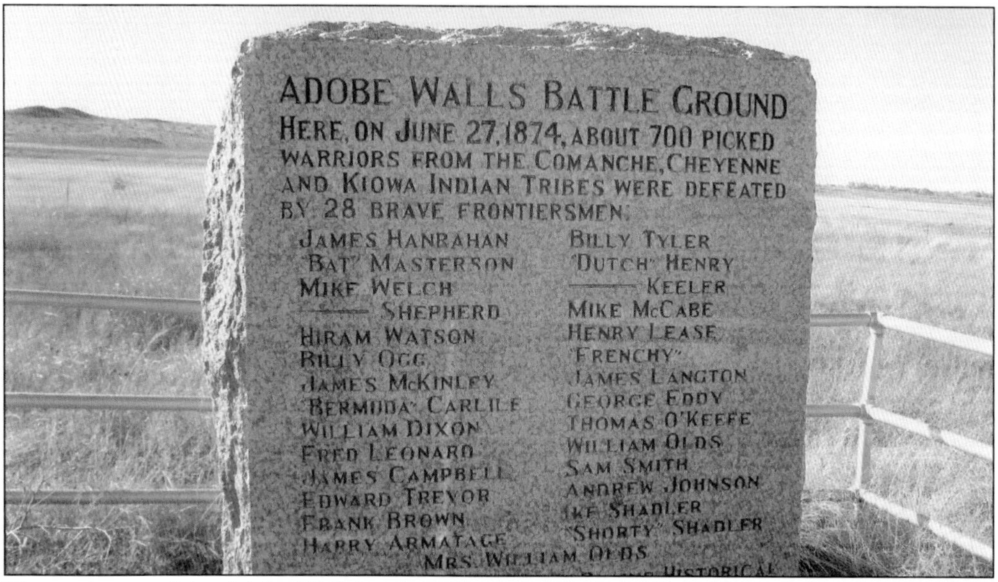

This is the site of the Adobe Walls battlefield near Stinnett, Texas, where Kiowa and Comanche, led by Quanah Parker, attacked a group of buffalo hunters and traders in 1874. The hunters battled with and defeated the Indians.

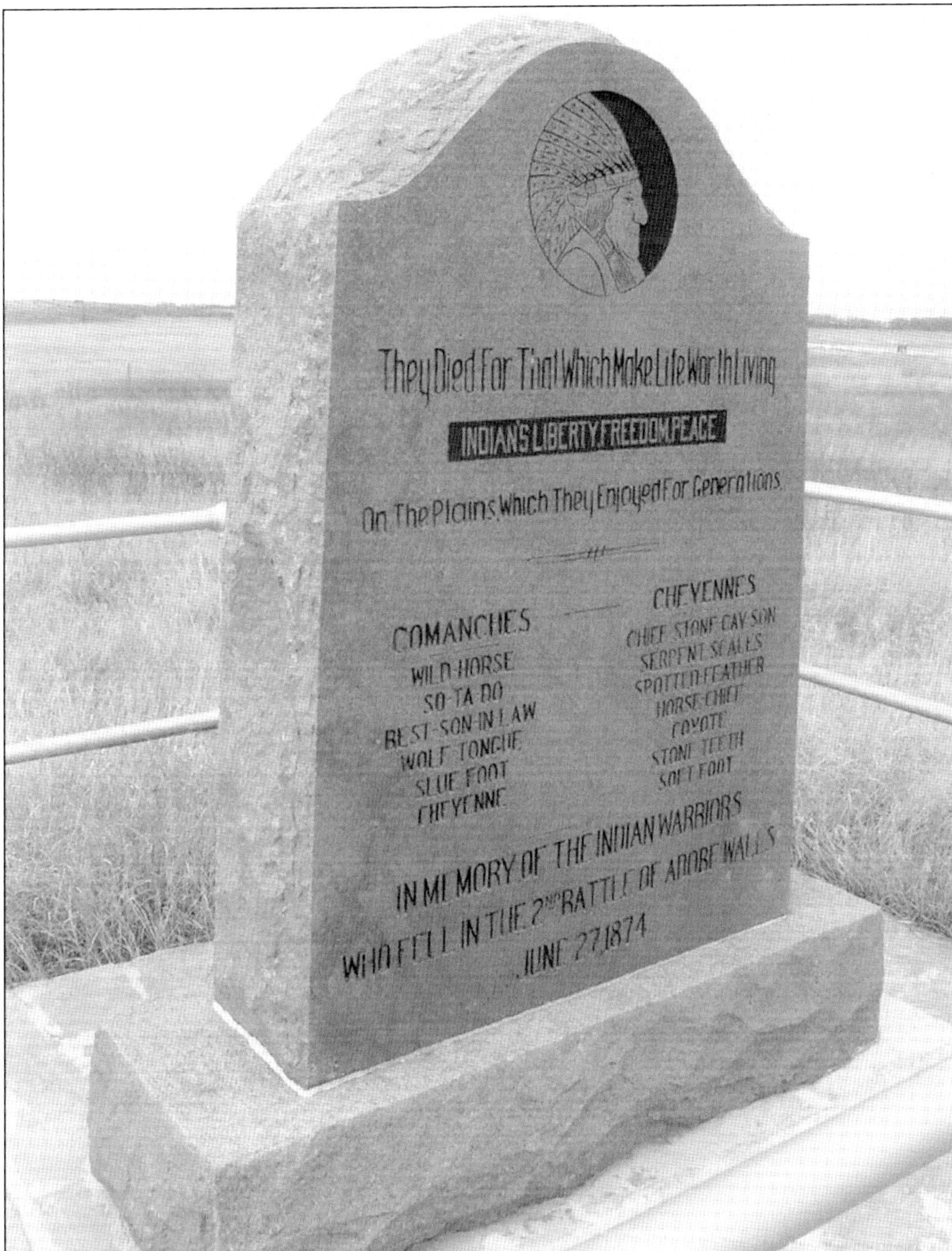

In 1864, the ruins of Adobe Walls were the site of a battle in which Col. Kit Carson led 335 soldiers and 72 Ute and Jicarilla Apache scouts against more than 1,000 Comanche, Kiowa, and Plains Apache. Two very different markers stand on the site expressing conflicting views of the battles and commemorating both the settlers and the Native Americans who died defending what they believed was theirs.

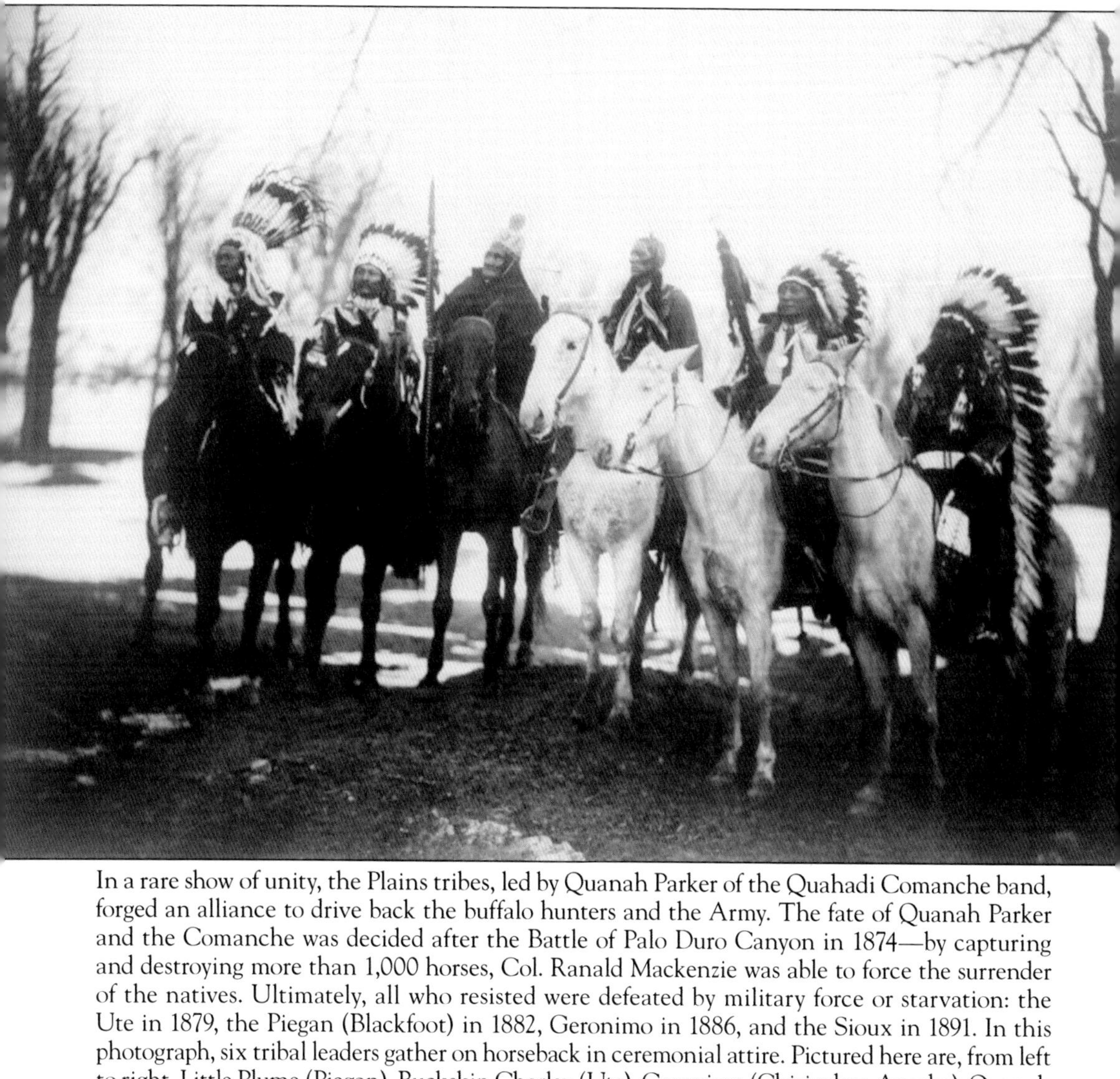

In a rare show of unity, the Plains tribes, led by Quanah Parker of the Quahadi Comanche band, forged an alliance to drive back the buffalo hunters and the Army. The fate of Quanah Parker and the Comanche was decided after the Battle of Palo Duro Canyon in 1874—by capturing and destroying more than 1,000 horses, Col. Ranald Mackenzie was able to force the surrender of the natives. Ultimately, all who resisted were defeated by military force or starvation: the Ute in 1879, the Piegan (Blackfoot) in 1882, Geronimo in 1886, and the Sioux in 1891. In this photograph, six tribal leaders gather on horseback in ceremonial attire. Pictured here are, from left to right, Little Plume (Piegan), Buckskin Charley (Ute), Geronimo (Chiricahua Apache), Quanah Parker (Comanche), Hollow Horn Bear (Brulé Sioux), and American Horse (Oglala Sioux). This photograph was taken by Edward S. Curtis around 1900. (Library of Congress.)

Two

Early Ranchers

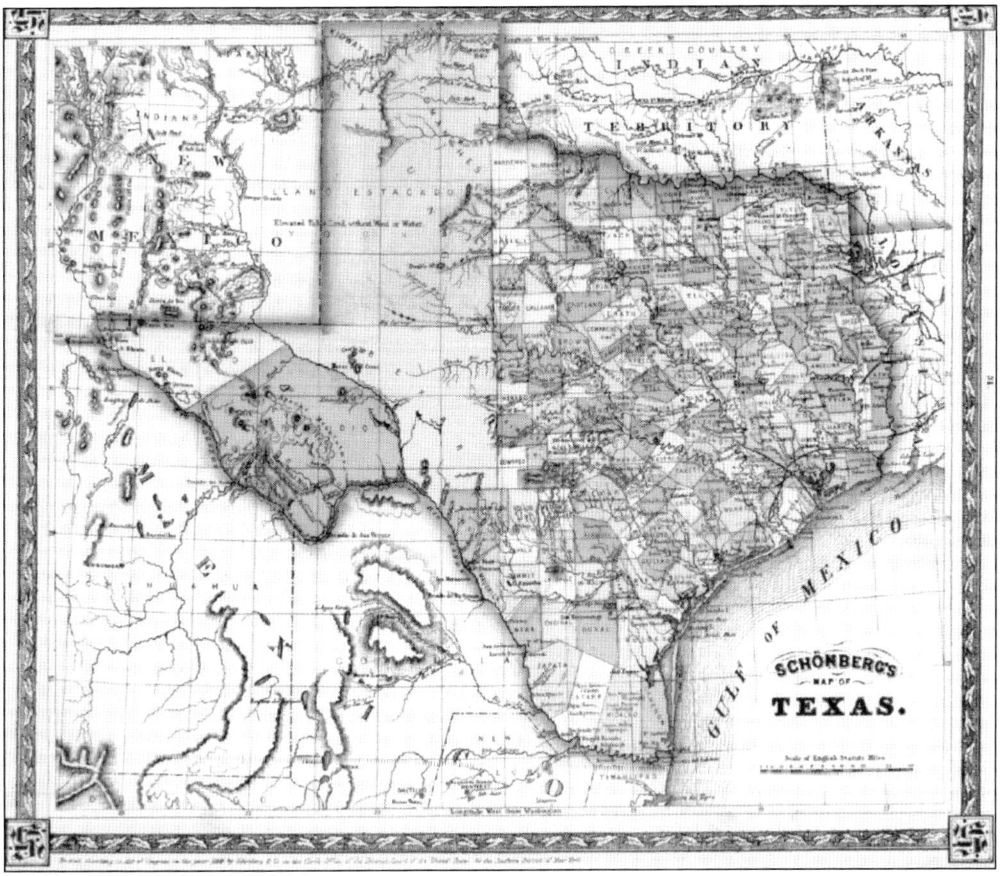

This c. 1866 Schönberg's map of Texas clearly shows the Panhandle Plains region. The Llano Estacado, described as "table land without wood or water," was the last part of Texas to be settled. Col. Ranald Mackenzie defeated the last Native American resistance at Palo Duro Canyon in 1874, and two years later, Charles Goodnight established the JA Ranch near the site where the battle had taken place. With the original inhabitants forced onto reservations in Oklahoma, the era of white settlement had begun. (David Rumsey Historical Map Collection.)

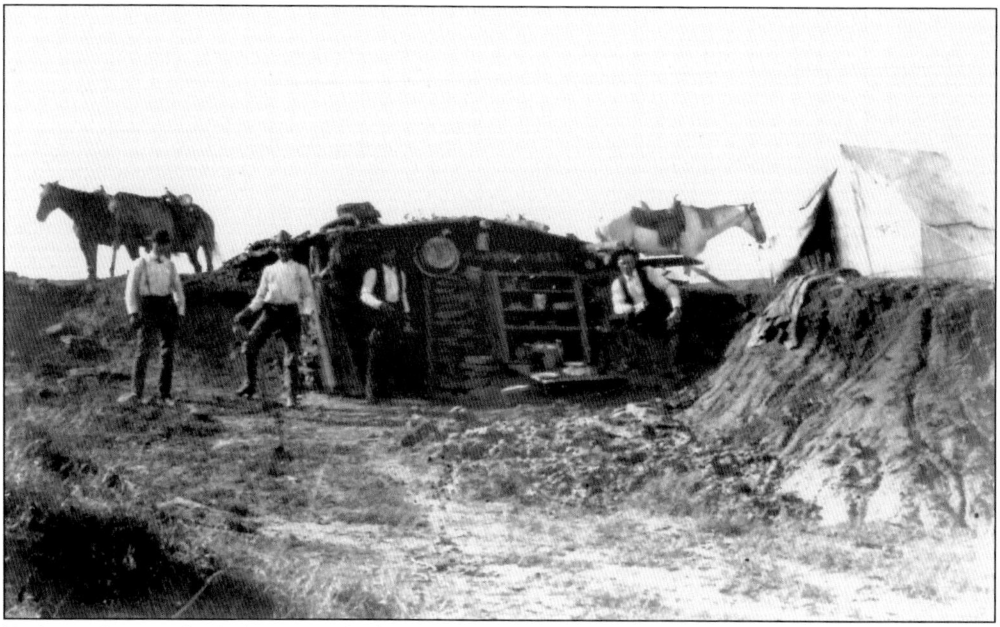

Early settlers made shelter out of whatever materials were available. Dugouts constructed and used as homes and businesses were abandoned when men moved on or better housing became available, and very few still exist. The owner of this dugout may have been a range cook based on the unusual "chuck box" attached to the front wall. The men in this picture are unidentified. (Clay County Historical Society, Henrietta, Texas.)

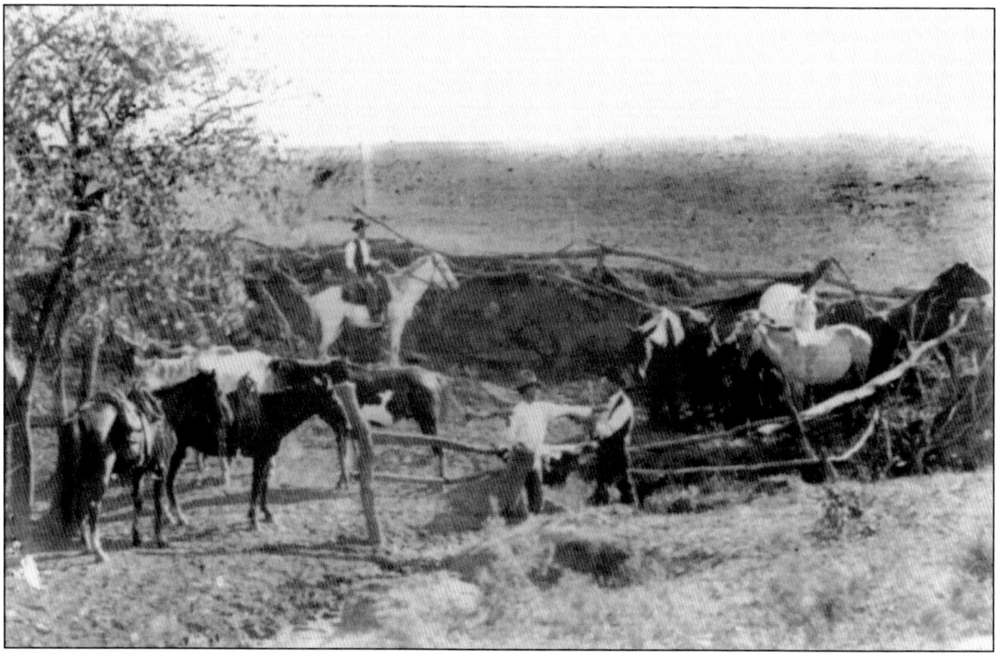

This makeshift pole corral, which is visible from the dugout in the photograph at the top of this page, indicates that the dwelling and adjacent corral were headquarters for a ranching operation. A cowboy is mounted on a white horse inside the corral, and two others are having a discussion near the fence. (Clay County Historical Society, Henrietta, Texas.)

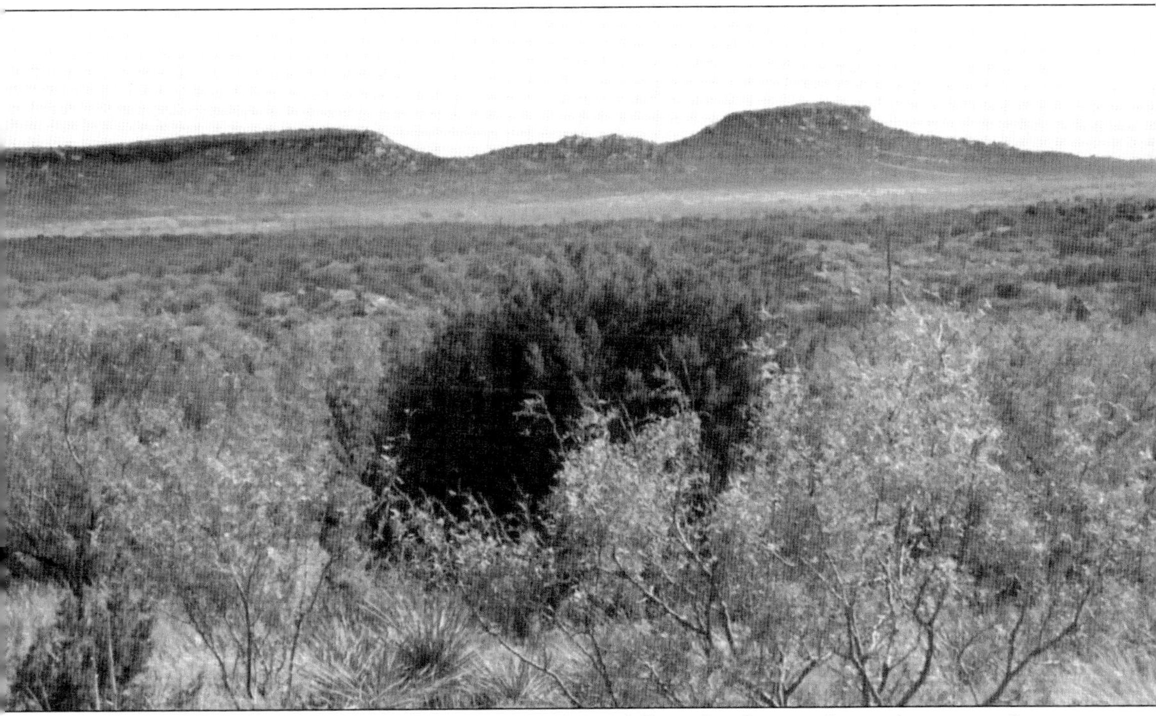

In 1875, Texas Ranger and Army scout Jim Jackson followed a Comanche raiding party from Coleman County into Kent County, a distance of over 150 miles. Along with Col. Ranald Mackenzie, he climbed Big Mackenzie Mountain. Jackson saw cattle-raising potential in the region, but he also caught sight of the Comanche. The Army chased the Indians northwest and, once within range, starting shooting at them, killing a number of Comanche and reclaiming stolen stock. This present-day view from Big Mackenzie Mountain is probably very similar to what Jackson saw, although the vast herds of buffalo are noticeably absent.

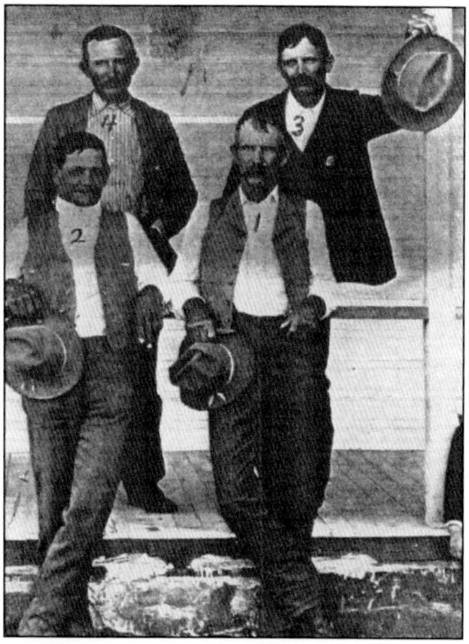

Jim Jackson was one of four sons-in-law of George Kindred "Uncle Kin" Elkins. They are, from left to right, (first row) Tom Deats and Jim Jackson; (second row) Ike Boren and John Cambell.

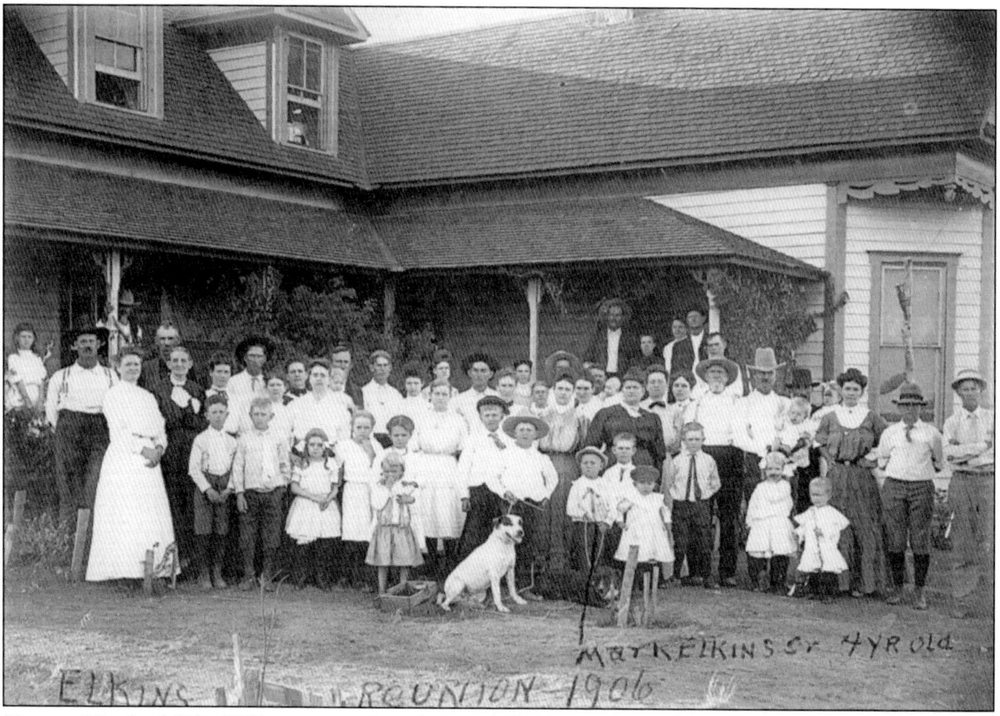

George Kindred "Kin" Elkins started in the cattle business around 1853, when his family came to Parker County from Illinois. He made his first cattle drive to Fort Leavenworth, Kansas, in 1857. After the Civil War, he trailed herds to New Orleans, and the family moved near Camp Colorado in 1867. When his son-in-law Jim Jackson drew his attention to Kent County, Kin Elkins told all of his friends and family, many of whom moved to join him. Others who followed Elkins's advice were Smokey Brown and the Long brothers, who established the famous OS Ranch. It might seem surprising that Kin Elkins had so many relatives willing to take a chance on the Panhandle Plains, but he had married three times and sired 19 children. This 1906 photograph was taken during a family reunion at Polar.

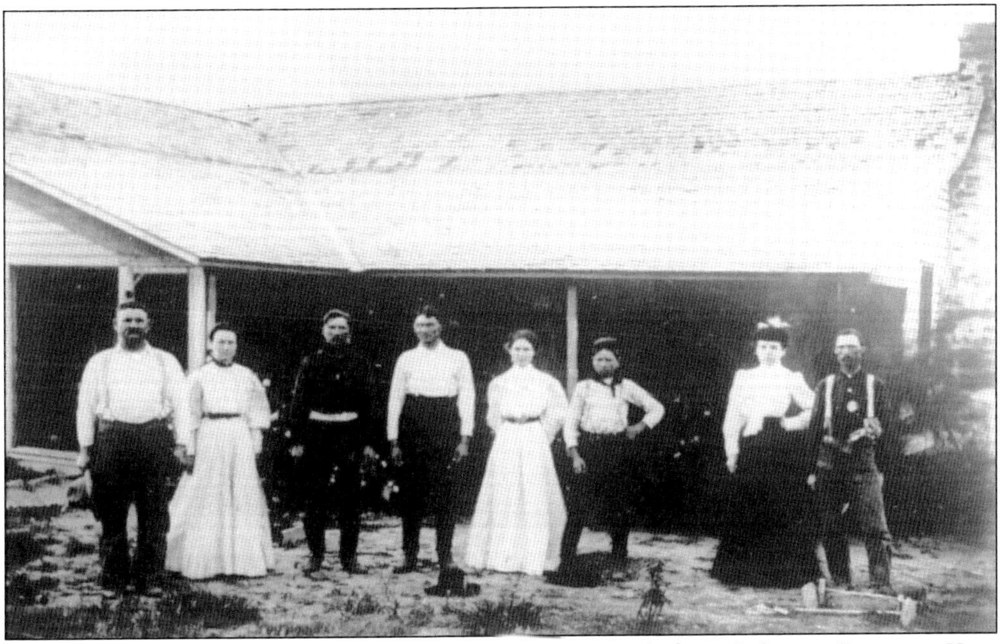

In 1876, George Elkins and Sam Gholson brought 5,000 cattle from Coleman County to Kent County. They headquartered just north of the mountains on Mackenzie Creek. Pictured here are, from left to right, George Elkins and his wife, Celia Amanda Elkins; Roy "Rip" Elkins; Alvin and Jettie (Elkins) Bettes; Earnest Bettes; and Sarah Sallie Elizabeth (Griggs) Elkins and her husband, Alvin Clay Elkins. (SCM.)

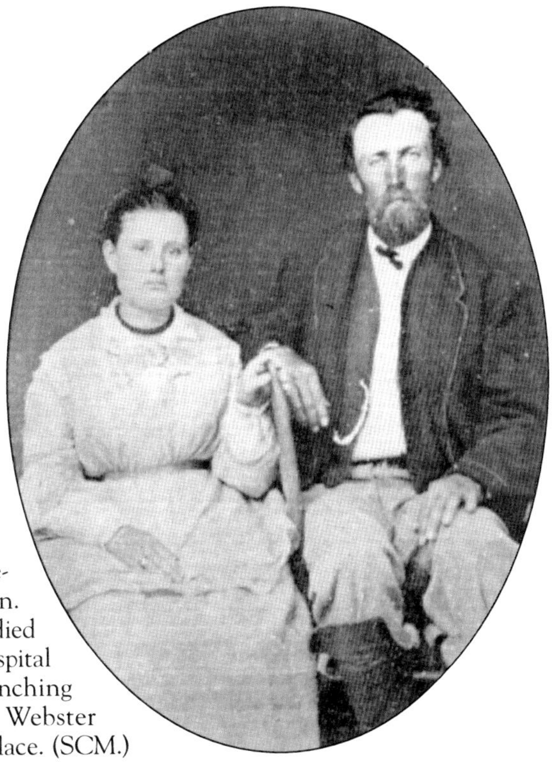

Clay Mann had to flee Parker County in 1866 after killing Hampton Pattilo, who had murdered his father, Matthew Mann. Clay went to Coleman County and a cousin's ranch. He soon had his own cattle, and he married Kin Elkins's oldest daughter, Mary (Mary and Clay are pictured at right). Clay Mann owned the "80" brand and ranched in Kent County before moving his operation to Mitchell County in 1879. Clay Mann was the biggest cattle operator in the West from 1882 to 1886, with cattle-freighting expenses of almost $1 million. Sadly, he liked to gamble and drink and died of acute alcoholism on July 21, 1889, in a hospital in Denver, Colorado. Mary continued ranching with the help of trusted friend Daniel Webster Wallace—better known as "80 John" Wallace. (SCM.)

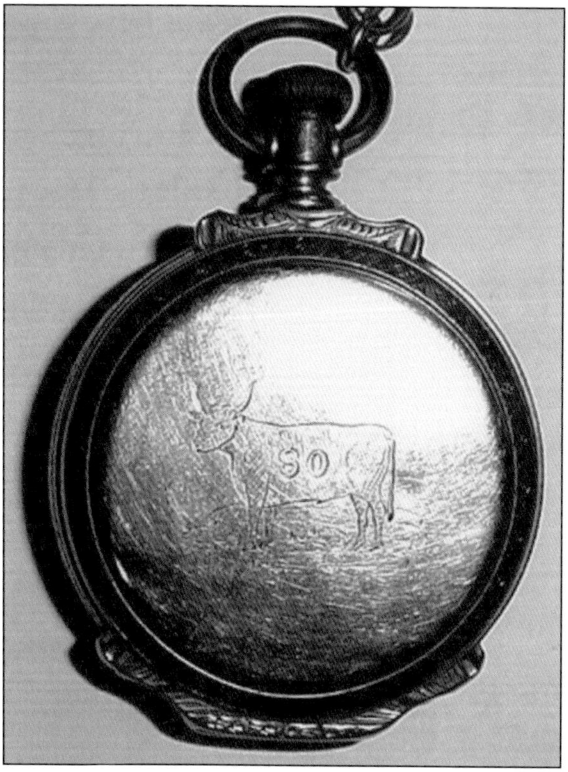

This is Clay Mann's 18-karat-gold watch. He had his name engraved inside the dust cover and a steer with the "80" brand engraved on the back of the case. The watch is now in the possession of one of Mann's great-grandsons in Colorado City.

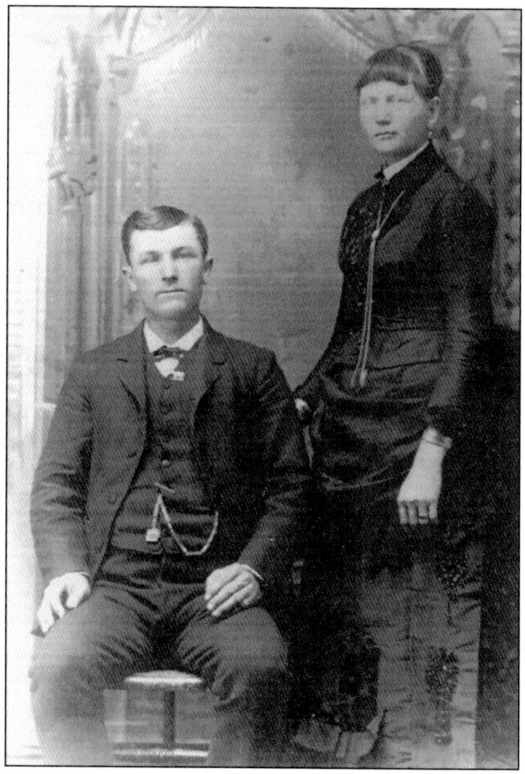

Boley Brown worked cow camps in Garza and Kent Counties in 1879 and built a dugout in Kent County for his bride, Martha "Matt" Garretson, in 1880. Boley increased his cattle herd by branding unclaimed strays. Matt would drive a wagon and maintain a fire inside of a pot to heat branding irons. Boley, riding horseback, would rope a cow and hold the animal until Matt branded it. The Browns' "24" ranch became one of the largest ranches on the Panhandle Plains, encompassing over 300,000 acres. (Don M. Jay Collection, SCM.)

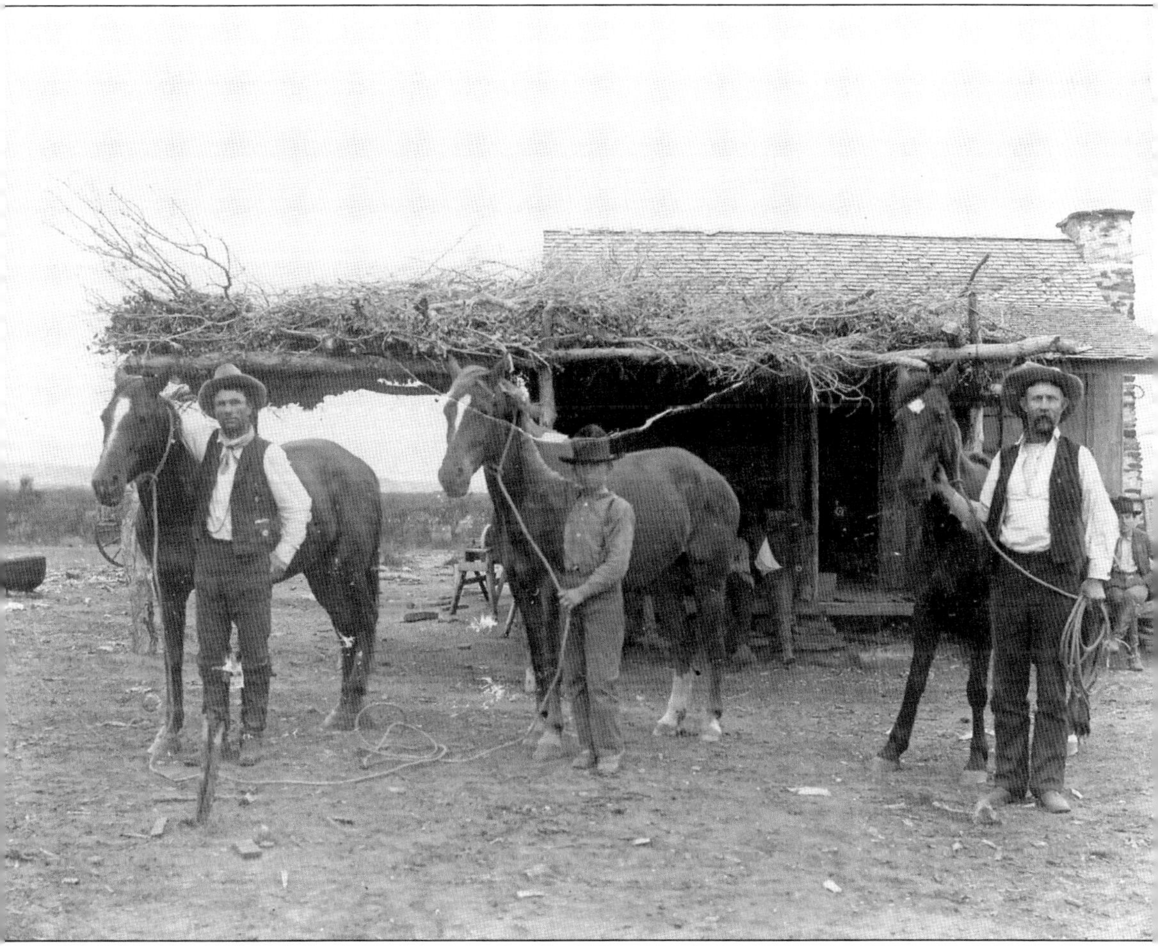

This is a line camp on Yellowhouse Creek in Kent County on the range of Boley Brown and his partner, I.D. "Pete" Scoggin. Note the brush arbor and unidentified men sitting on the porch. This range was joined by the Spur ranch north of the Salt Fork, the OS Ranch to the west, Clay Mann's big "80" to the south, and the Circles Bar "0-0" to the east. Posing here with their horses are, from left to right, Boley Brown, his son Chalk Brown, and Scoggin. (Don M. Jay Collection, SCM.)

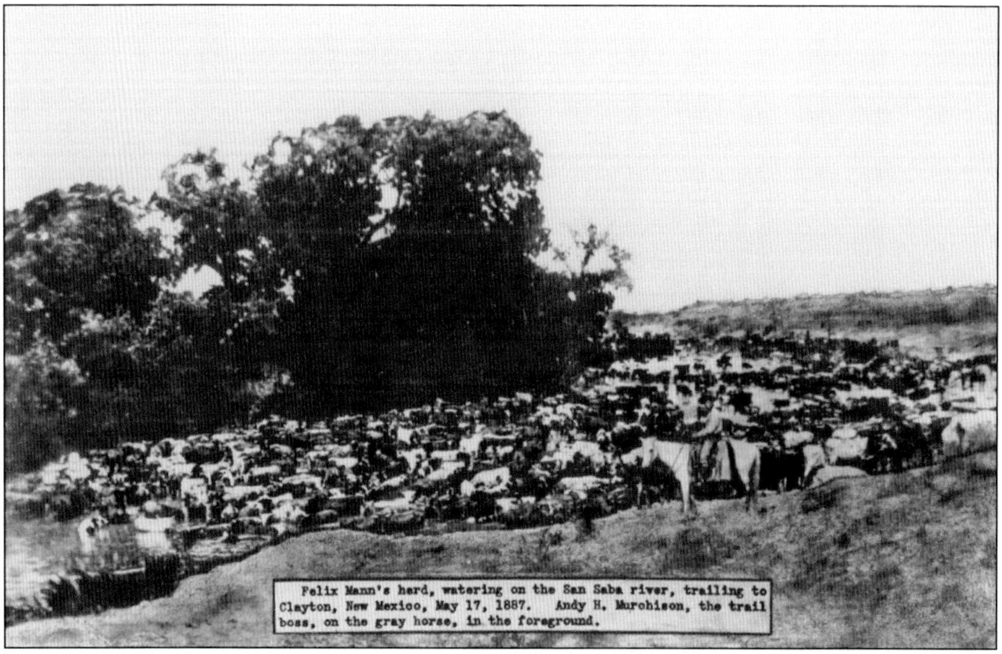

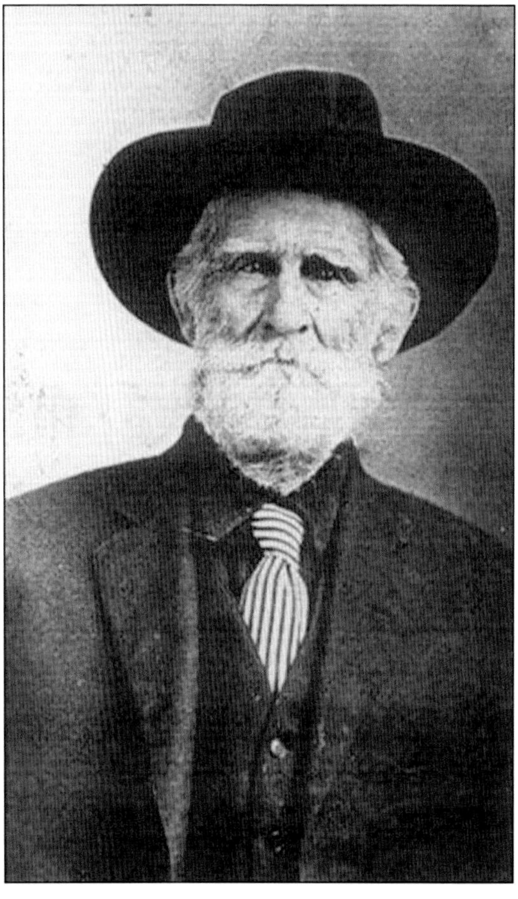

Felix Mann ranched farther south of his cousin Clay Mann. The cattle herd pictured here is being watered during a trail drive to New Mexico. Felix and Clay partnered as cattle operators, bringing cattle to Eastern markets and shipping from Amarillo and Colorado, Texas. (N.H. Rose Collection, University of Texas at Austin.)

Sam Gholson was an early rancher on the Texas Plains. He and his brother Frank joined the Rangers for about a year until their father found them and took them home. They were probably the only Texas Rangers who were discharged for being underage. Sam also fought the Native Americans.

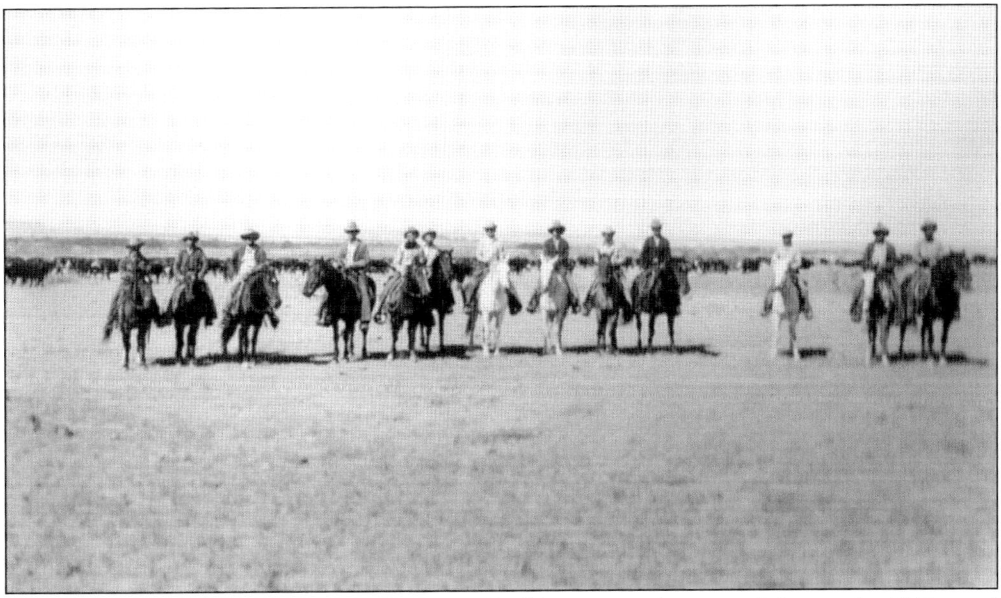

The OS Ranch had few bosses over the years. Bud Boren was the ramrod during the 1890s, and Sam Elkins, son of the famous Texas Ranger and Indian fighter Kin Elkins, was boss for many years under the ownership of Wilson E. Connell. In this photograph, Sam is third from left, and Ad Jones is fifth from left. When Connell died, the ranch was divided among four of his children. Another heir received a ranch near Polar, while his son Alan received a ranch near Midland. While the OS became a smaller ranch, it earned national fame as a site for calf-roping and art shows, drawing crowds of 20,000 or more every weekend. One regular attendee was Reba McEntire, the famous singer and actress. (Garza County Historical Museum.)

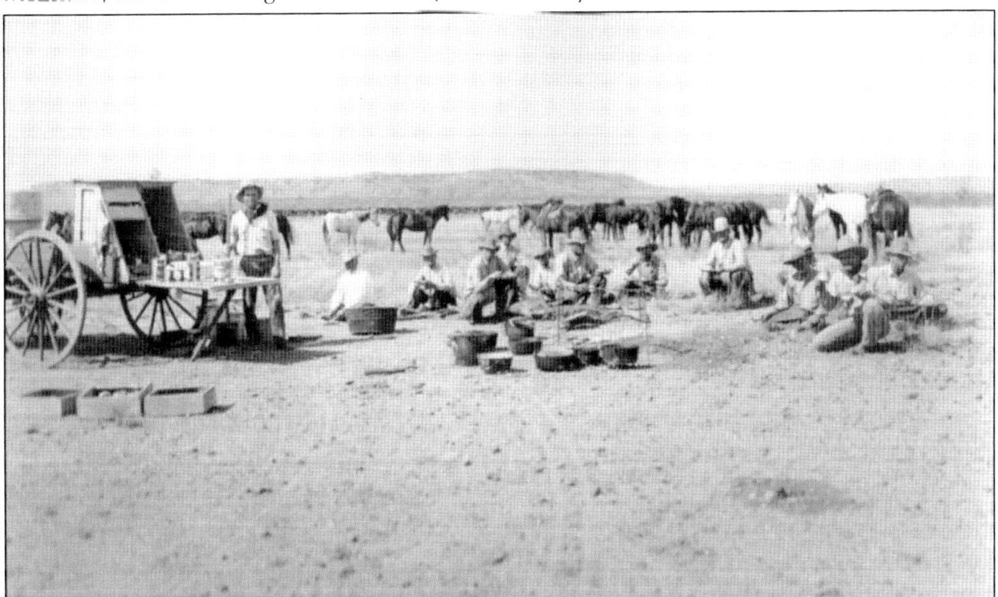

The OS cowboys had big roundups every year. This one took place on the OS range at Sand Creek, southeast of Post. Range cook B.R. Kennedy (far left) is setting up camp and starting dinner from the chuck box. The cowboys are tending the stock. (Garza County Historical Museum.)

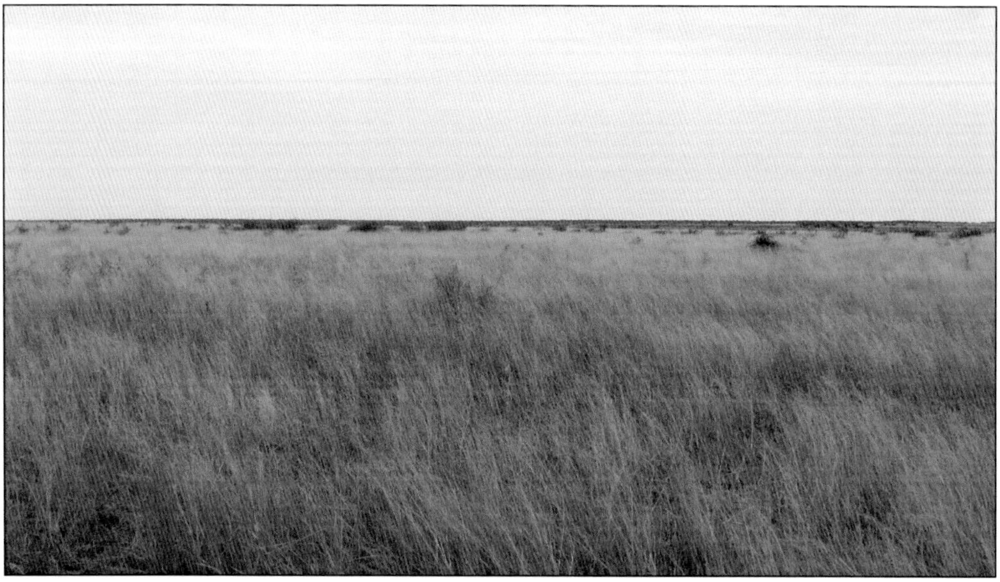

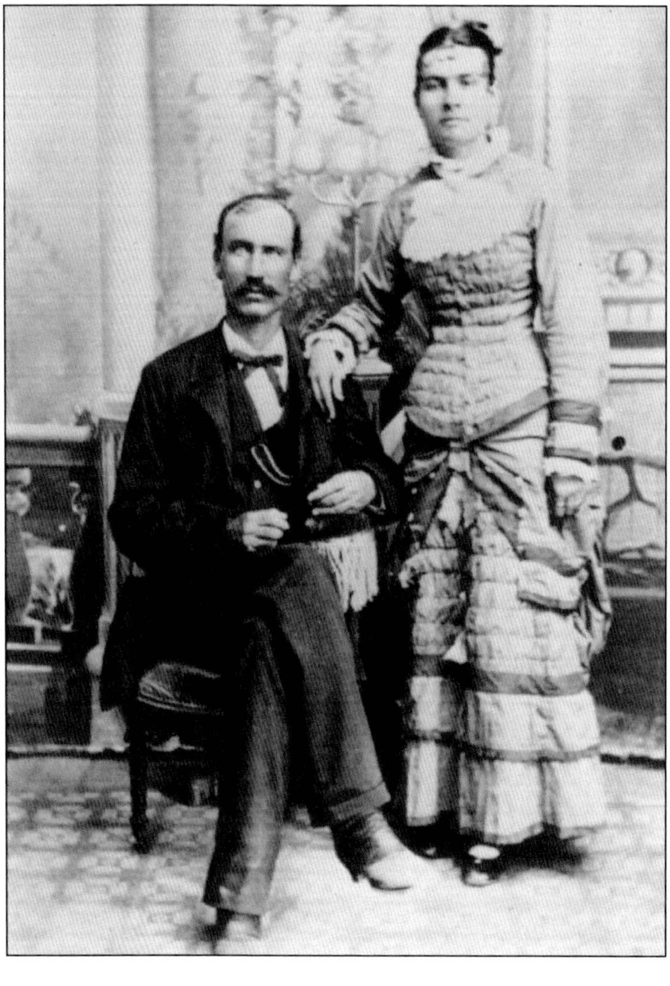

In 1879, the Long brothers, Andy and Frank, were listed as owners of the land along the Salt Fork of the Brazos River in Garza County. Richard Overall and nephew Frank Sharp herded cattle near present-day Fluvanna and sold their herd to the Longs. The Kentucky Cattle Company, to the north, sold another herd to the Longs, who combined the herds and branded their cattle in honor of Overall and Sharp, starting the OS Ranch. The ranch was sold to W.E. Connell in 1901. Today's range looks much the same.

Andrew Jackson "Andy" Long was born in 1848 in Lavaca County and moved to Sweetwater, Nolan County, in 1877. He married Queen Ila Boren, daughter of Isaac and Mary Queen Cave Boren, on August 11, 1881. They maintained a residence in Sweetwater and made trips to the OS Ranch as needed.

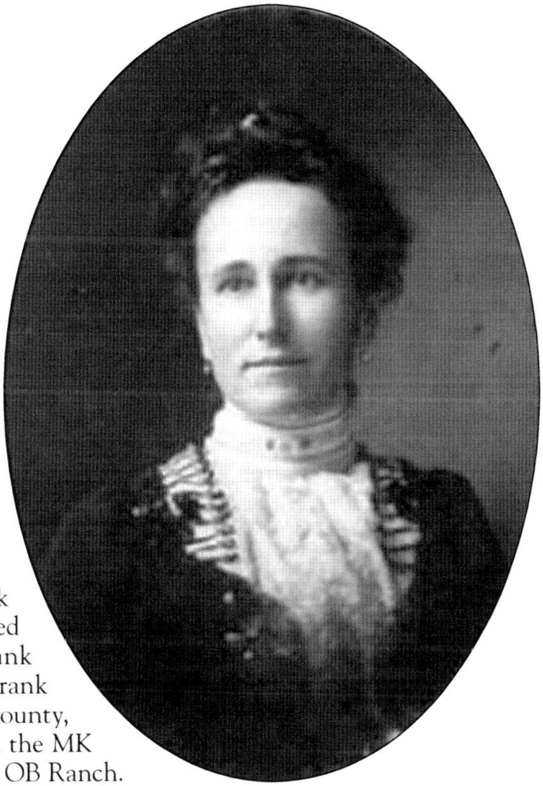

Francis Marion "Frank" Long (below) was born on November 20, 1856, in Caldwell County. He moved to Taylor County in 1875 and became partners with his brother Andy. Combined, the two men had 1,200 head of cattle, which they moved to Oak Creek in Nolan County. In 1879, they moved their herds to Garza County. In 1881, Frank married Flora Temple Linn Long (right). Frank later operated the OB Ranch in Fisher County, which he sold in 1901 and then purchased the MK Ranch in Borden County, renaming it the OB Ranch.

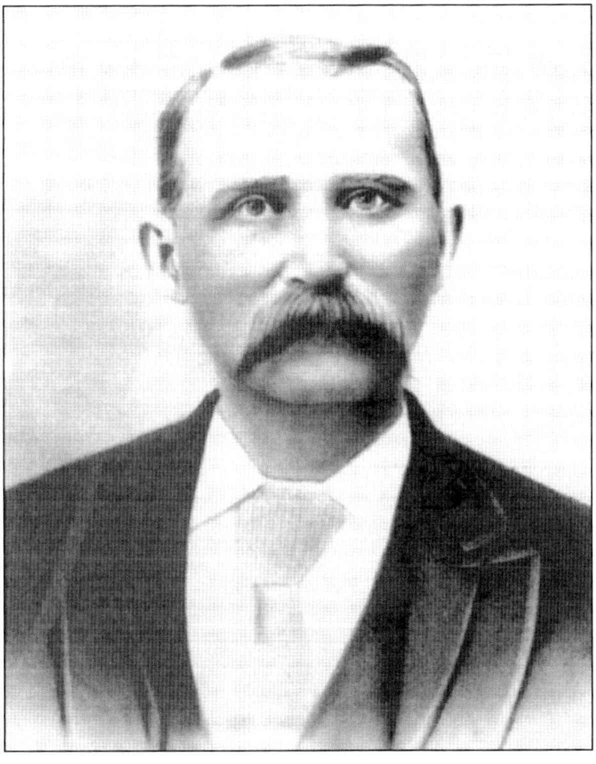

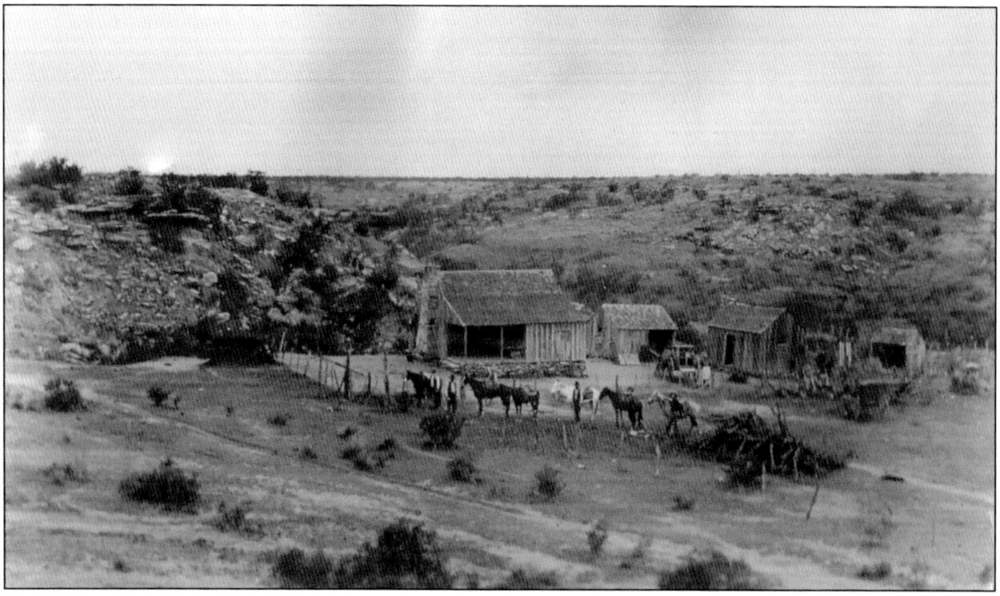

This ranch headquarters and surrounding land was purchased by the Long brothers and became part of the OS Ranch. Here, cowboys are about to mount their horses for a day's work. The cook is loading supplies for the chuck box. The building behind the cook is the bunkhouse. The main house has a rock foundation. (Garza County Historical Museum.)

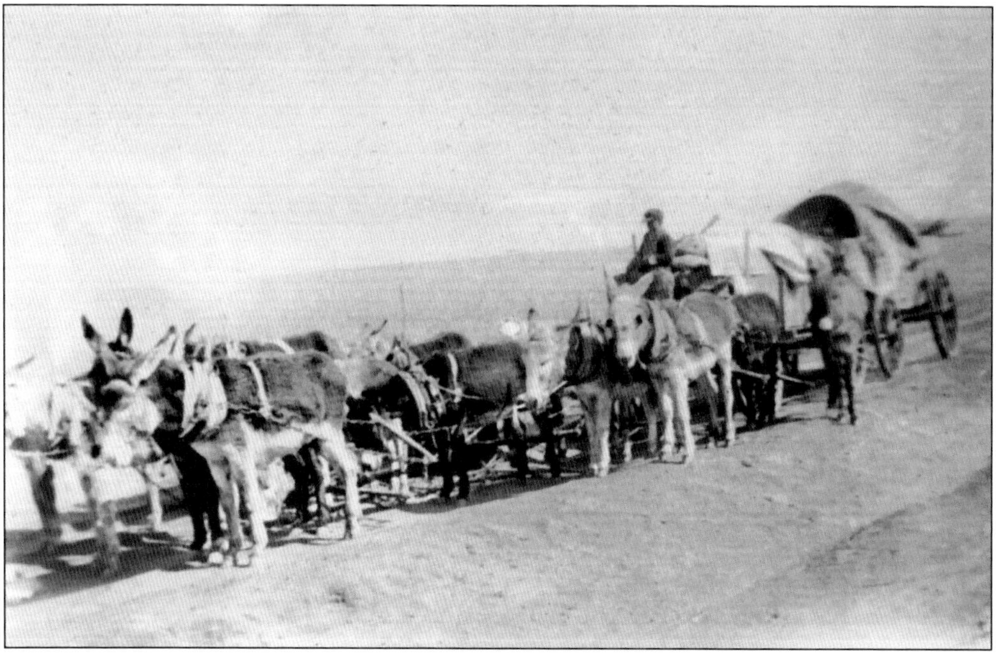

There were no towns in the Panhandle Plains region for many years. Before the railroad came to the area where Abilene was established, ranchers had to haul freight from far-off Weatherford. After the railroads came to Colorado, Texas, it became a supply point much closer to the ranchers on the plains. This freight outfit is being pulled by a team of Missouri jacks. (SCM.)

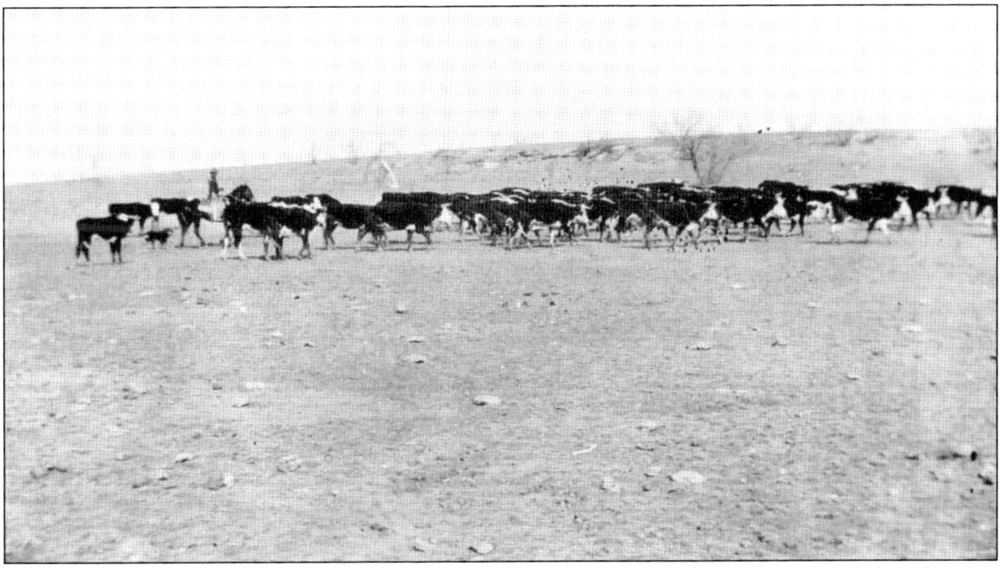

Horses were not the only working animals on early cattle ranches. Here, Joe York and his dog round up cattle before driving them to the holding pens. (SCM.)

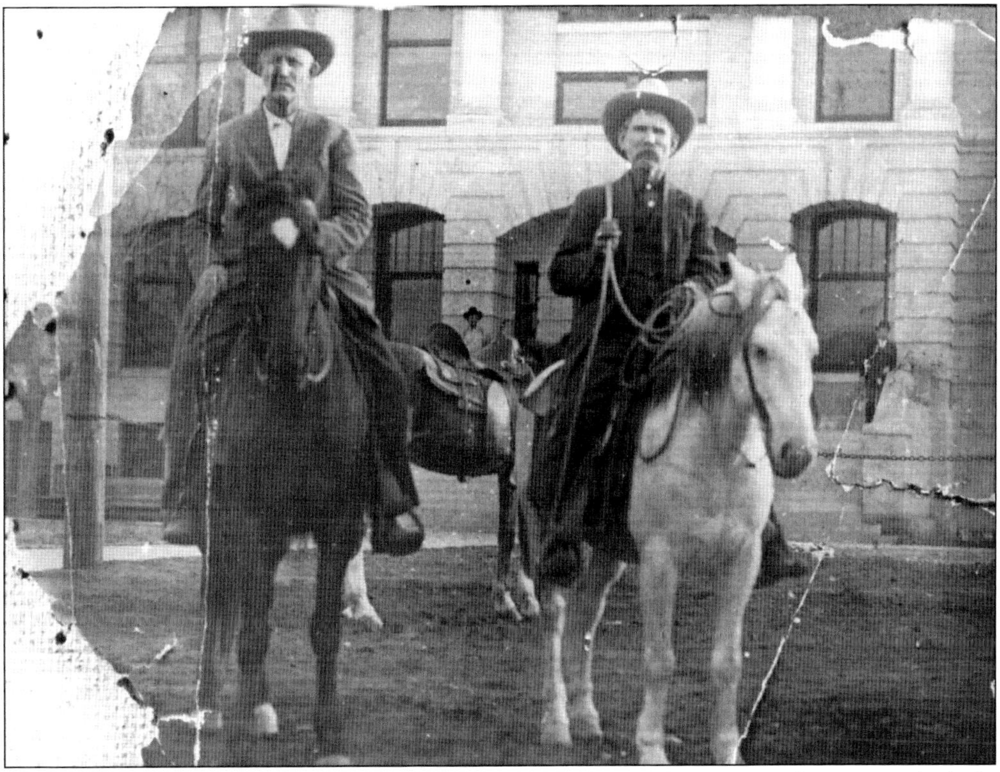

I.D. "Pete" Scoggin and Boley Brown ran the "24" ranch in Kent County. After Brown died of a heart attack in 1911, Pete continued in the ranching business and became an operator, buying and shipping cattle to the markets. He was on the board of directors at the Snyder bank and was a prominent figure in both Kent and Scurry Counties. This 1912 photograph shows W.D. Sims (left) and Scoggin in front of the Scurry County Courthouse. (SCM.)

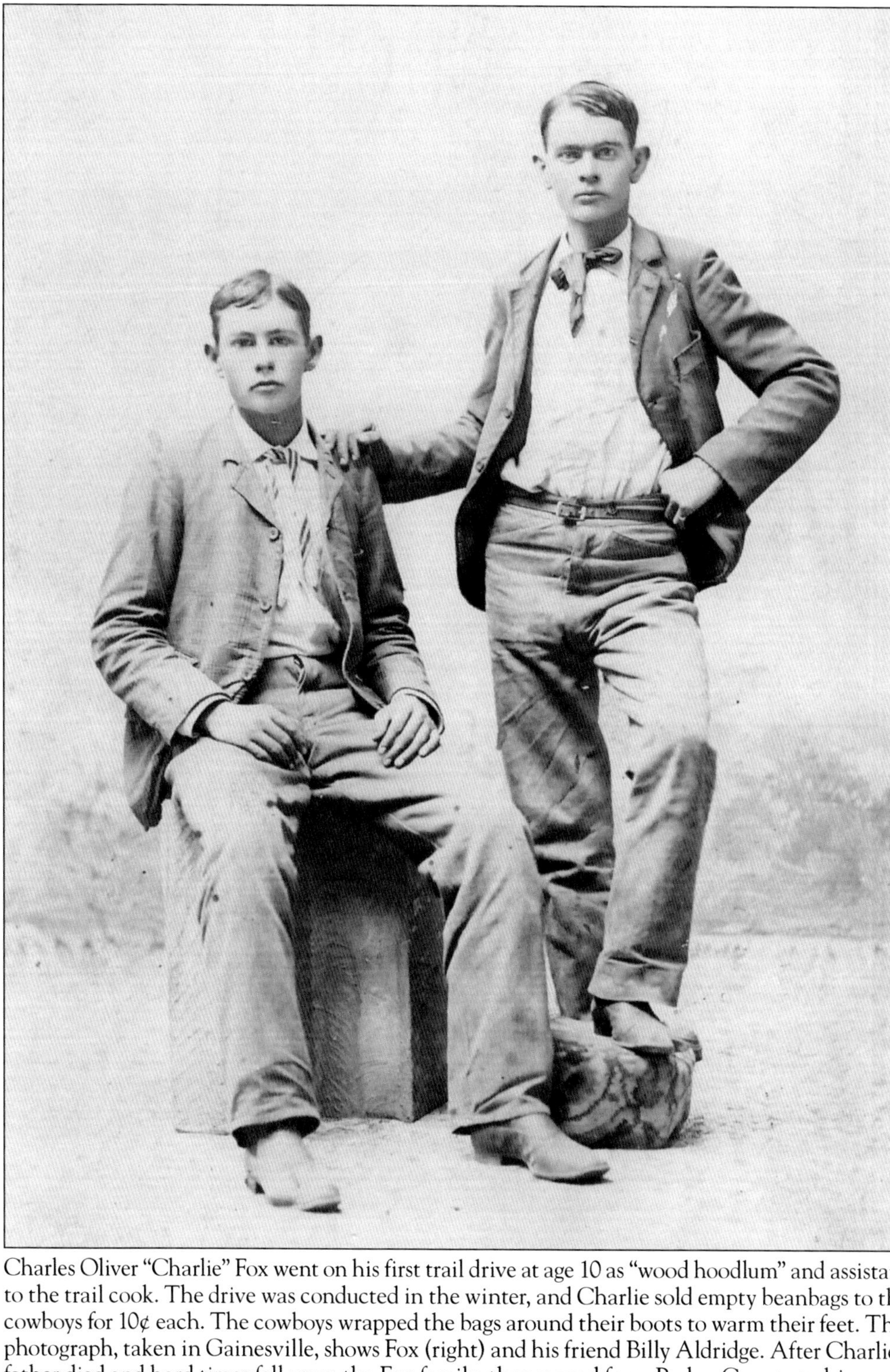

Charles Oliver "Charlie" Fox went on his first trail drive at age 10 as "wood hoodlum" and assistant to the trail cook. The drive was conducted in the winter, and Charlie sold empty beanbags to the cowboys for 10¢ each. The cowboys wrapped the bags around their boots to warm their feet. This photograph, taken in Gainesville, shows Fox (right) and his friend Billy Aldridge. After Charlie's father died and hard times fell upon the Fox family, they moved from Parker County to his uncle Boley Brown's "24" Ranch in Kent County. (Don M. Jay Collection, SCM.)

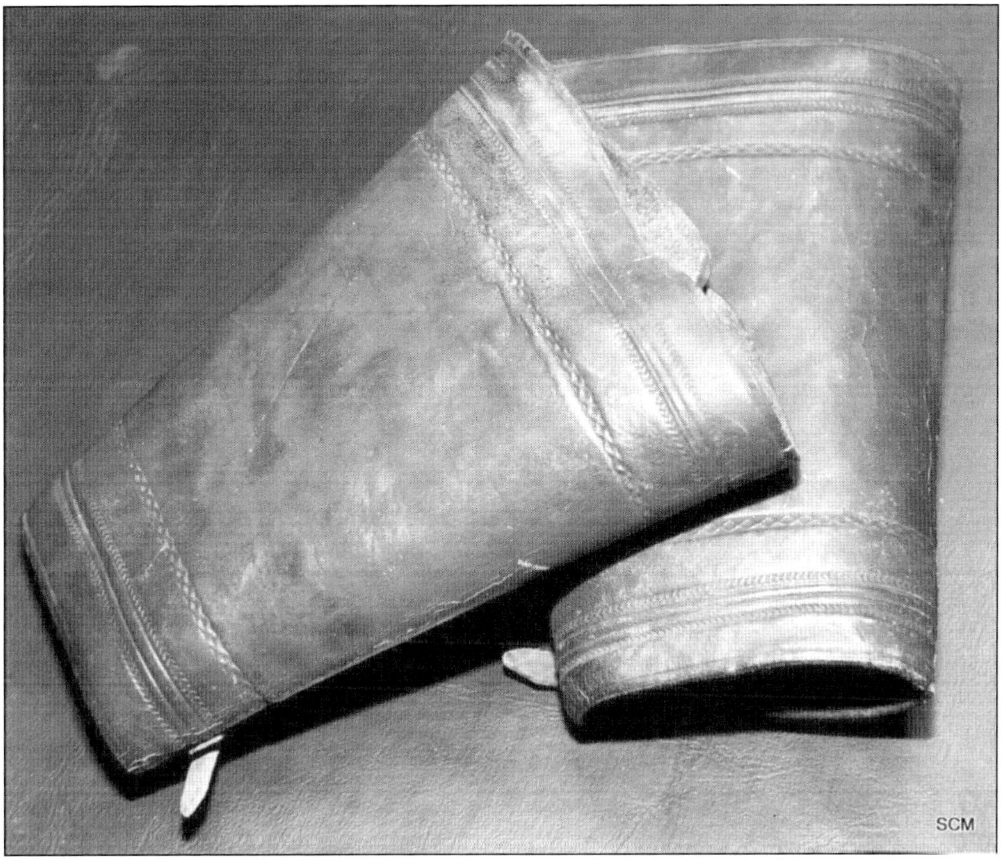

These leather wrist cuffs belonged to Charles Oliver Fox. (Don M. Jay Collection, SCM.)

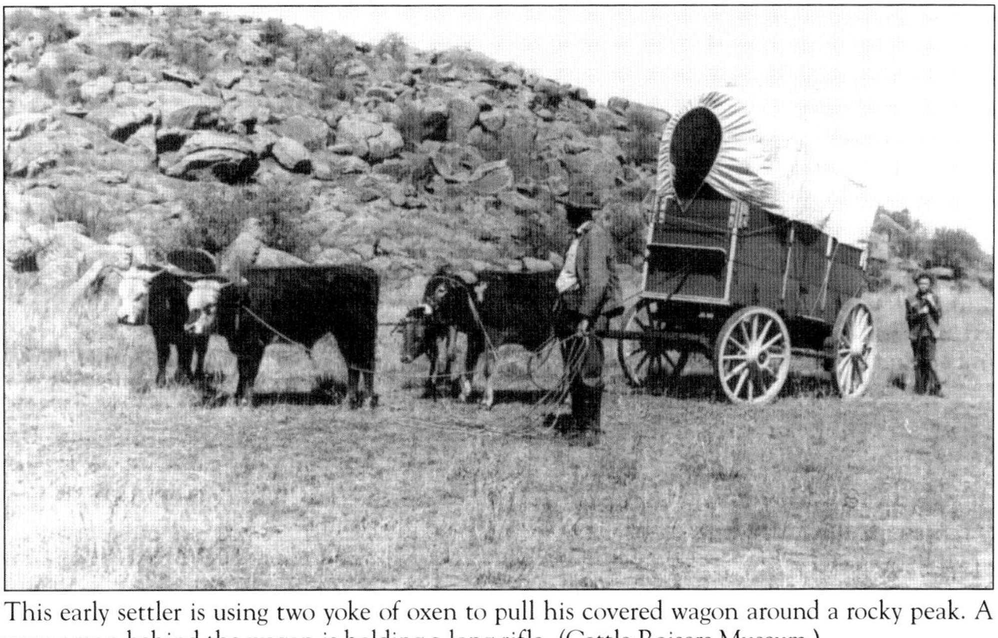

This early settler is using two yoke of oxen to pull his covered wagon around a rocky peak. A young man behind the wagon is holding a long rifle. (Cattle Raisers Museum.)

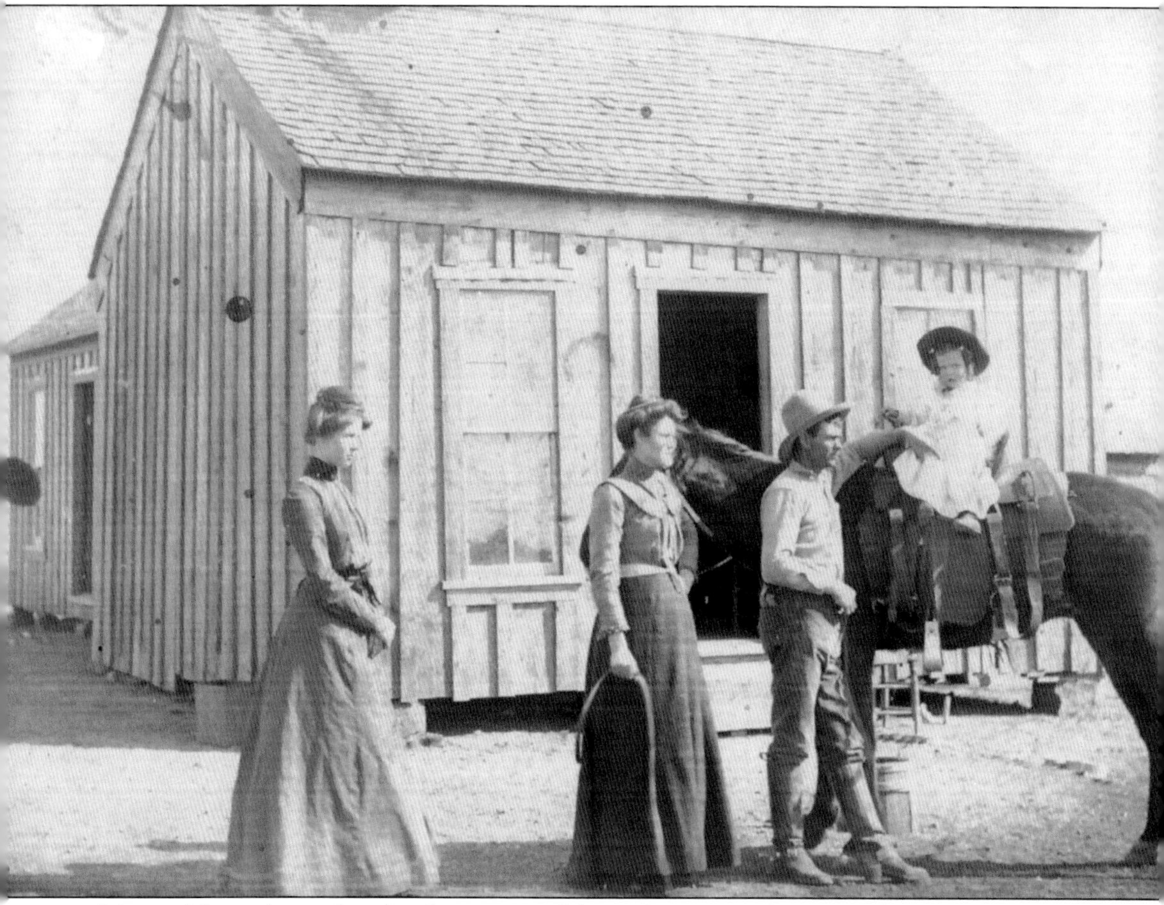

Many of the early ranchers lived in tents and, later, dugouts. In the 1880s, the Texas Legislature passed the four-section law, which dissolved open-range ranches, and homesteaders in Garza and Kent Counties hauled lumber from Colorado, about 70 miles to the south, to build box and strip homes. Pictured here are, from left to right, Gussie Hardin Snowden, Martha and Charlie Addie, and Gussie's daughter, Billie Boley. (Don M. Jay Collection, SCM.)

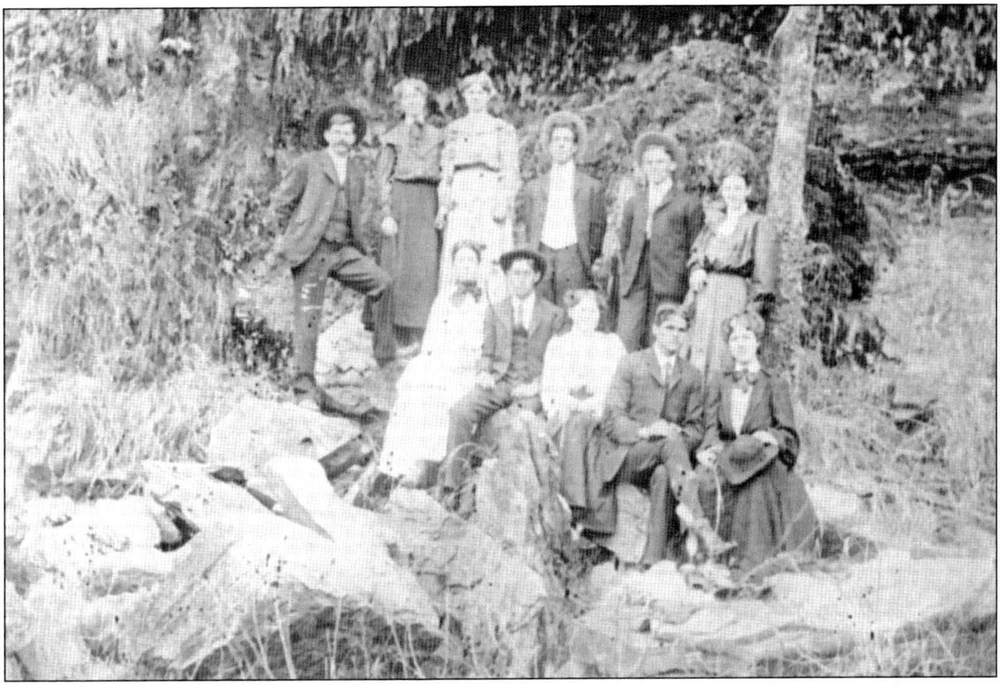

The Camp Springs site in eastern Scurry County was important to the Comanche and other Native American tribes. Arrowheads and other archaeological finds prove that this natural spring had been visited by humans for thousands of years. Early ranchers also saw its benefits, and in 1878, sheepherder W.H. Camp moved to this area near Spring Creek. A post office was established for the town of Afra, which was later renamed Camp Springs; the water source made this one of the first settlements in the area. Pictured here are early residents of Camp Springs, which eventually grew to a population of 50 around 1920.

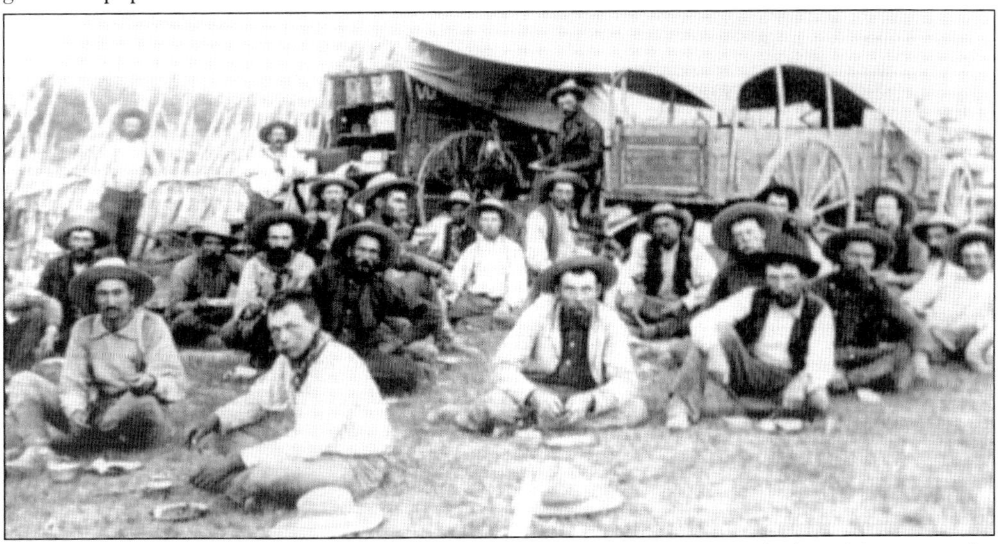

This 1877 photograph was taken when Jim Neighbors drove 3,500 cattle from Mexico to the Panhandle. Here, the drivers have stopped for chuck and rest. Note the temporary corral behind the chuck wagon. Harry Clark is in the left foreground (with his hat on the ground), and Jim Neighbors is in the center foreground. (Amarillo Public Library.)

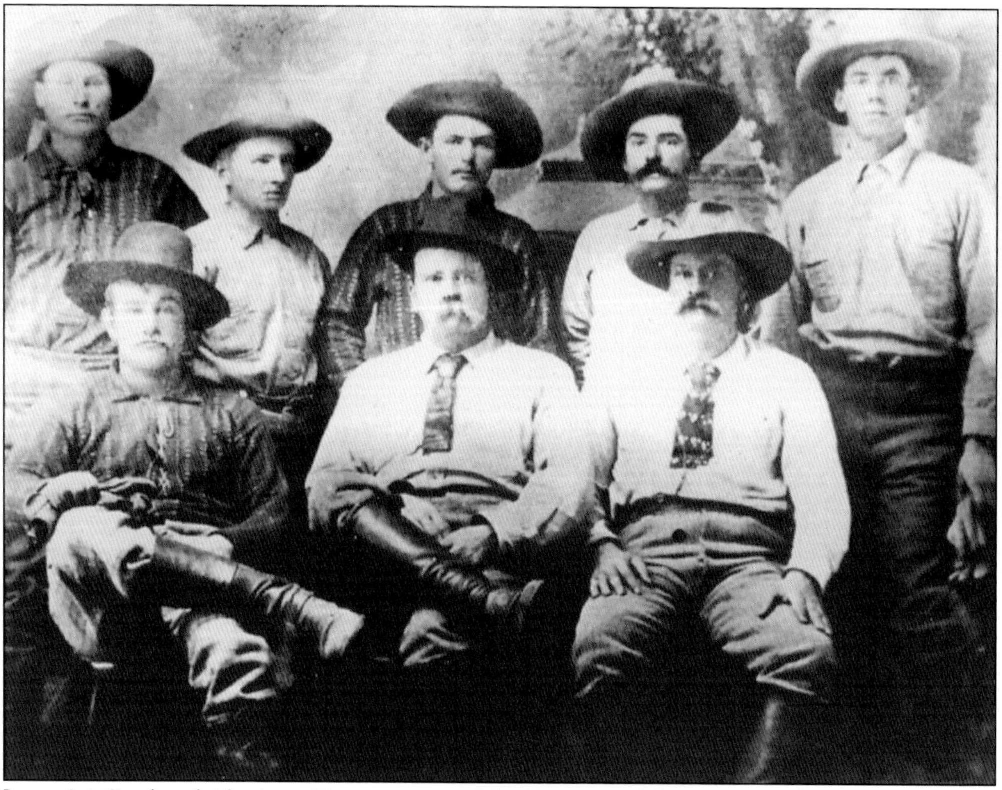

James McCord and Abraham Nave, owners of the Square and Compass ranch, were not present for this photograph of the ranch workers. The *Borden Citizen* newsletter of June 1971 displayed this image and named the cowboys as follows, from left to right: (first row) ? Dennison, J.D. Mitchell, and Jim Mitchell; (second row) ? Pressley, ? Whatley, Frank Crossland, Austin Bouchier, and Jim Weatherford. The Mitchells, who were brothers, later became ranchers in the upper Panhandle. (Garza County Historical Museum.)

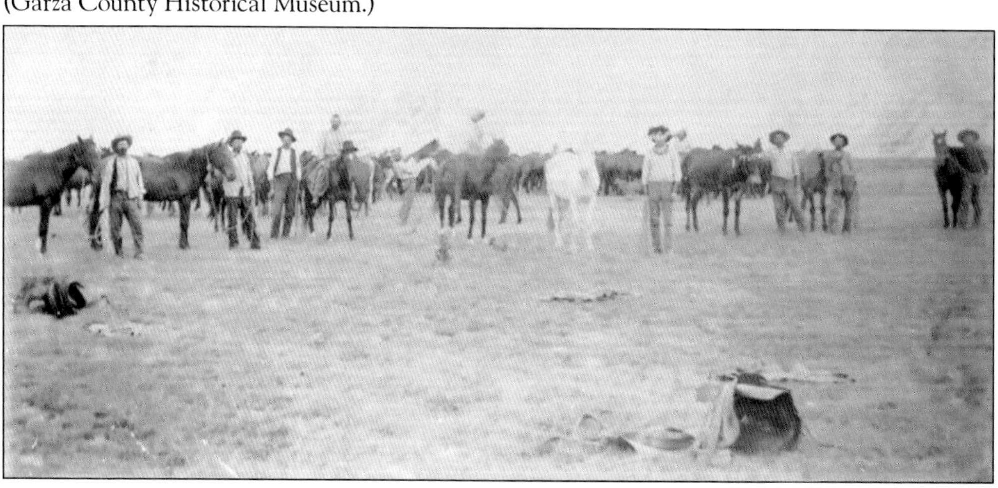

The Magnolia MK Ranch was one of the largest in Borden County. The cowboys shown here are on a trail drive. Wagon boss Jack Rogers is at far left. The unidentified cowboy fourth from the left decided to loan his hat to his horse. Cowboys were notorious for playing practical jokes such as placing a rattlesnake in someone's bedroll. (Borden County Museum.)

The only man identified in this photograph is James Henry Lundy (first row, center). Lundy was a cowboy for the Bar L Ranch in Scurry County in the 1880s. He named his son Earl after a good friend, who may be the man seated to his right. This photograph was probably taken in Dodge City, Kansas, at the end of a trail drive around 1885. (Jan Lundy.)

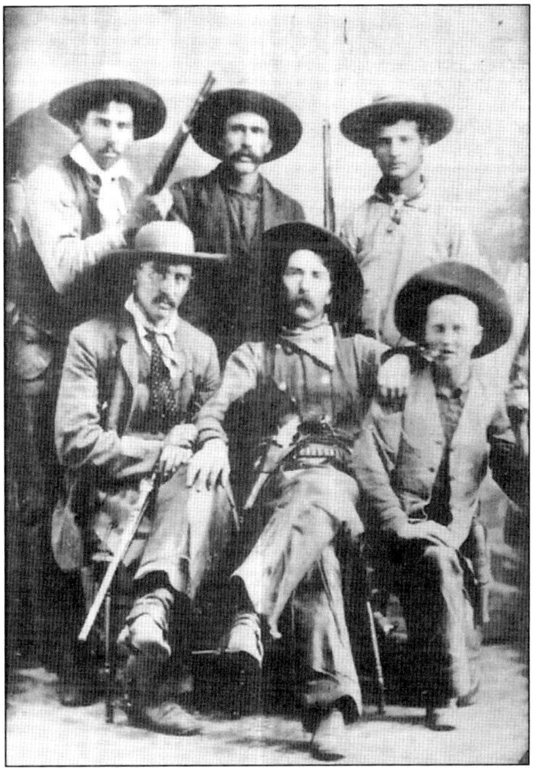

Major Willa V. Johnson established a number of ranches on the Panhandle Plains and was a ranching associate of Col. Ranald Mackenzie. Johnson had already formed the Kentucky Cattle Company and the Two Buckle Ranch in Crosby County when, in 1883, he formed the Magnolia MK Ranch a few miles east of Gail. It was one of the largest ranches on the Plains, with some 500 sections located mostly in Borden County. Johnson's headquarters were in Louisville, Kentucky. He is buried with his wife, Lilly, in Colorado City, Mitchell County.

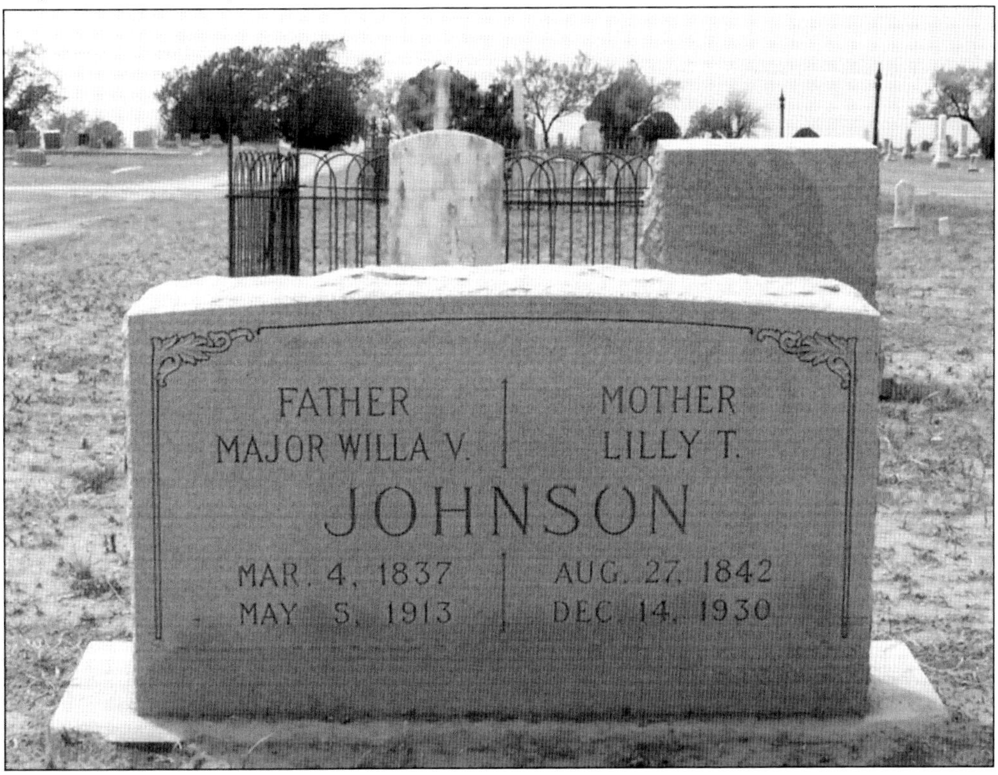

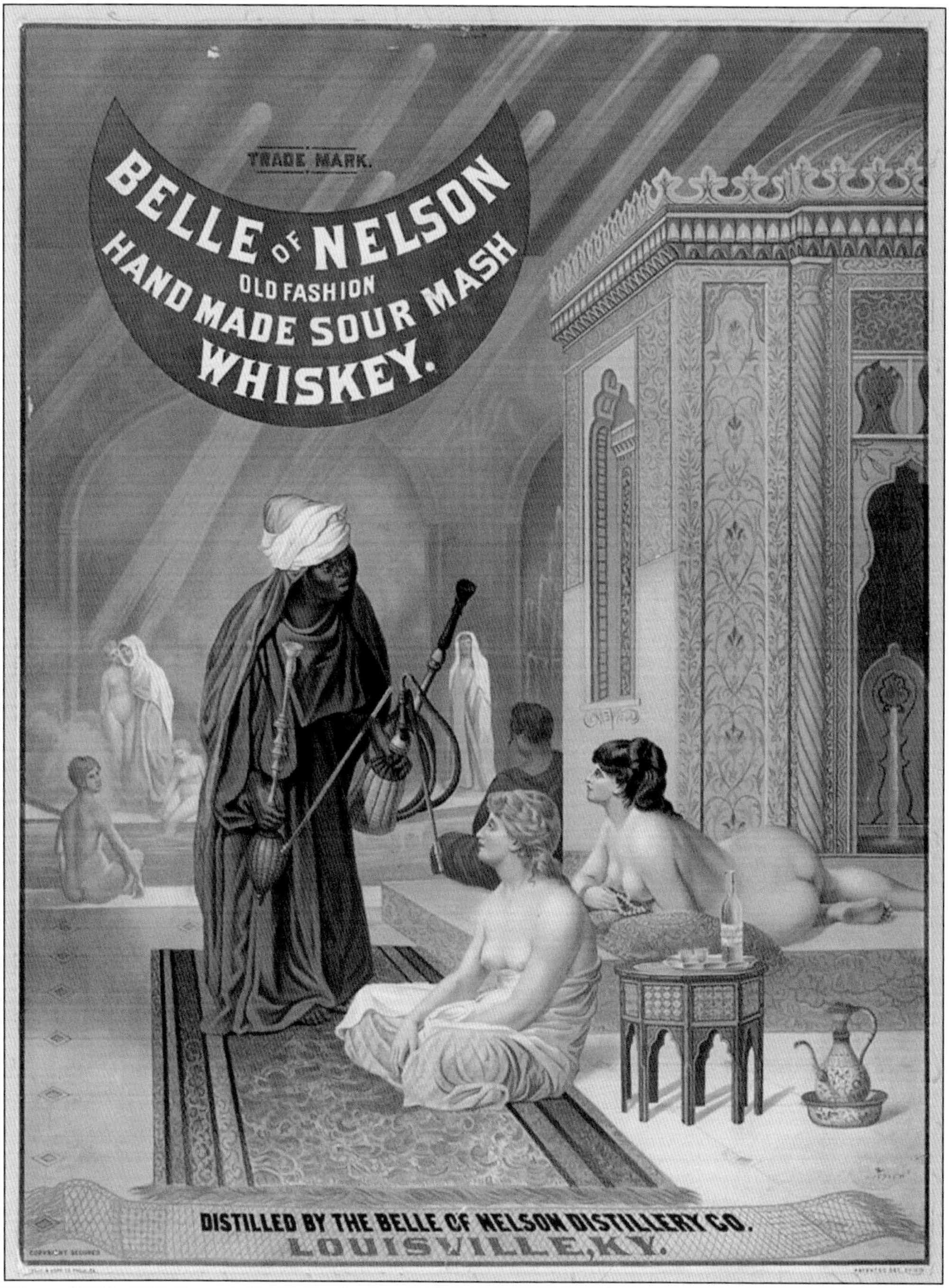

Major Willa V. Johnson had another interest—whiskey. The Belle of Nelson was a Kentucky distillery company founded in 1869. The company distilled the brands 1901, Belle of Nelson Whiskey, and Hill and Hill Bourbon, a 16-year-old bourbon bottled by American Medicinal Spirits Corporation. The Belle of Nelson distillery was owned by Bartley, Johnson & Co. (Library of Congress.)

Three

The End of the Open Range

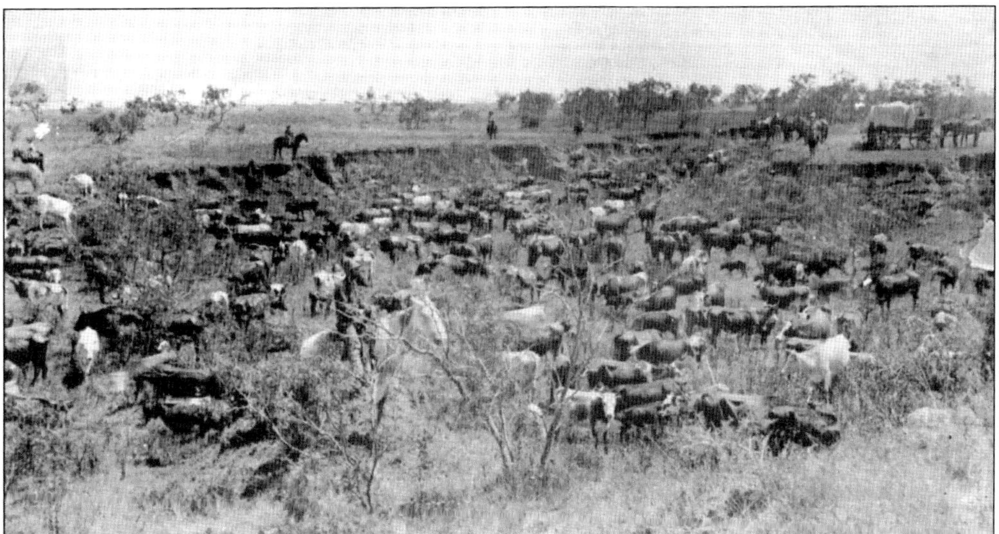

Part of the attraction of the Panhandle Plains was the free and open range. It enabled men to take chances without substantial financial investments, and many of the ranchers who arrived early became very wealthy, securing the land closest to valuable water sources for themselves. Richard Miller came out of Alabama and settled in Borden County before 1900. He was a major rancher in Borden and Garza Counties. In this photograph, a large herd of cattle grazes on the Miller ranch. The men on horses are, from left to right, Homer, Clyde, Ed, and Bill. Standing in front of the wagon are Richard's wife, Alice, and the Miller children, Lillie and Charles. Richard Miller is in the arroyo with his cattle. (SCM.)

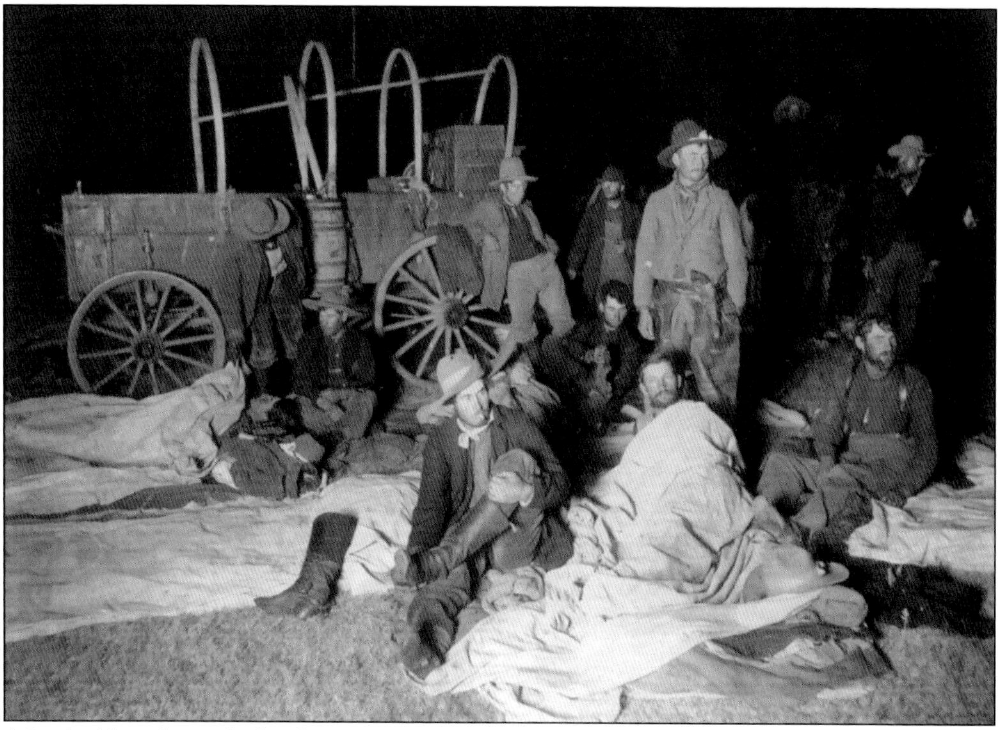

After bedding down the herd on a trail drive, these cowboys ready for bed, placing their bedrolls close together. One cowboy is already asleep, and guards are being selected to ride herd during the night. Although fictional accounts imply that all cowboys were gunfighters, only one of these men appears to have a pistol. (Cattle Raisers Museum.)

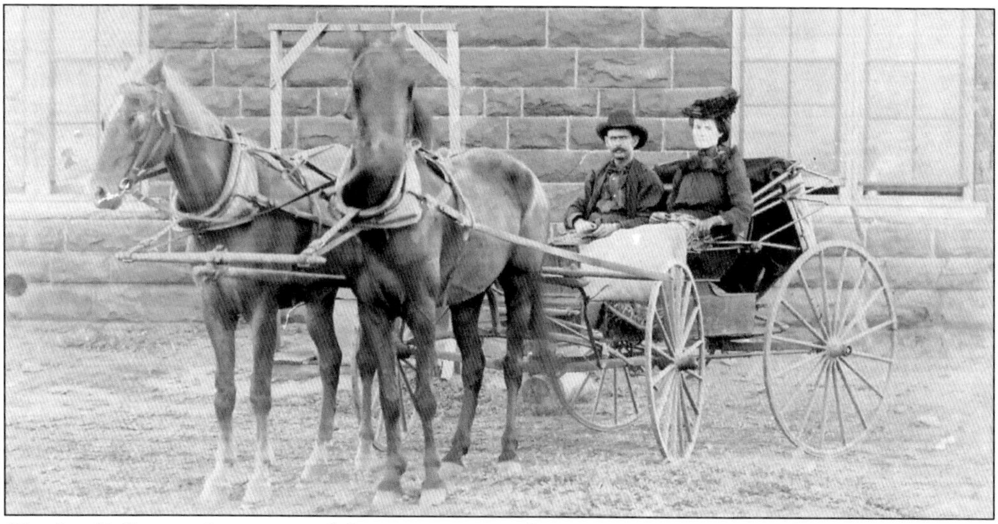

Charles O. Fox made many trail drives as a young boy. He recalled making $10 a month on his first drive, on which he served as "wood hoodlum." The next year, he went up the trail as the horse wrangler for $15 a month, with free grub and the open prairie for a bed. In later years, he became a livery stable owner, mail contractor, and even tried his hand at gold mining at Cripple Creek, Colorado. Here, he and his wife, Fannie Hardin Fox, sit in a buggy pulled by a handsome pair of horses. (Don M. Jay Collection, SCM.)

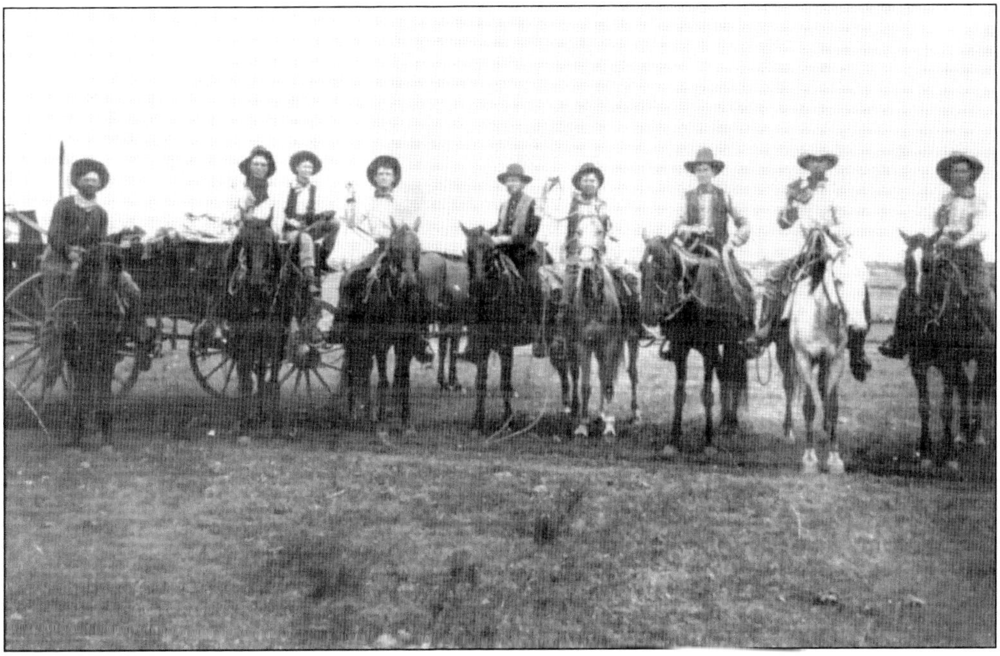

These OB Ranch cowboys are returning from a 175-mile trail drive to the Red Lower Camp and heading back to headquarters in Borden County. Pictured here are, from left to right, Tom Benton, Lee Wooten, Jim Jolly (cook), Walter Jolly, Bud Boren (trail boss), Homer Miller, Will Ware, Charley S. Brown, and Tom Smith. The photograph was taken on June 26, 1906, at Tahoka in Lynn County, Texas.

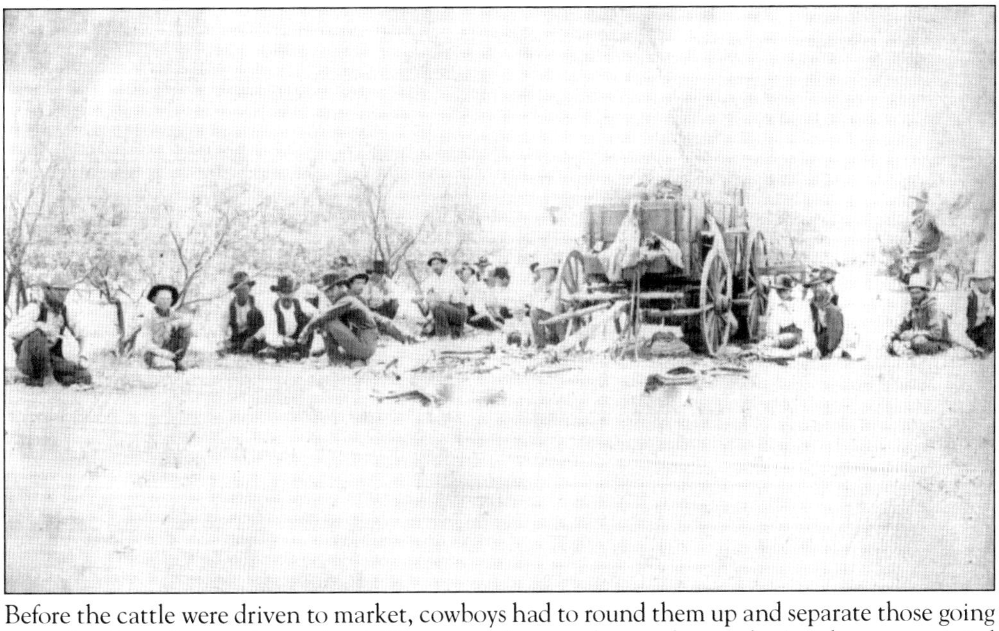

Before the cattle were driven to market, cowboys had to round them up and separate those going to market from those to be retained. The wagon boss made sure the rancher's orders were carried out. After the roundup, the trail boss took charge of the herd and assigned a crew to trail them to market. This group of unidentified cowboys was working a roundup for the "24" Ranch. (Don M. Jay Collection, SCM.)

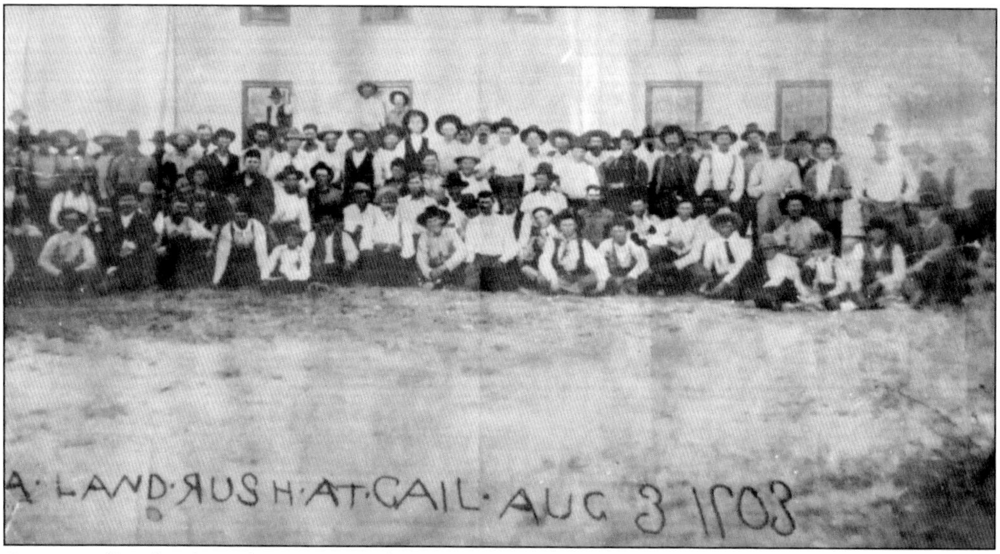

A group of land rush settlers is pictured in August 1903 at Gail (Borden County) in this photograph. In the early years of settlement, ranchers preferred the open range, without fences or other boundaries, and disliked farmers taking over grazing land. Farmers were sometimes called by the derogatory name "nesters" by ranchers, who took offense to Texas's four-section homestead law passed in the 1880s. In Borden County and elsewhere, fights between ranchers and farmers were common, with initial settlers attempting to drive the newcomers away. There were two factions: the cowboys, representing the ranchers, wearing blue armbands, and the homesteaders (pictured above), wearing red armbands. The homesteaders eventually got their land, but a lack of rain soon sent them packing. (Borden County Historical Museum.)

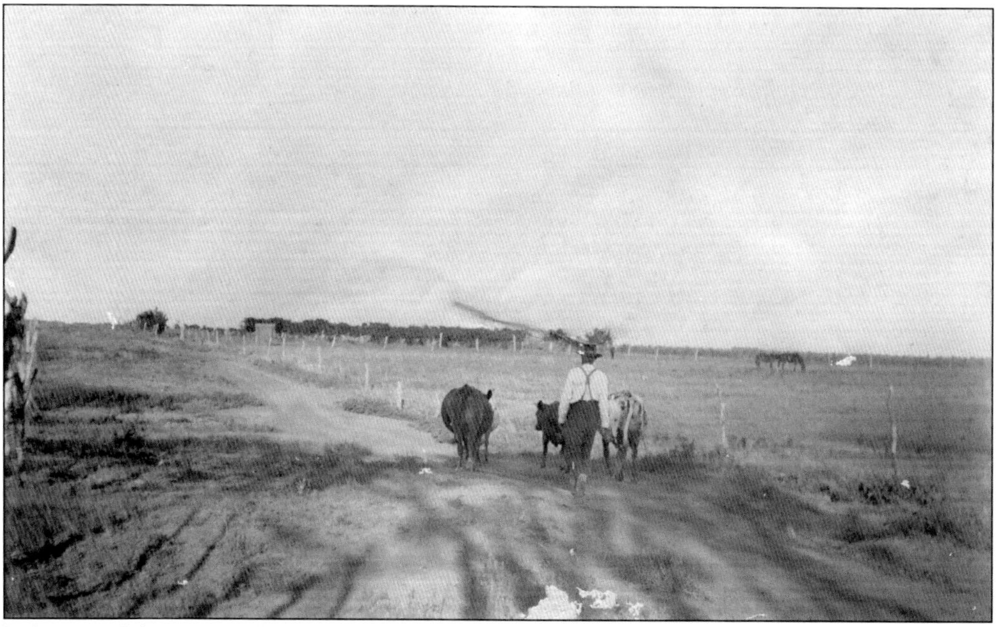

Relatives of the Nation family, who settled in Scurry County, lived in Cache, Oklahoma, and sent this postcard, which shows their family farm, in 1909. Hundreds of miles separated the two families, but the Great Plains looks much the same from the Dakotas south to Texas. (SCM.)

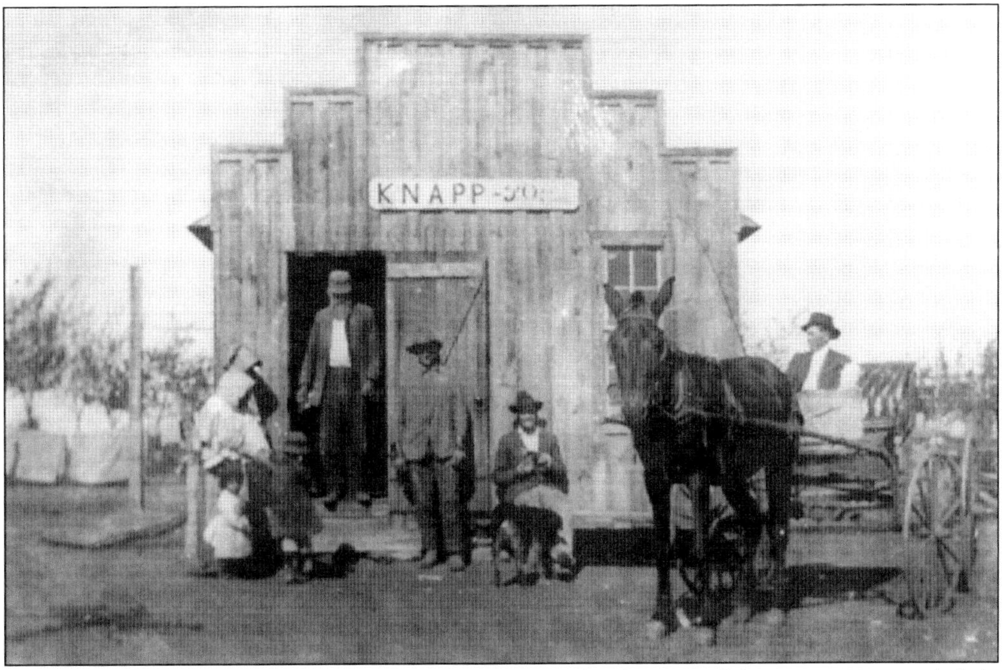

In this 1890 photograph, Herman Von Roeder stands in the doorway of the store at Knapp. At left, nearest to the store door, is Mrs. Herman Von Roeder. Standing in front of her is an unidentified Mexican woman and her little girl. To the right of the doorway are Sam Bruce, Rover (dog), and C.N. Von Roeder (sitting). In the buggy is Clyde Willis, from Durham. Willis carried the mail from Ira to Durham, meeting the carrier from Colorado City every day; Willis's yearly holiday was either July 4 or December 25. Page 108 of this book contain an image of this store as it looked 60 years later. (SCM.)

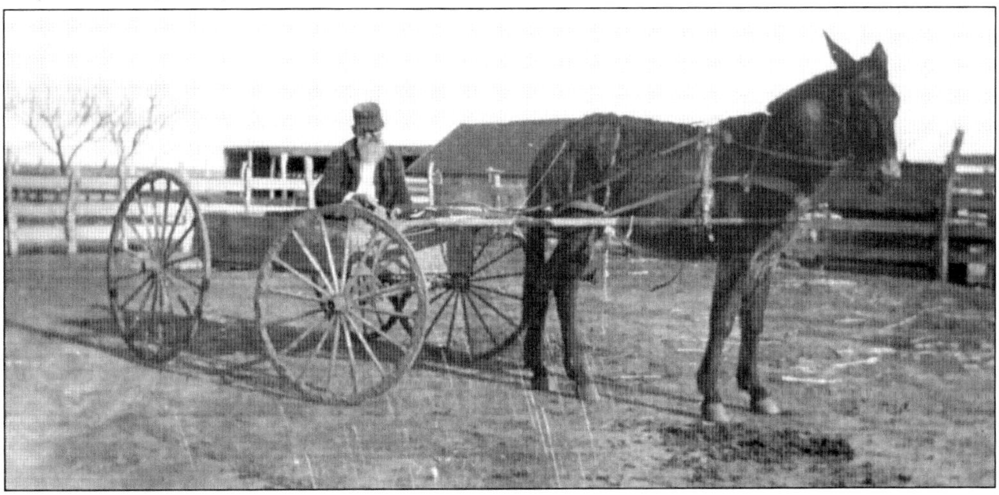

Rather than giving up when his early cotton crops were destroyed, Clemens Von Roeder began breeding tougher cotton. By 1923, he was producing a long staple, big boll cotton and had introduced strains that resisted hail, windstorms, and rust; this cotton, still grown today, is known as Western Stormproof. In this photograph, Herman Von Roeder is at work on the family farm 15 miles west of Snyder. Like many others who settled in West Texas, Herman was a Confederate veteran. (SCM.)

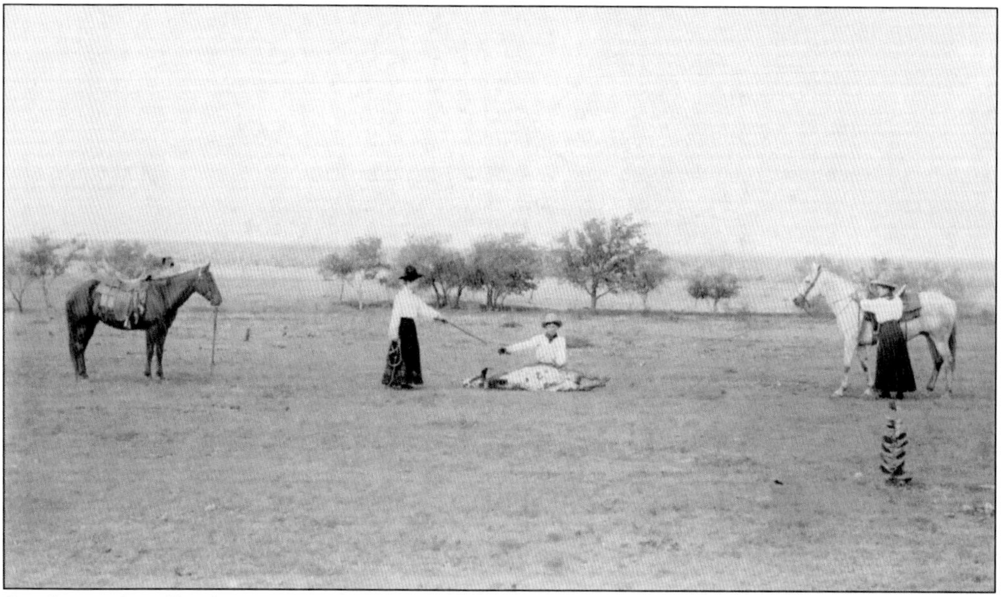

On the Panhandle Plains, a woman's work was never done. At left is Martha Hardin, cousin of the gunfighter John Wesley Hardin. She has heeled a calf and is holding the branding iron. Nonnie Rodgers, son of the famous Texas Ranger, Norman Rodgers, is holding the calf while his sister Jettie (right) keeps the rope taut. (Southwest Collection, Texas Tech University.)

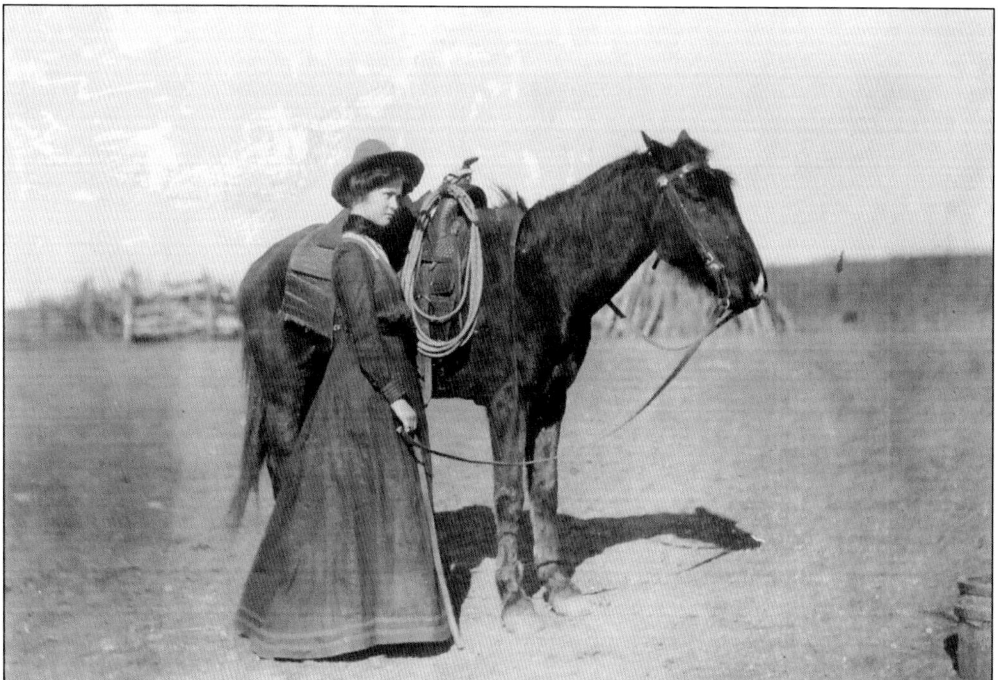

Like all of her sisters, Fannie Hardin Fox was a hardworking cowgirl. During a time when there were few women in West Texas, the Hardin girls worked wherever they were needed whether on the ranch or in the home. Sidesaddles would not do for these active ladies. (Don M. Jay Collection, SCM.)

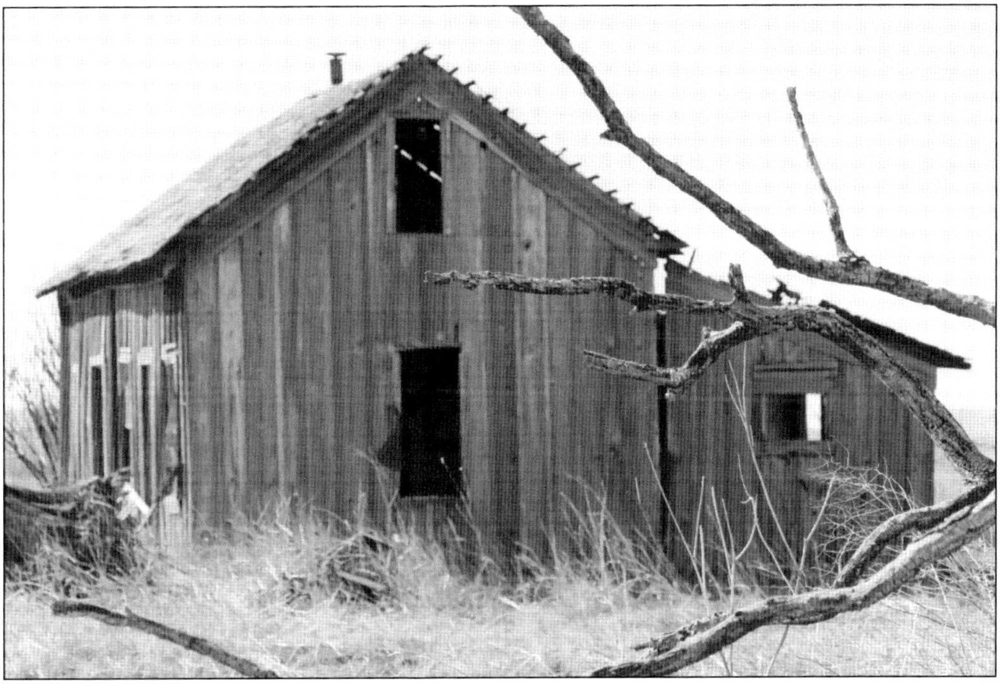

This old homestead still stands in southern Garza County on land owned by the descendants of "Bud" Boren, who built the house in 1902 with lumber he hauled from Colorado City, Texas. As he started building with the first wagonload, his brothers went to Roscoe in Nolan County and returned with a second load of lumber.

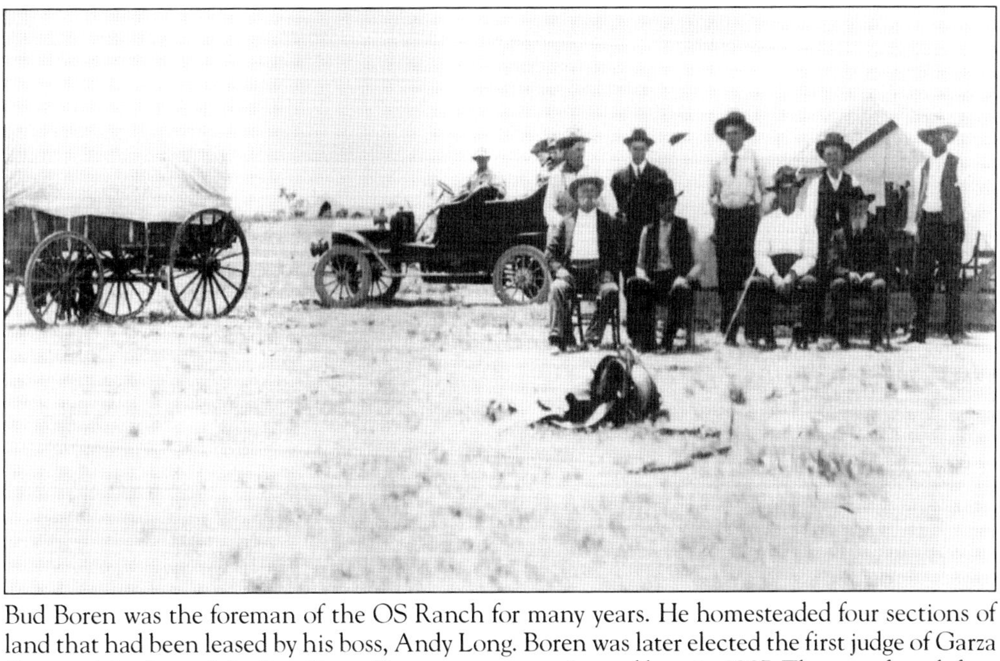

Bud Boren was the foreman of the OS Ranch for many years. He homesteaded four sections of land that had been leased by his boss, Andy Long. Boren was later elected the first judge of Garza County. Members of the first Garza County court are pictured here in 1907. They are, from left to right, (first row) S.C. Wilkes, L.F. Barrow, Walter Roy, and ? Davis; (second row) W.E. Alexander, Hal Murrey, Bud Boren, B.F. Wilkes, and Oscar Kelly.

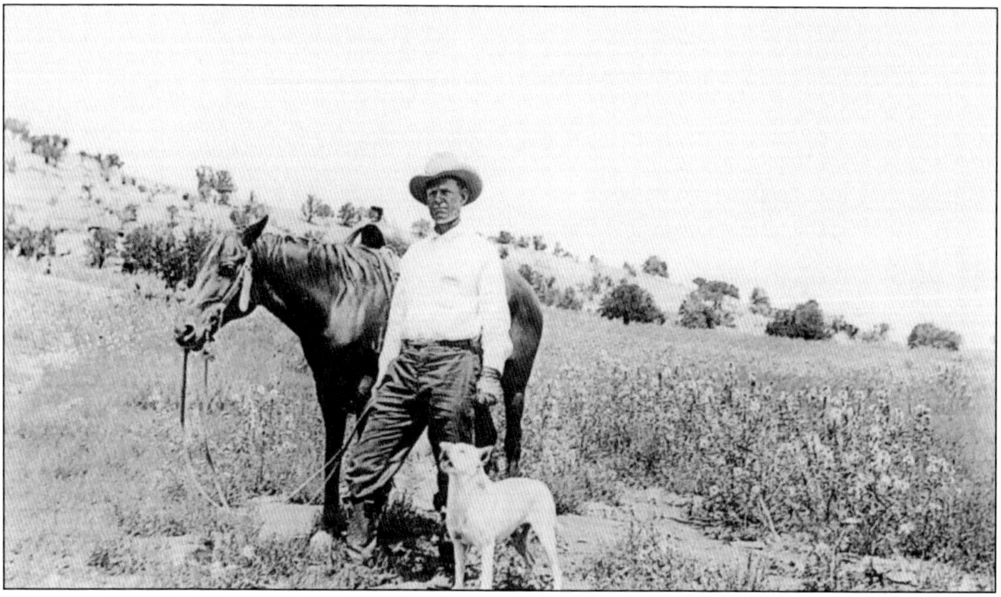

Many cowboys had dogs to help them herd cattle. Here, Henry Elkins stands beside his favorite cutting horse and his dog, Booger Red—the unusual name appears often in West Texas. It originated as a nickname for Samuel Thomas Privett Jr., a famous bronco rider who established the SP Ranch in Erath County and, by the age of 12, had begun his career breaking horses. More than a few dogs and horses were named for him, most of which had reputations of being especially ugly or tough.

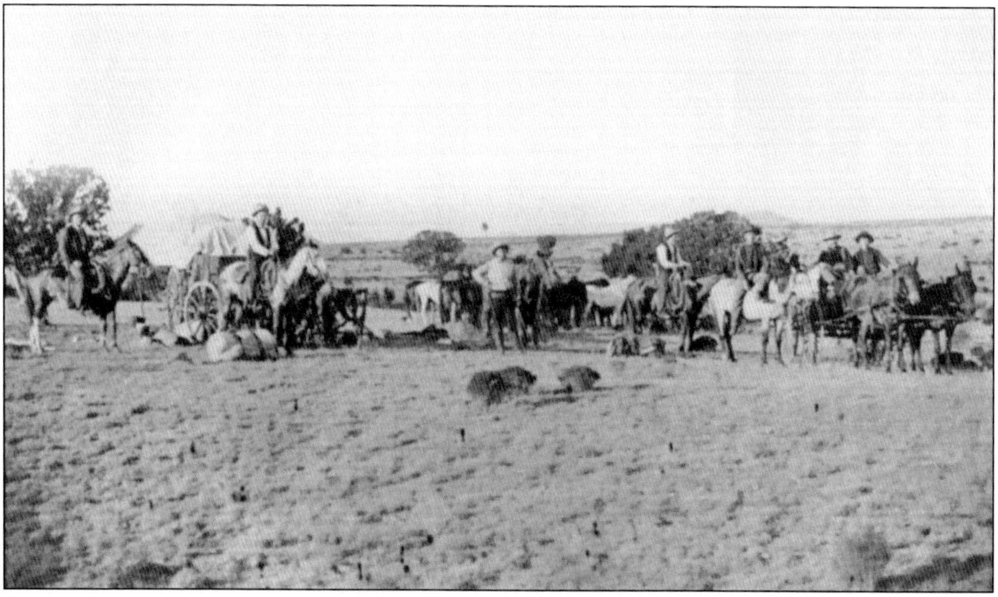

W.C. Bishop and George N. Fletcher established the "0-T-0" Ranch around 1887 on Fletcher's range in Dawson County. The ranch consisted of 200,000 acres. These cowboys are setting up a roundup camp and have gathered about 12,000 cattle. Pictured here are, from left to right, Gip Akins, Charlie Nivvins, Eldridge Ingle (of Ensley—now Birmingham, Alabama), Paul Dalmont, V.P. Baker, Eulis Dalmont, Harry Morgan, B.A. "Bill" Oden (foreman), and other unidentified men. (University of Texas at Arlington Library.)

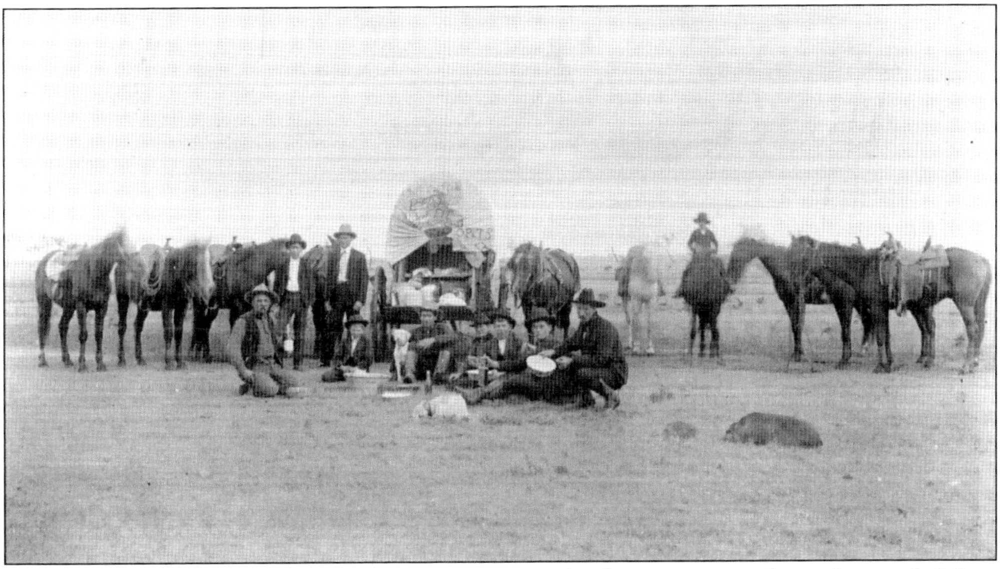

Bill Pitts was a stock farmer in Scurry County. During the dry seasons, ranchers often trailed their cattle to better ranges in Mexico, New Mexico, and Wyoming. Pitts is pictured here kneeling at left. He is wearing a pistol and holding a quart of whiskey in his left hand. The words "Bill Pitts outfit, N.M. [New Mexico] or bust" are written on the wagon canvas, along with a "Spade" brand. (SCM.)

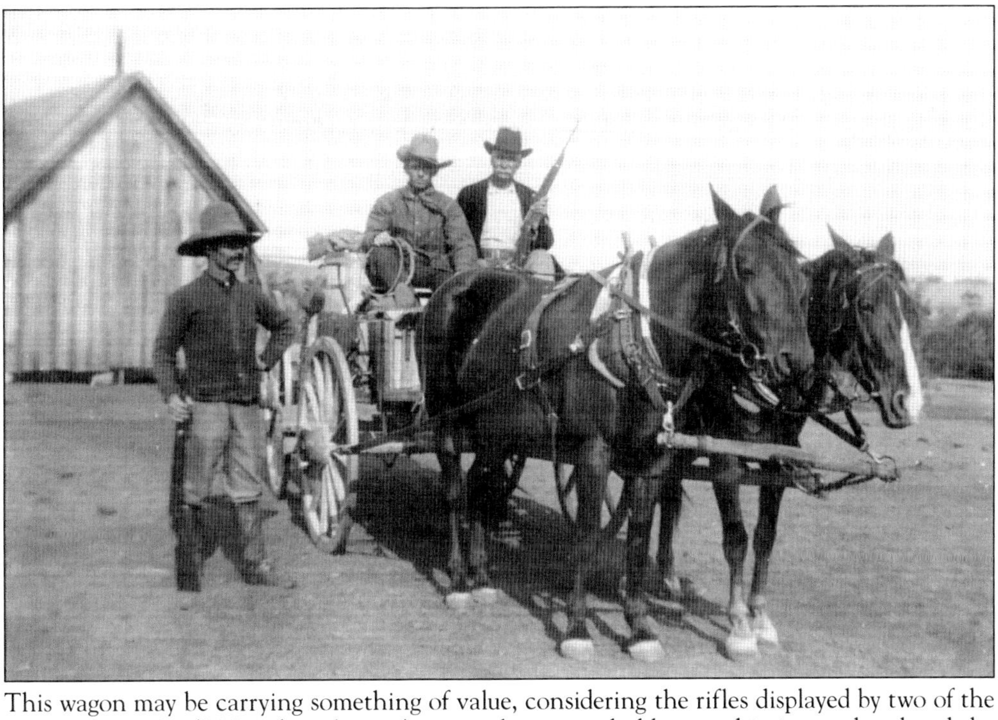

This wagon may be carrying something of value, considering the rifles displayed by two of the men. Marion "Red" Hamilton (center) sits in the wagon holding a whip in one hand and the reins in the other. The man sitting next to him is believed to be his brother-in-law Bill Nichols. The man at left, also holding a rifle, is Marion's older brother Ben Hamilton. Ben was a stock farmer in Scurry County. (SCM.)

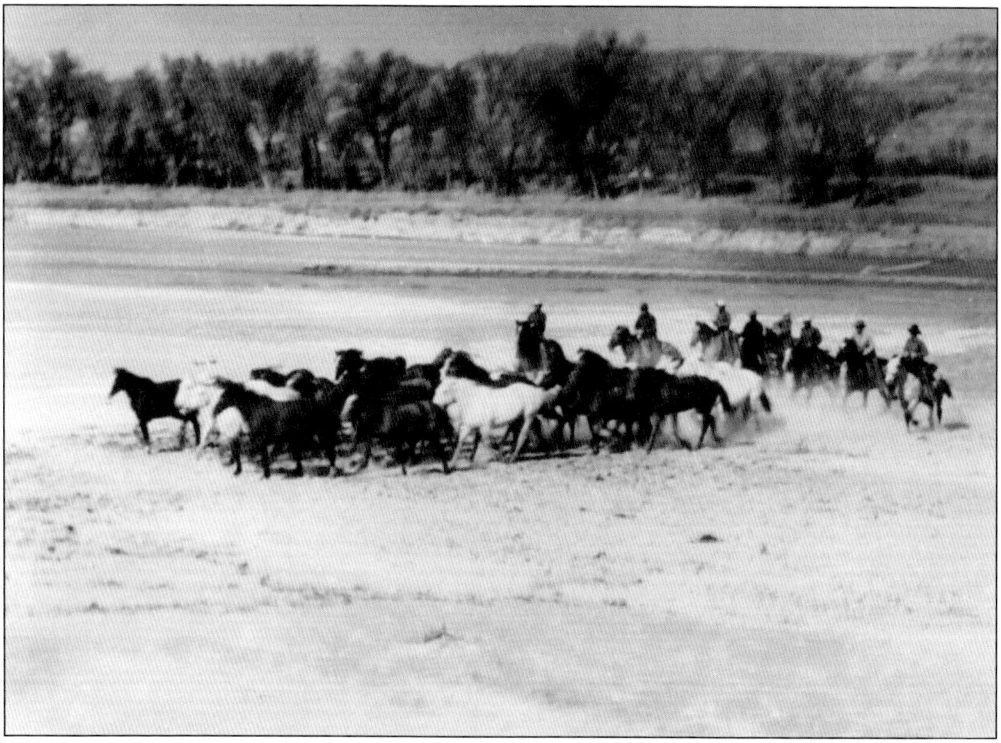

The first wild horses in the Americas were of Spanish stock, having been brought by the conquistadores. Like the Native Americans, early ranchers rounded up mustangs (from the Spanish *mesteño*, meaning "stray"). These cowboys are driving a herd of wild horses toward a home range to be corralled, branded, and saddle-broken. (Cattle Raisers Museum.)

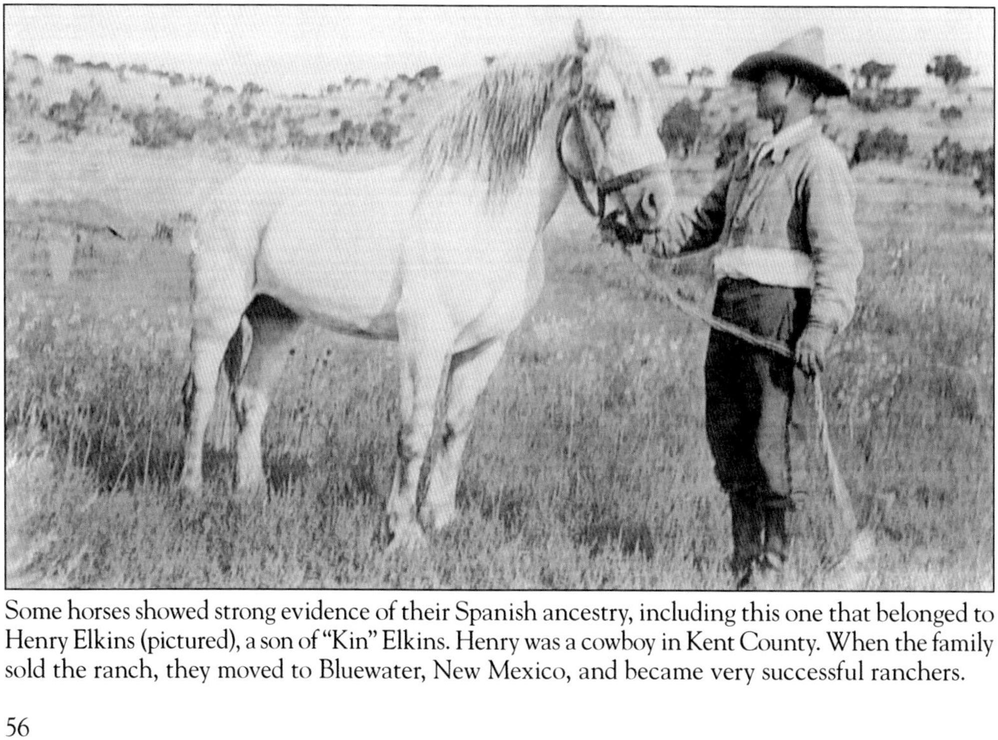

Some horses showed strong evidence of their Spanish ancestry, including this one that belonged to Henry Elkins (pictured), a son of "Kin" Elkins. Henry was a cowboy in Kent County. When the family sold the ranch, they moved to Bluewater, New Mexico, and became very successful ranchers.

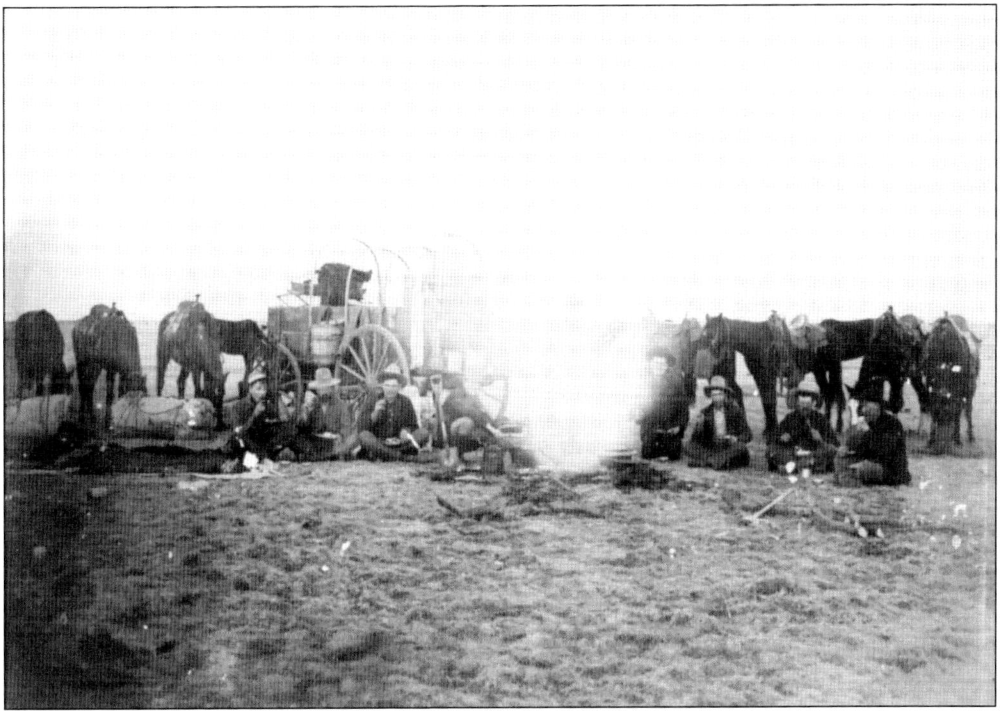

These cowboys are having chuck during a "24" range roundup in Kent County. The fire is still blazing as the cowboys dig in. (SCM.)

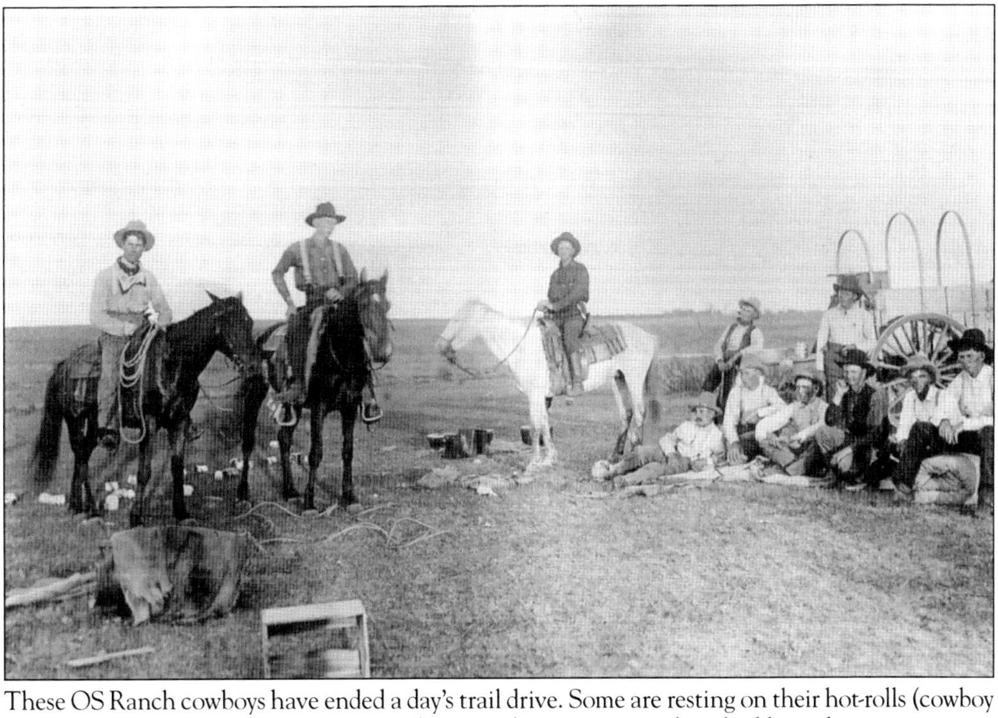

These OS Ranch cowboys have ended a day's trail drive. Some are resting on their hot-rolls (cowboy slang for bedroll) at the chuck wagon. The camp host appears to be a bad housekeeper, as empty cans and other items are scattered around the camp. (Garza County Historical Museum.)

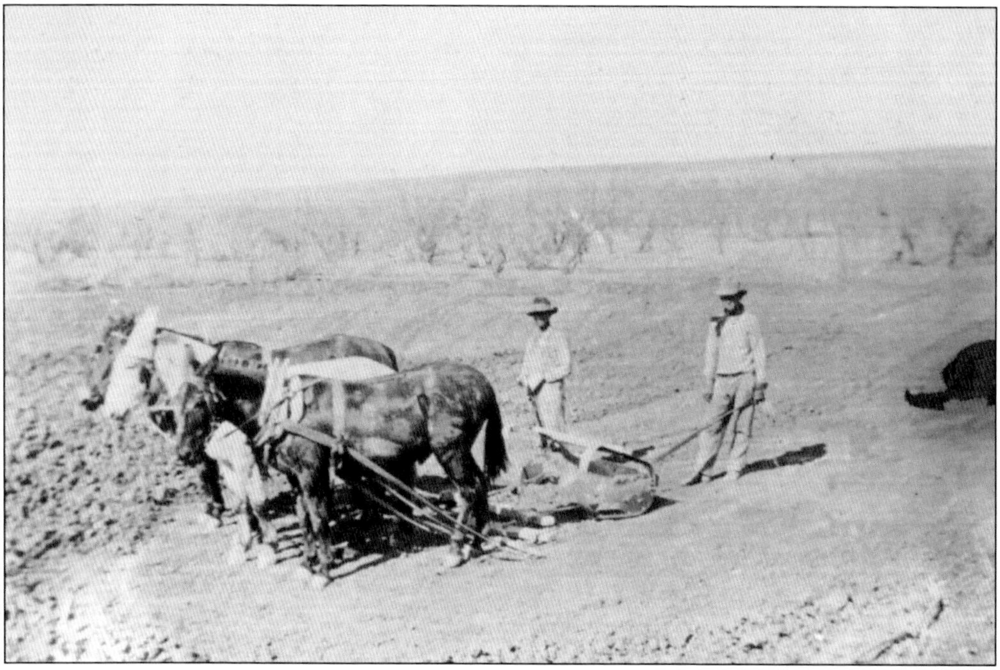

Ranchers needed stock tanks to catch and store rainfall on their range. They learned to build them with a piece of earth-moving equipment called a Fresno Scraper; these men, owners of the York ranch in Borden County, are using one to scoop away topsoil and move it behind them to make a dam. (SCM.)

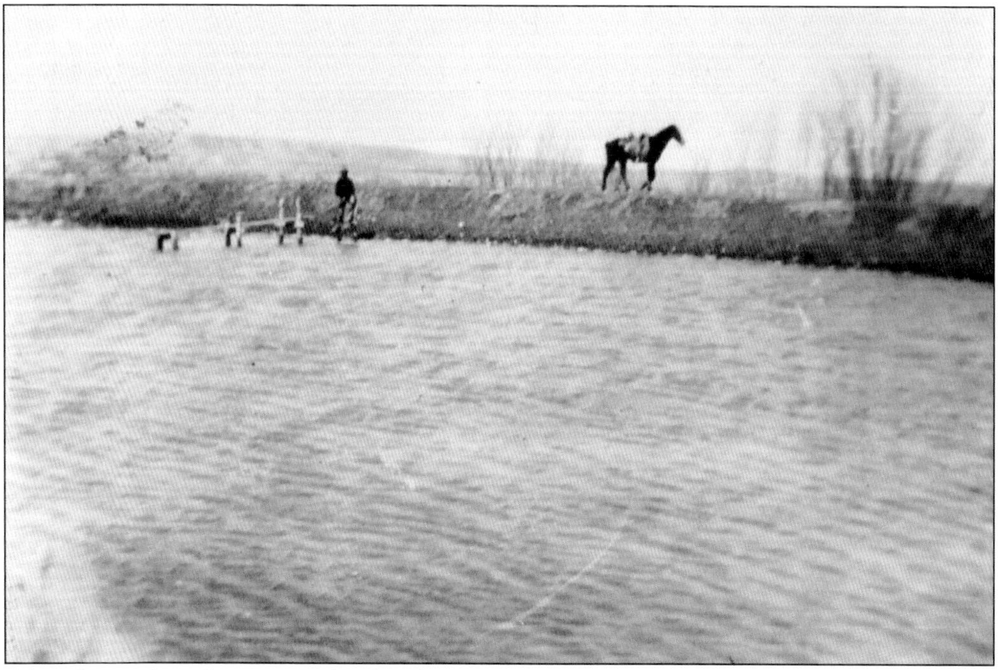

After the stock tank was completed, a few years later, it became a large watering place for the cattle. Here, Joe York has dismounted to take a look at the tank from the wooden dock while his horse walks along the crest of the dam. (SCM.)

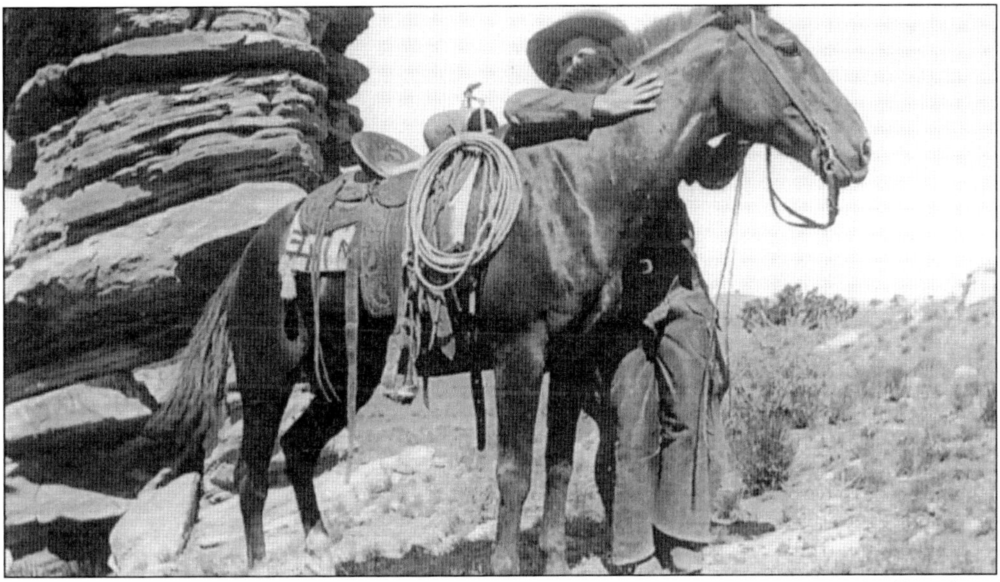

As barbed wire cordoned off ranches, ranchers sometimes had trouble getting thrill-seeking cowboys to do the necessary work. Mark Elkins (pictured) was the youngest son of George Kindred "Kin" Elkins. He grew up in the shadow of Mackenzie Mountain. As a young man, Mark did roundups for the OS Ranch and John Slaughter. He then rode to Crosby County and was hired to fix windmills; along with working on wells, this was a job that many cowboys would not take. Of course, even Mark had his limits; according to his unpublished autobiography (which he wrote in 1971), when he was told to get an axe and start chopping firewood for the winter, he quit and rode off, telling the foreman: "Cowboys don't chop wood."

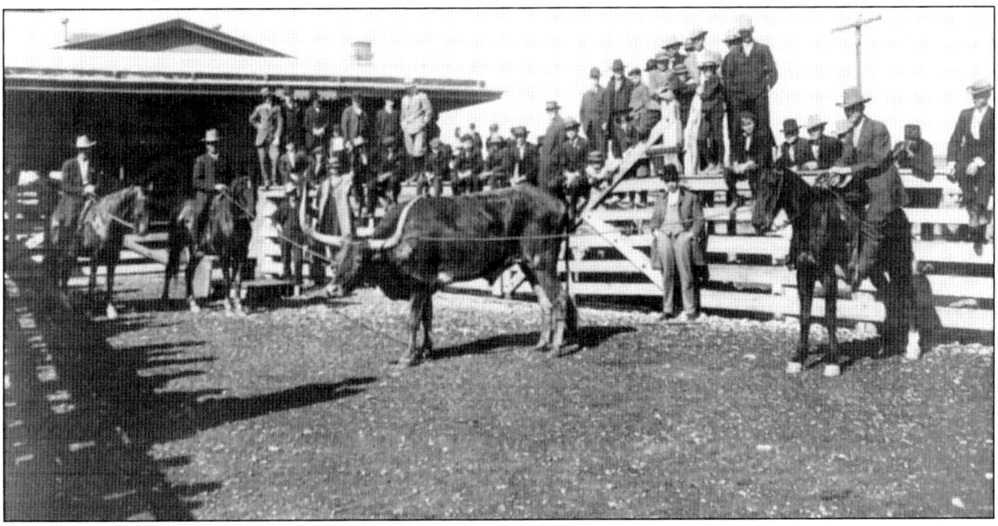

Before the Civil War, the longhorn was virtually the only breed of cattle in Texas. Longhorns are still considered by many to be the iconic Texas steer. The hardy breed could survive on little grazing and water, which made them ideal for long trail drives. Closer railheads made it possible for ranchers to raise new breeds of cattle such as Herefords, which had a greater muscle-to-bone ratio, resulting in more saleable meat. Today, few genuine longhorn cattle still exist. In this c. 1915 image, three cowboys rope a longhorn in the stock pens near Fuller Cotton Mill in Snyder, Scurry County. (SCM.)

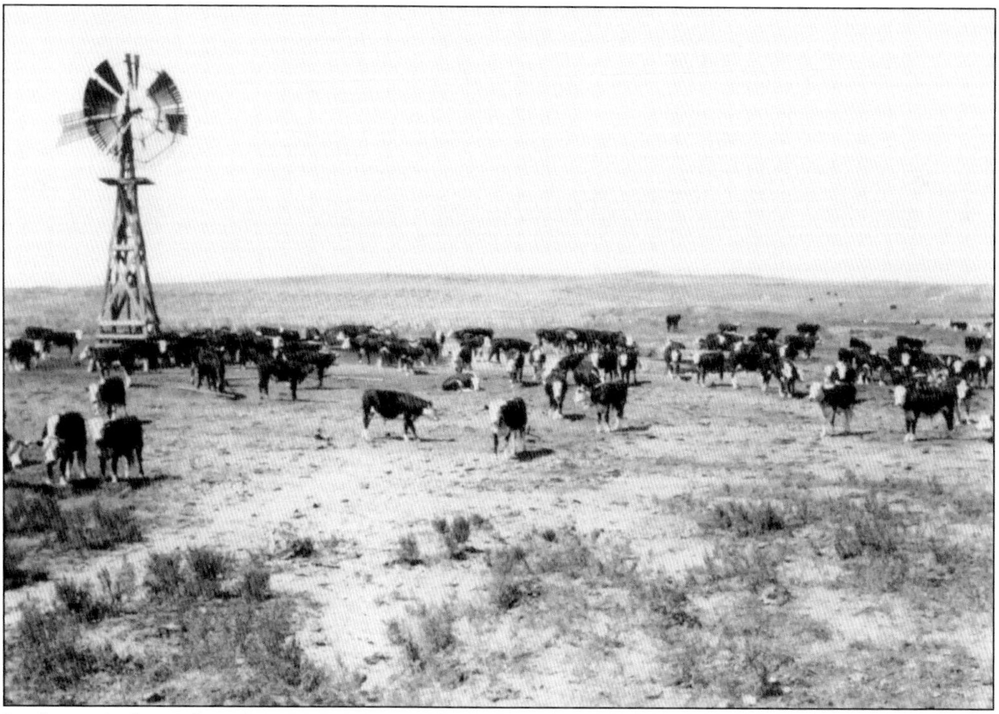

In the early days of settlement, springs and streams were adequate to support the sparsely settled lands. When the water-pumping windmill was introduced to the region in the late 19th century, water became easier to access. This photograph shows cattle drinking near a large wooden windmill. (Cattle Raisers Museum.)

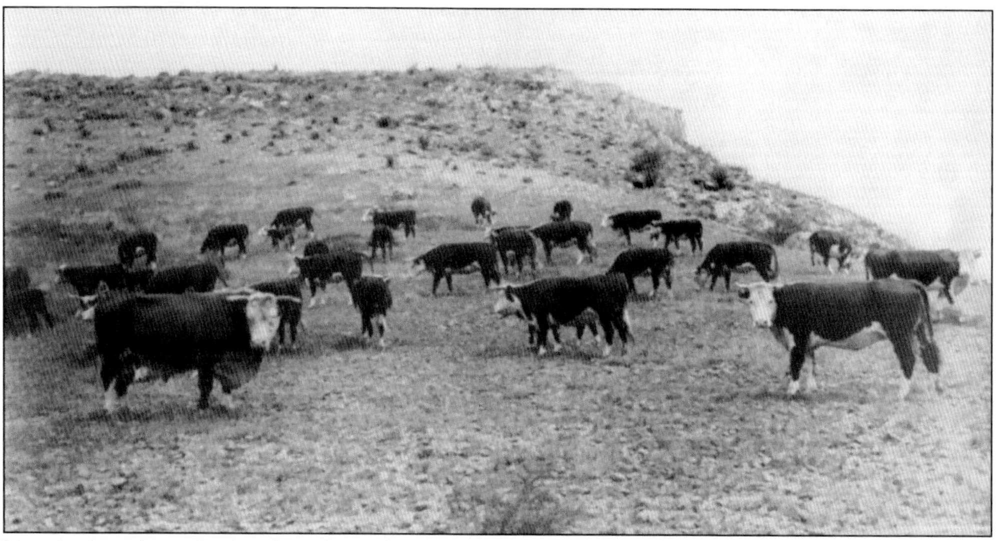

Hereford cattle and other breeds gradually replaced the rugged Texas longhorns as more fences were erected on the plains. As cattle drives became shorter, ranchers could afford to raise animals for the meat they could produce rather than their ability to survive on limited grazing and harsh terrain. These cattle belonged to W.B. Mitchell. (Cattle Raisers Museum.)

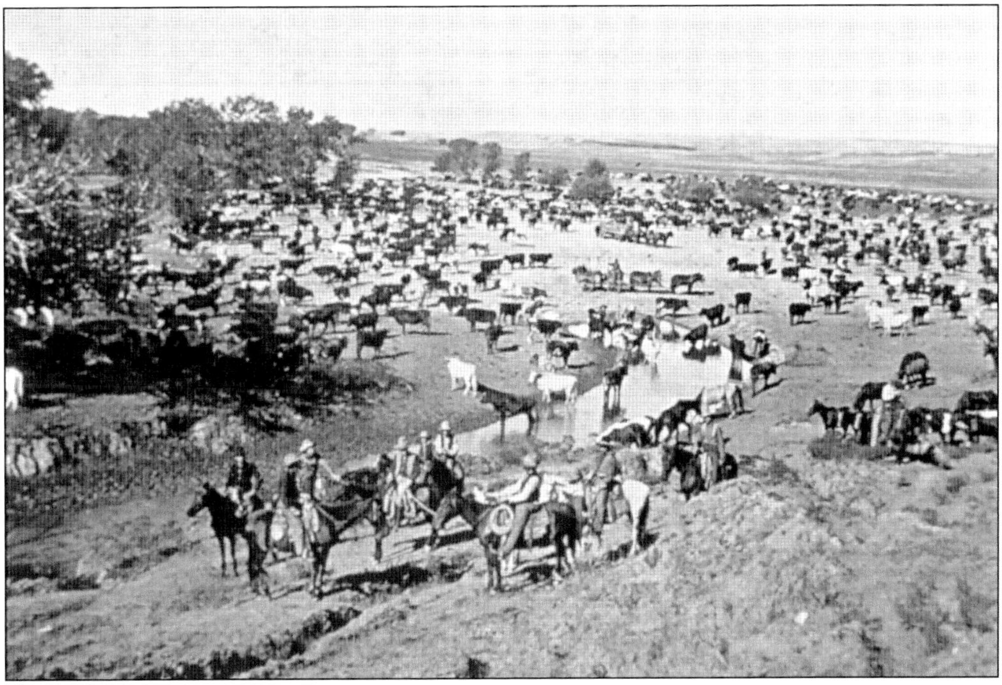

While water was an issue to Panhandle Plains ranchers, it was much more plentiful in the early years. Even so, drought years were more frequent than wet years. Of these OS Ranch cowboys, only "Bud" Boren, the ranch foreman, is identified—he is the fourth man from the left. The cowboys are watering the herd at Green Tank. In later years, a major highway cut through the tank, and someone established a rest stop on the site. (SCM.)

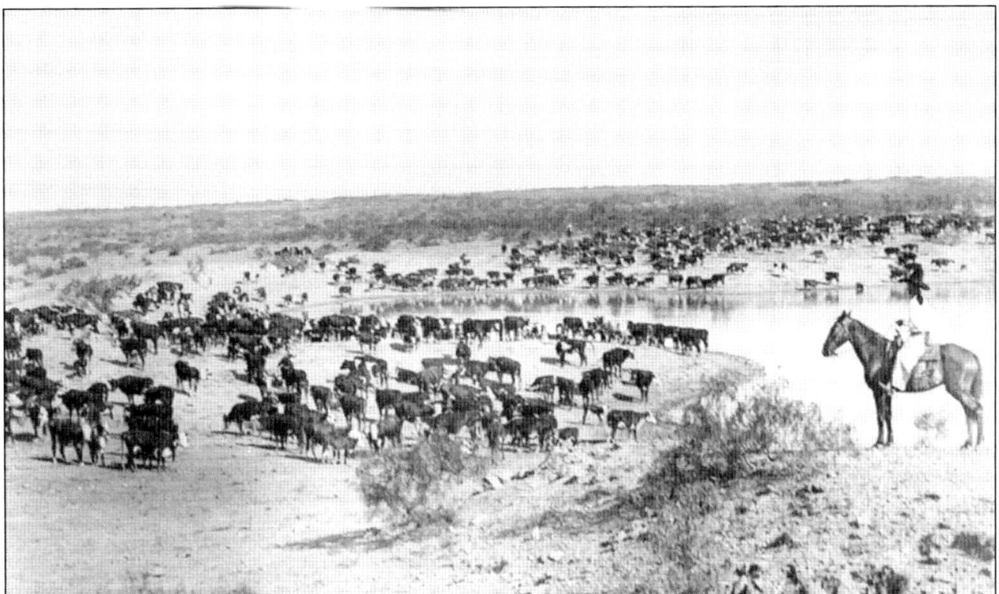

Here, a cowboy waters a large herd of cattle at a stream. The landscape of the Panhandle Plains, which is mostly flat, features natural depressions called playa lakes. These areas retain water during wet years. (Cattle Raisers Museum.)

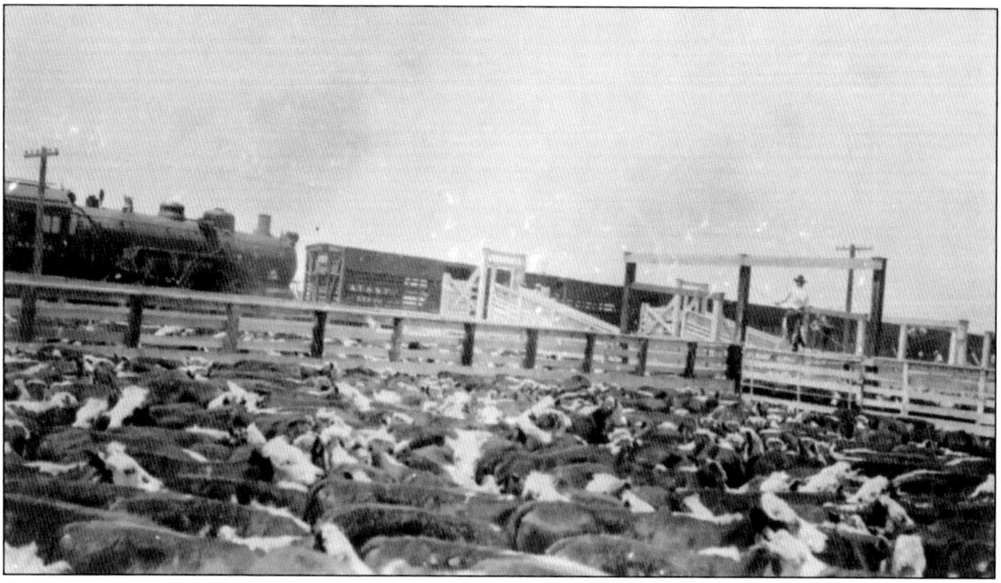

Cattle markets were in the northeastern United States, and the most efficient and economical means to get them there was by rail. Many of the ranchers on the Panhandle Plains drove to the railheads in the new town of Colorado, located to the south in Mitchell County. This herd of Hereford cattle belonged to the Winston family of Scurry County. (SCM.)

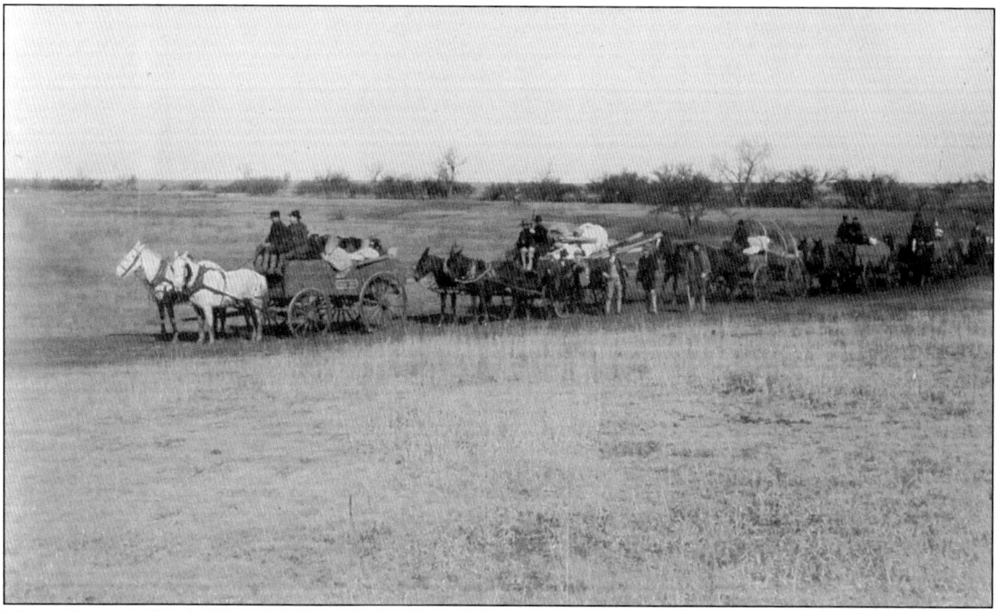

The Chicago, Rock Island & Pacific Railway, which operated from 1852 to 1980, laid tracks in 14 states. In 1887, an act of Congress granted the railroad right-of-way across Indian Territory into North Texas and down to Galveston. Lines also went from Liberal, Kansas, to El Paso, and from Memphis, Tennessee, west into New Mexico Territory. This wagon train, made up of a survey crew, traveled across Arkansas, Oklahoma, and Texas around 1902. When the tracks reached the site a few miles west of Dallas, two of the surveyors dropped their instruments and established the town of Irving. The rest of the crew continued westward. One of them was town cofounder J.O. Schulze. (Charles and Catherine Schulze Collection, Irving, Texas, Public Library.)

Four

Town and Country

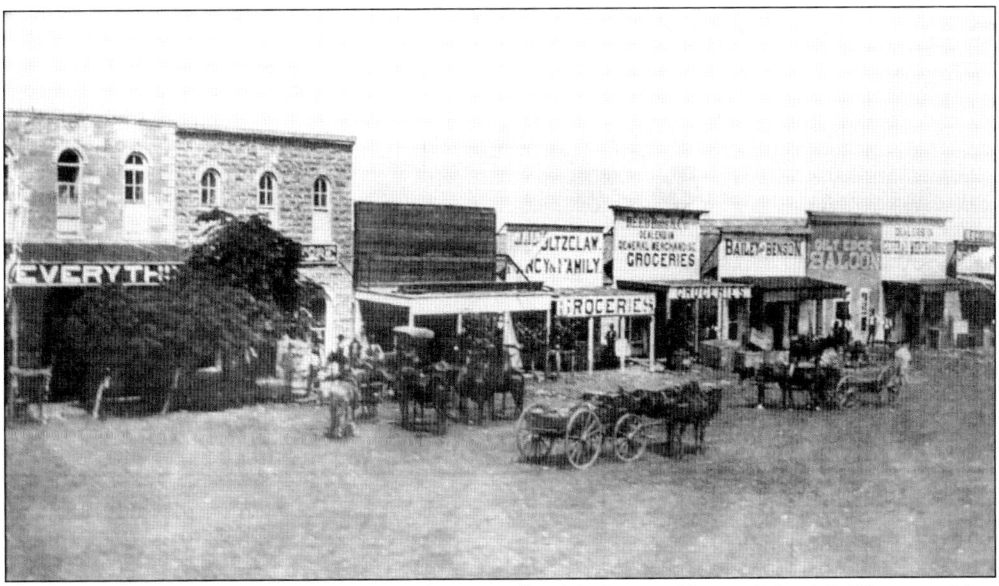

This 1882 image is the earliest known photograph of Coleman, Texas. John M. Elkins and his brother, "Kin," were responsible for taming this wild town during the 1870s. John remained in Coleman County, and Kin moved his family to Kent County in 1881 after his son-in-law Jim Jackson reported the tall grasses of free range. Most of the businesses shown here are mercantile stores, although one imagines that fun could be had at the Gilt Edge saloon. (Ronald Henderson.)

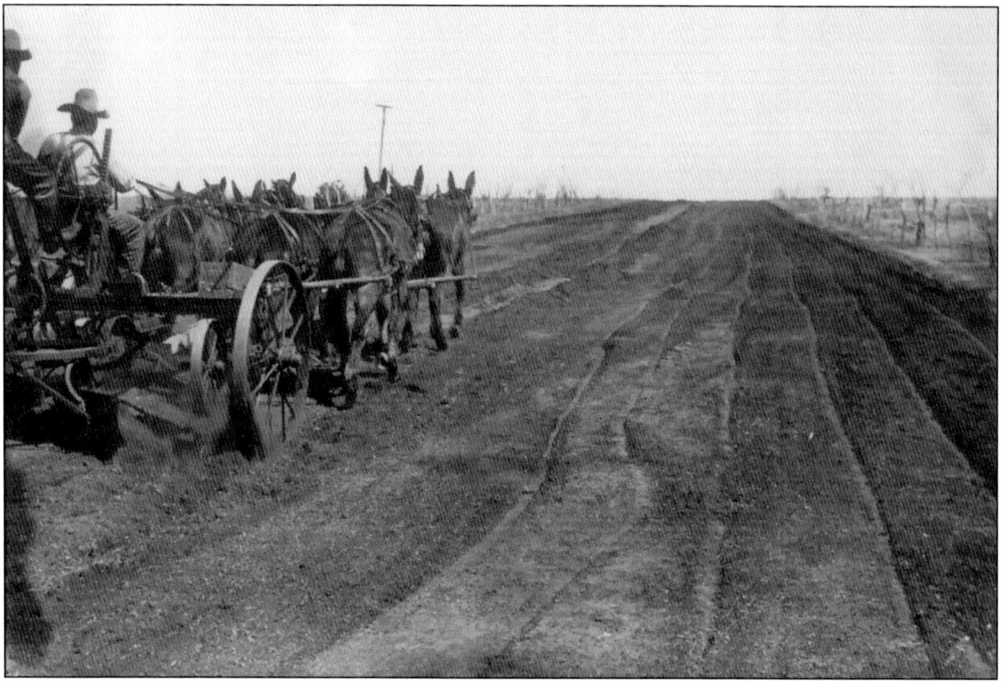

This piece of equipment was used around 1920 as the very first road grader in Kent County. The driver had to handle the eight-mule team pulling the contraption, while another man rode behind him in an elevated seat to control the depth and angle of the blade. (Don M. Jay Collection, SCM.)

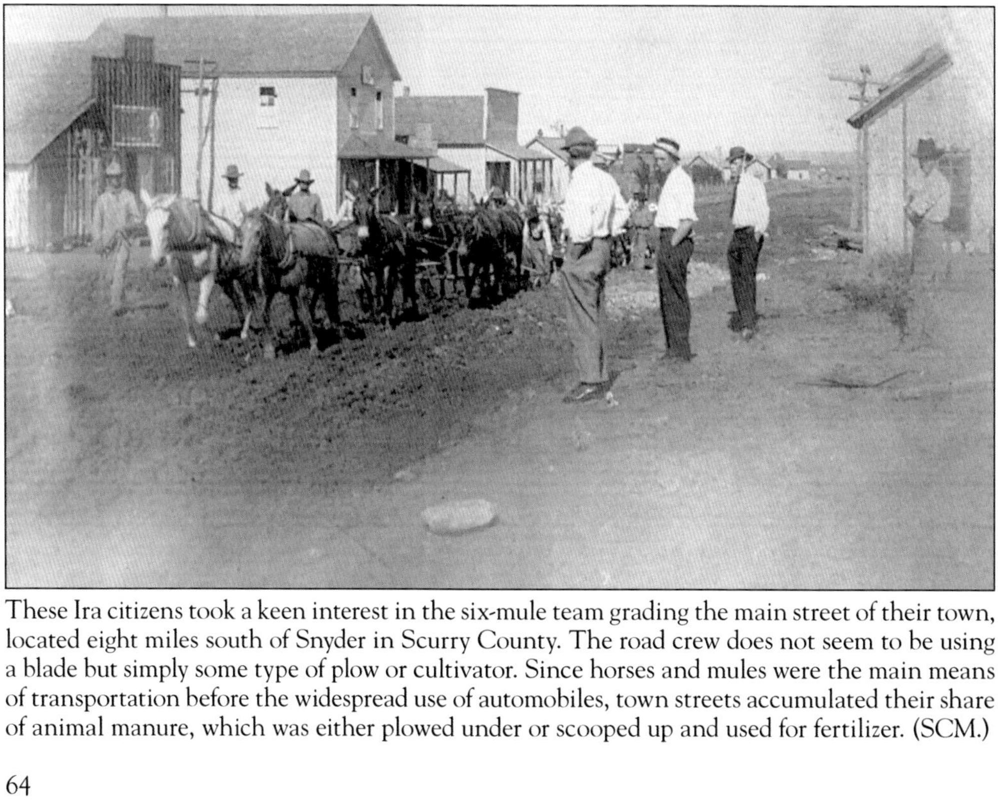

These Ira citizens took a keen interest in the six-mule team grading the main street of their town, located eight miles south of Snyder in Scurry County. The road crew does not seem to be using a blade but simply some type of plow or cultivator. Since horses and mules were the main means of transportation before the widespread use of automobiles, town streets accumulated their share of animal manure, which was either plowed under or scooped up and used for fertilizer. (SCM.)

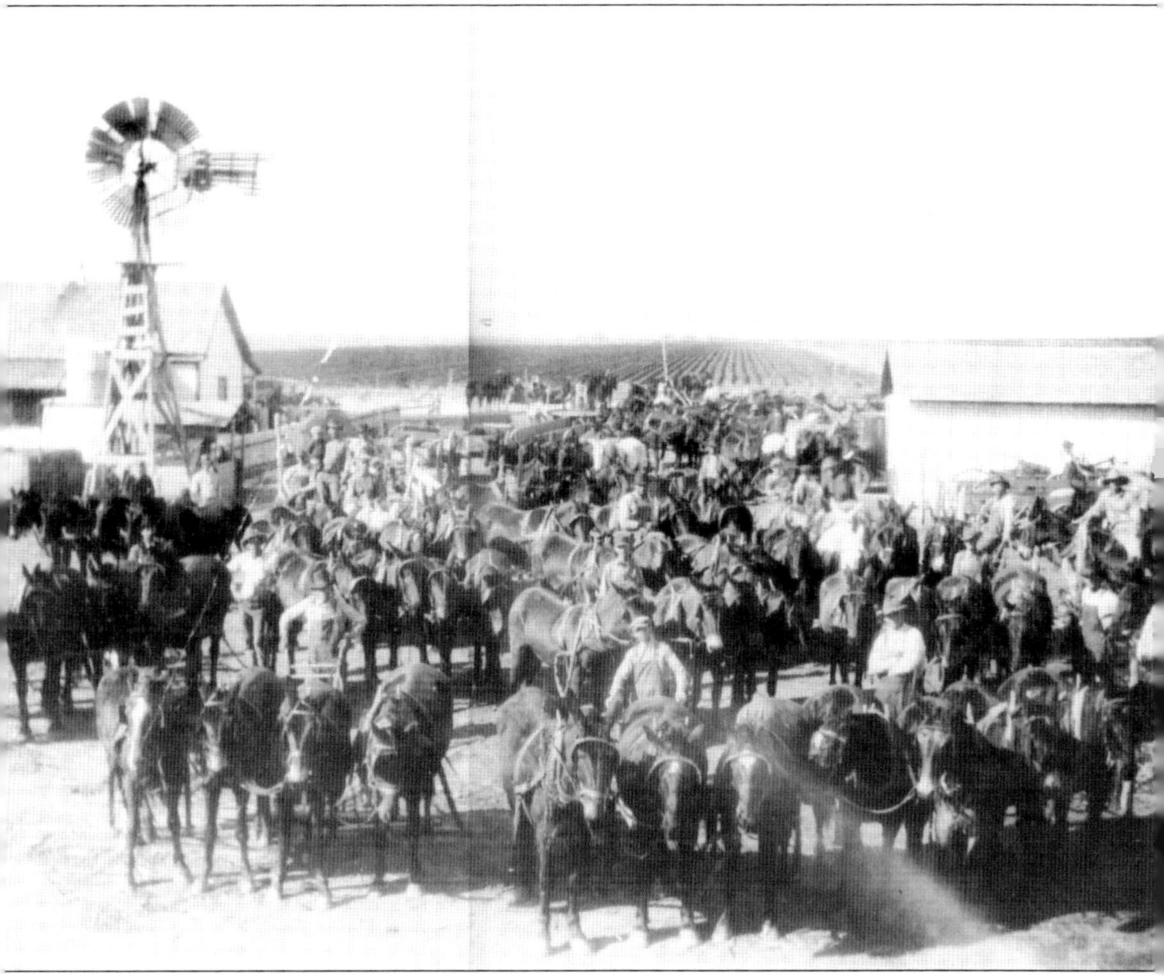

There were a lot of mules in Scurry County, and Joe Middleton claimed that he had gathered every one of them for this photograph. Before the invention of automobiles and modern farm equipment, mules were used for hauling freight, building roads, and farming. Early settlers liked mules because they were hardier and more sure-footed than horses. (Randy Hays.)

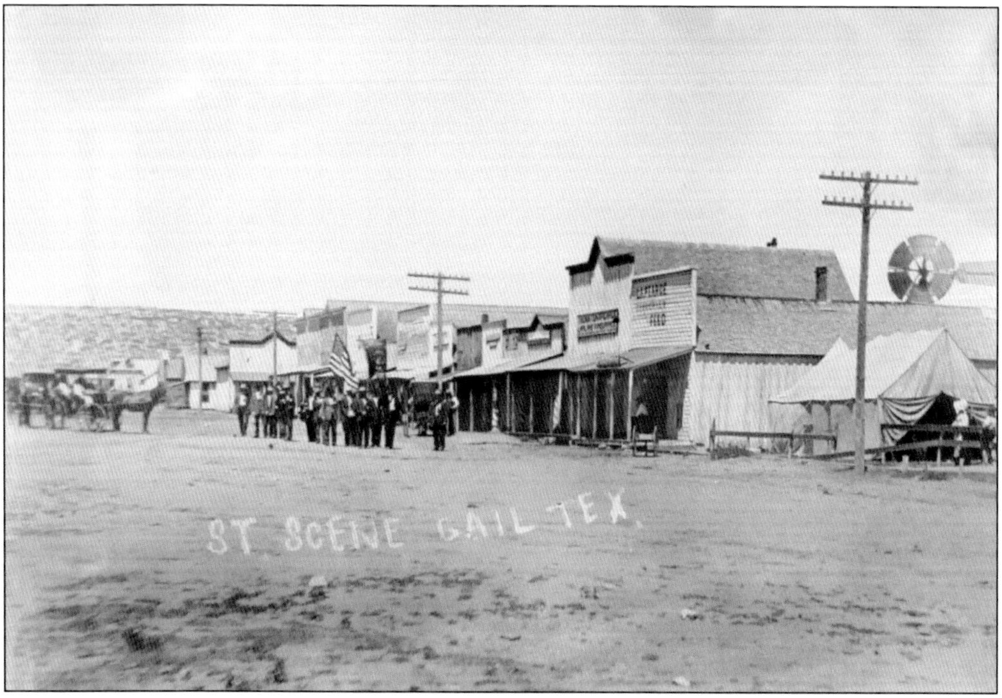

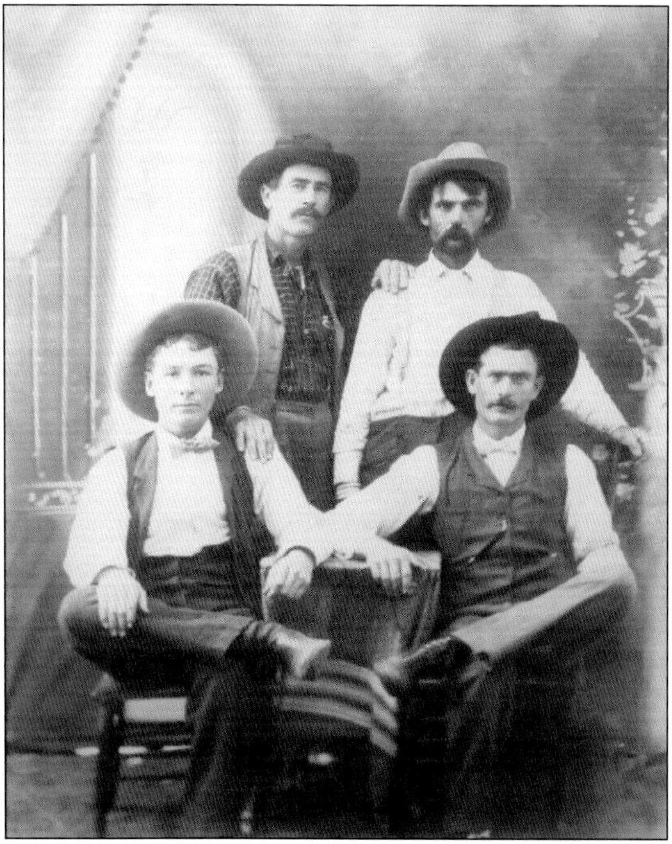

These men are marching down the main street of Gail, possibly to celebrate the Fourth of July, around 1911. The livery and the L.A. Pearce Feed Store are next to the tent. (Borden County Historical Museum.)

A new face in town was sure to draw lots of attention. Towns were especially anxious to attract residents with useful skills, such as blacksmiths and doctors. These early residents of Borden County, identified by their occupations, are, from left to right, (first row) Samp Morrow, rancher, and Jim Craig, lobo (wolf) trapper; (second row) Will Clark, deputy sheriff, and Jim Winslow, identified as a "drifter." (Borden County Historical Museum.)

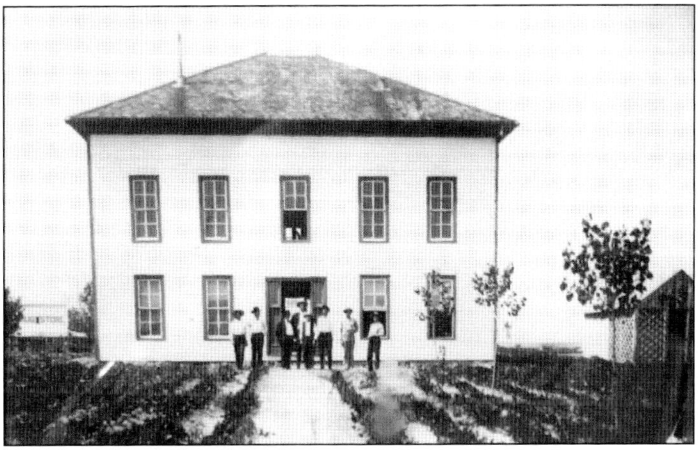

This is the first courthouse in Borden County, erected at the county seat of Gail in 1891. Those identified in the photograph are, in no particular order, W.A. Clark (deputy sheriff), L.A. Pearce (merchant), and Henry Hollar. Uncle "Scalper" Smith's watermelon patch is visible in front of the building. (Borden County Historical Museum.)

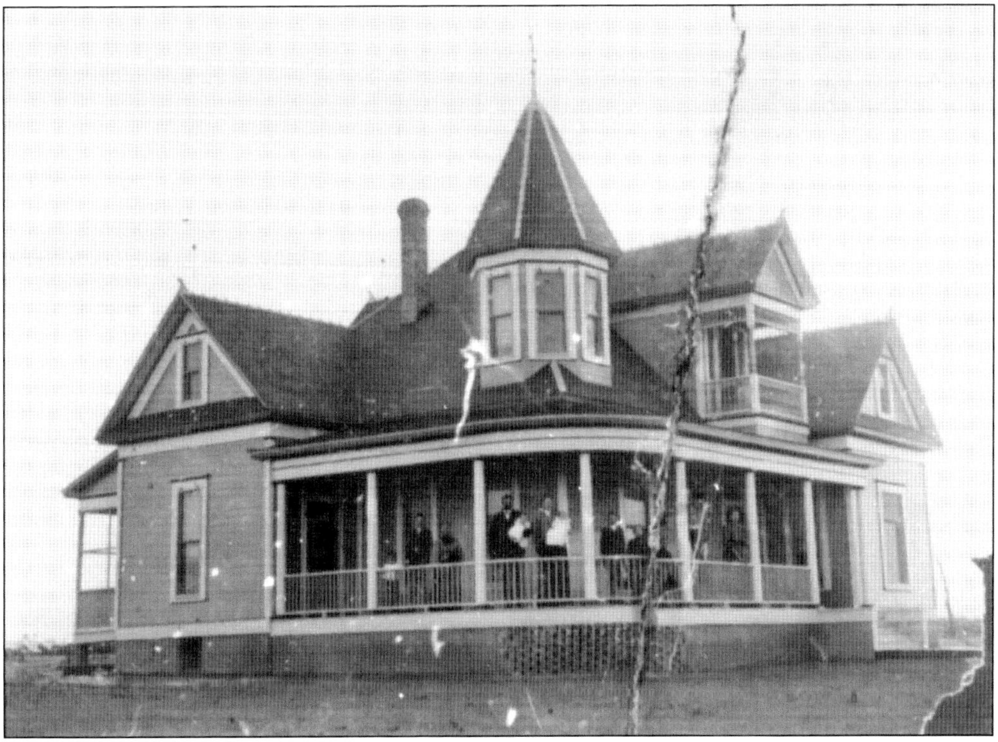

The house in this photograph was built by Mr. and Mrs. William Thompson in 1908. A palace by the standards of the time, it had 10 rooms, 52 windows, and glass doors. Like all good houses, this one had a lightning rod. The total cost of construction was $2,500, and the carpenters were paid 10¢ per hour. There were nine children in the Thompson family, and William's mother lived with the family. Pictured here on the porch are, from left to right, Albert, Edward, grandmother Thompson, William (holding twin Oran), Kate (holding twin Ora), Elvin, Mary, Virginia, Nell, and Alma Thompson. The house was located one mile south of the Snyder courthouse in Scurry County. (SCM.)

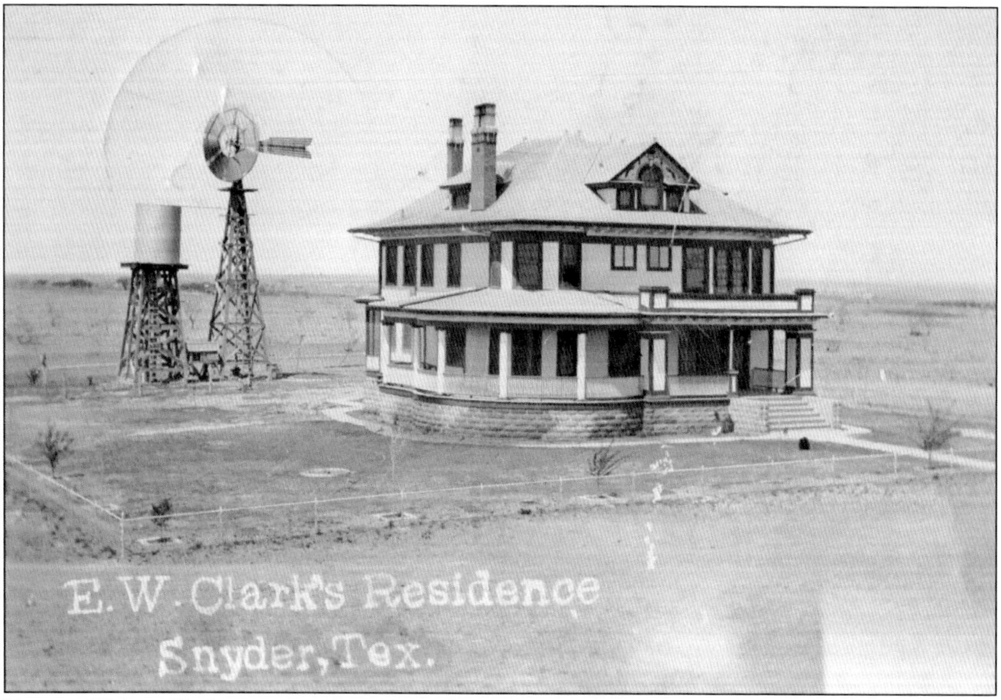

Eugene Walter Clark, a native Texan, was born in Denton County in 1860. In 1884, he herded cattle for John Chisum in New Mexico. He started his own herd three years later, moving it to open range on the Texas–New Mexico line. In 1901, he, W.E. Connell, and John Scarborough bought the OS Ranch in Garza County, one of the largest ranches in the country. Clark married Lillie McCormick in 1895. He was a major stockholder, director, and vice president of the Snyder National Bank when it was organized in 1905. His house, built in 1908, still stands at 2306 Thirty-second Street in Snyder. Modified very little from its original form, the house was designated a state historic landmark in 1964. (SCM.)

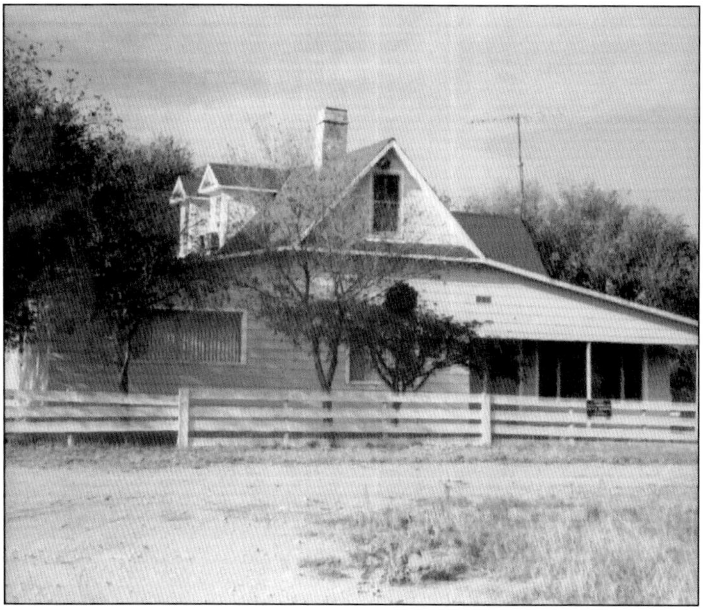

George Kindred "Uncle Kin" Elkins, a Confederate veteran and fighter of Native Americans, moved his family from Coleman County to Polar, Kent County, in 1879. He built this house 22 miles north of Snyder in 1902. In 1917, he sold his ranch to Leroy Spires and moved to Bluewater, New Mexico, with a cattle herd, wagons, and a Model T car. This photograph was taken by T. Dudley Cramer in 1971. (SCM.)

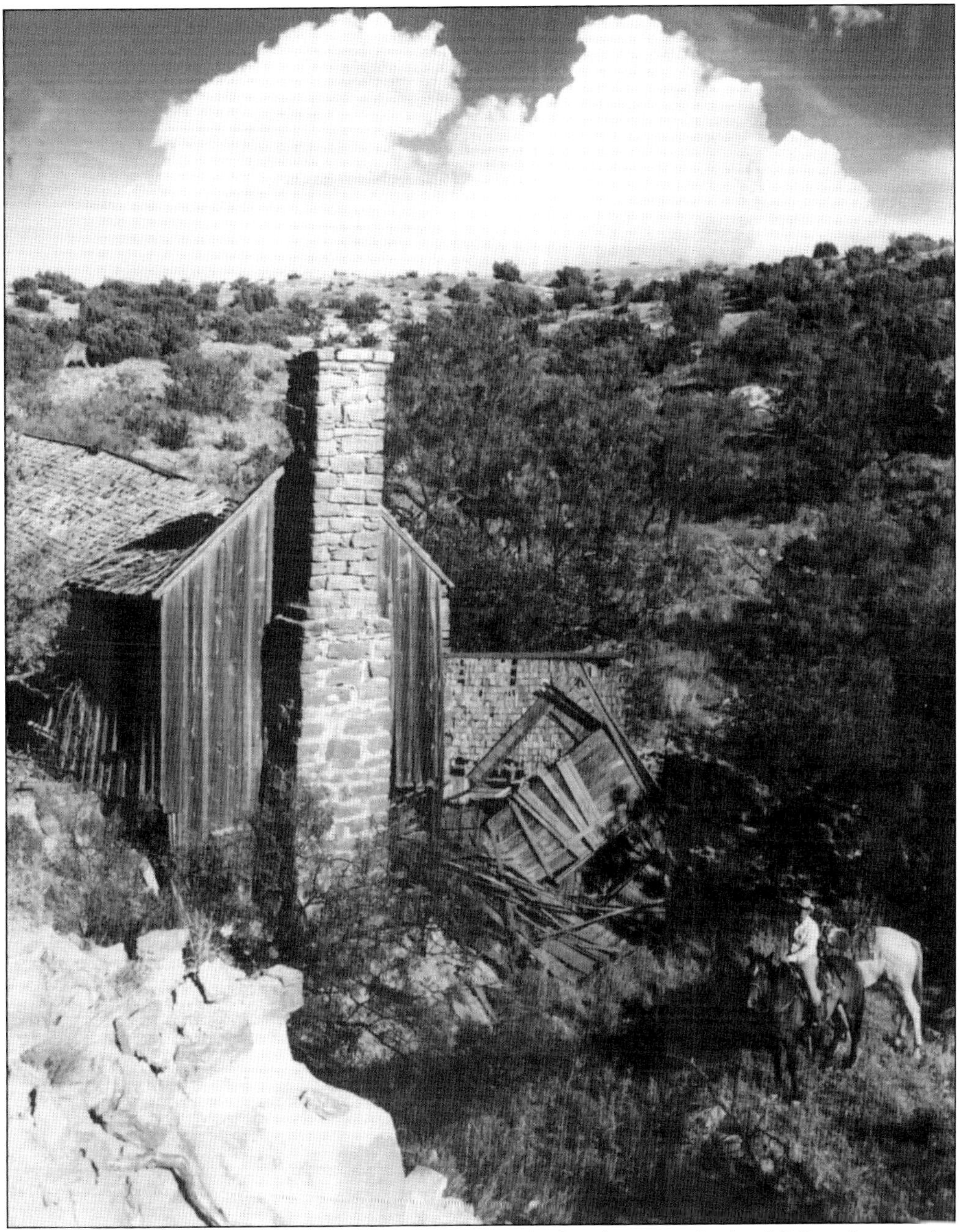

L.H. "Red Buck" Pruitt built this house in 1895 as the headquarters for his LP Ranch near the Scurry-Kent county line. In 1924, Roy Elkins became foreman of the ranch. He and his family lived in the house for many years. Joe York is visible at right on horseback next to the abandoned house. This photograph was taken by T. Dudley Cramer in 1971. (SCM.)

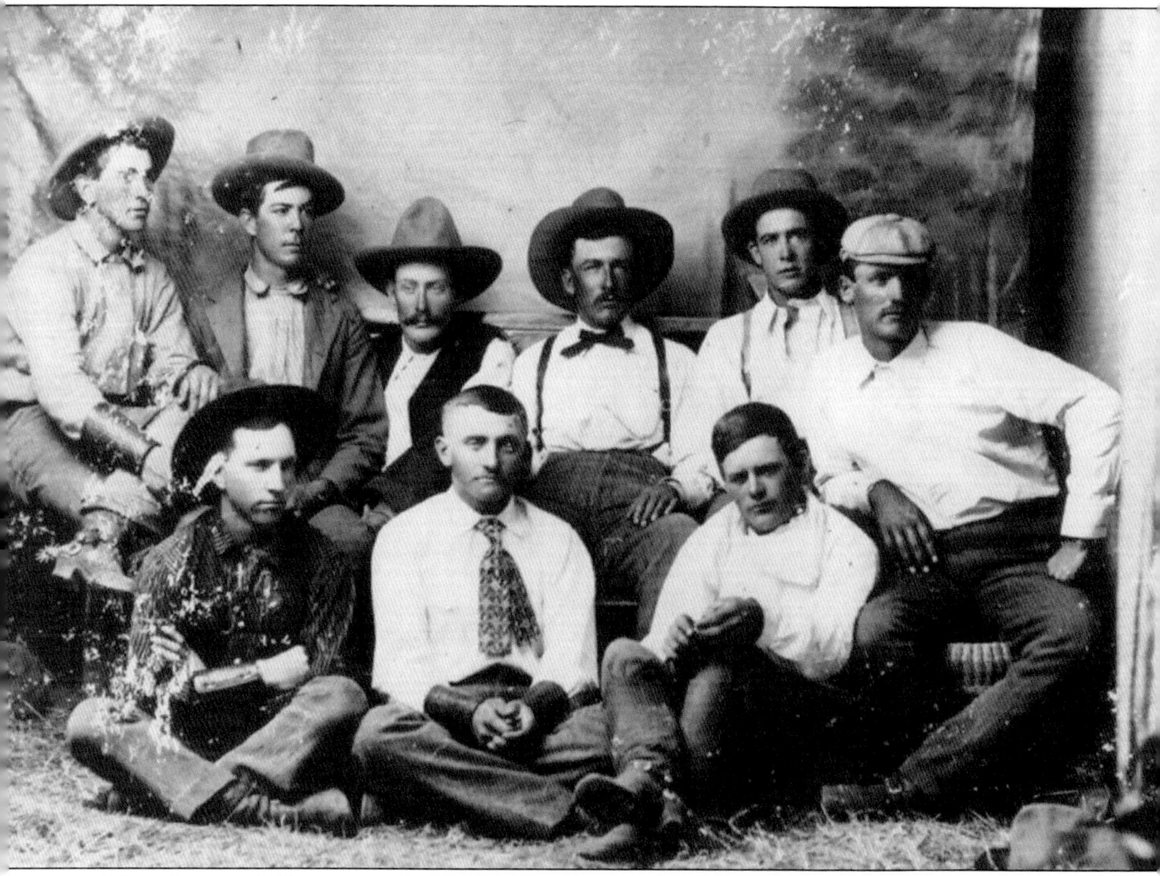

These Lipscomb County cowboys are posing for a studio photograph. Practical cowboy clothing, such as leather cuffs, is visible, along with new fashions from East Coast cities, such as the newsboy cap worn by the man at far right. (Wolf Creek Heritage Museum.)

Only a bold cowboy would dare to wear these flashy gal leg spurs. Hollywood often associates cowboys with gamblers and saloon girls, but in reality, they spent very little time in the towns. A lonely night on the range under the stars was a much more common evening for a cowboy. Even when they did enter civilization, cowboys usually had very little money to spend. (SCM.)

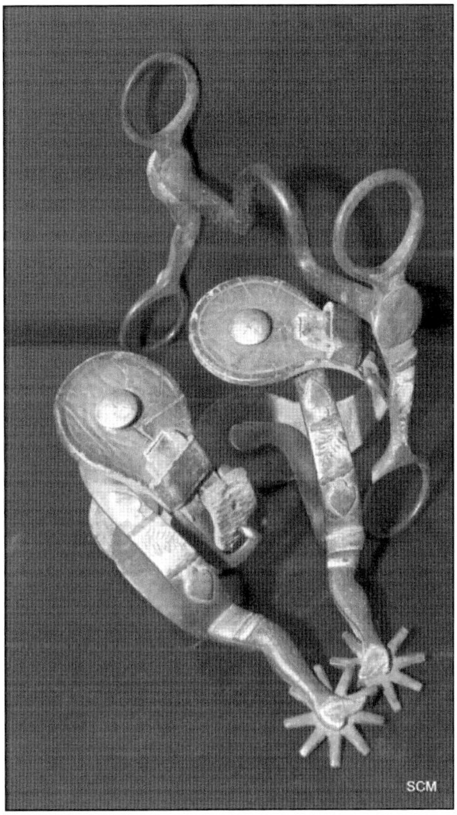

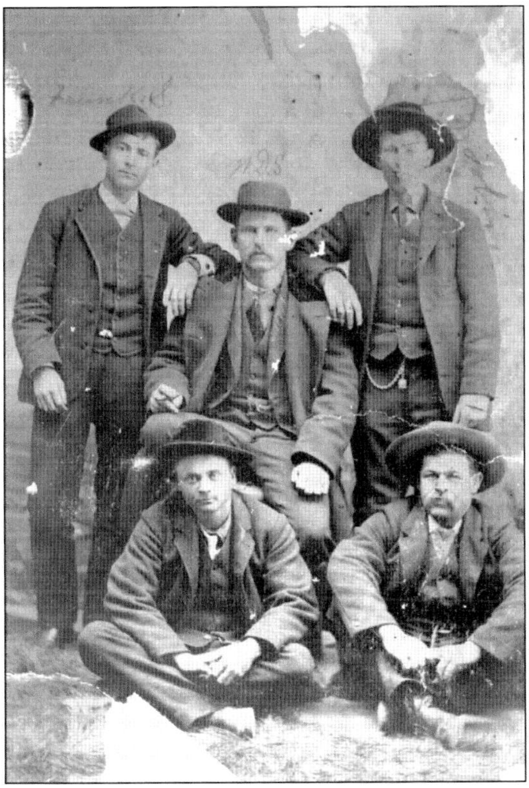

Frank Sims (standing at left), W.D. Sims (second row, center), and John Sims (standing at right) were in Cheyenne, Wyoming, when this photograph was taken in 1884. The two men seated in front are unidentified, but were probably employees of W.D. Sims. The Sims family primarily ranched in Scurry County, but, like many families, they spread throughout the plains. Long cattle drives allowed young cowboys to get a firsthand look at potential rangeland they might acquire for themselves. Having many relatives to call upon also meant that family problems did not always stay within one town or county. (SCM.)

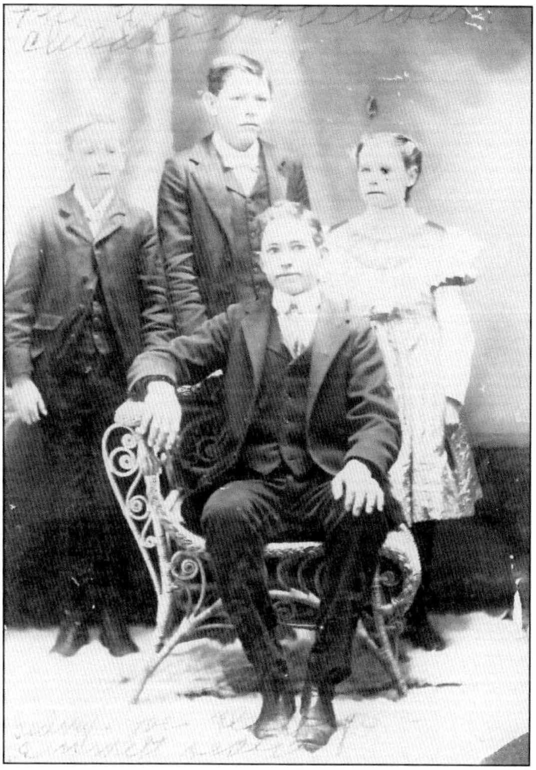

The Johnson-Sims feud, known as "the last blood feud in Texas," began in 1916 when Gladys Johnson and her brother Sid shot and killed Gladys's husband, Ed Sims. The feud involved shootings and thefts of courthouse documents in multiple counties and included a veritable "who's who" of the region. In the spring of 1917, Texas Ranger Frank Hamer (best known for shooting the famous gangsters Bonnie and Clyde) married Gladys Johnson. The four children of W.A. Johnson are pictured here around 1903. They are, from left to right, Sidney, Joe, Emmett (seated), and Gladys. (SCM.)

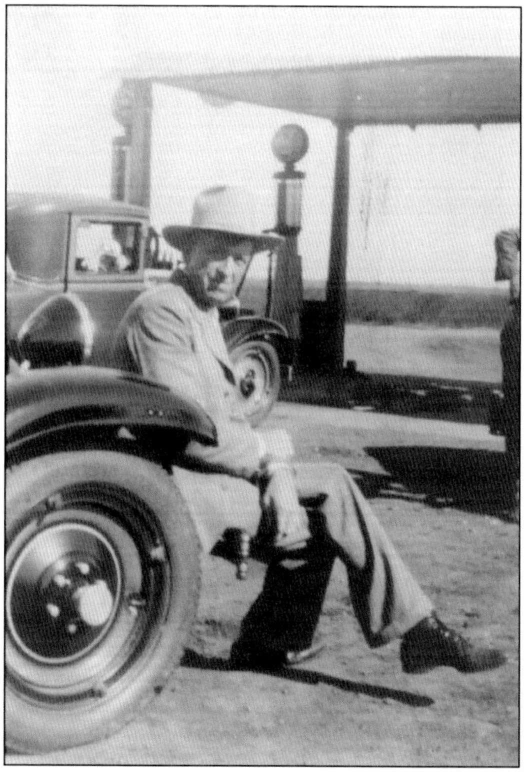

R.I. Goodall (pictured) served eight terms as sheriff of Kent County. In March 1918, Sion "Si" Bostick, along with two accomplices, fired a shotgun through a window of the Clairemont Hotel, fatally wounding Judge Cullen Higgins. Goodall and town marshal Charles O. Fox pursued the shooter, and as Bostick traveled to his own house north of Post, Fox tracked him and arrested him. Bostick was moved to Sweetwater for better protection while Texas Rangers investigated. After they interviewed Bostick, he was found hanged in his cell with his feet touching the floor. Ironically, his death was ruled a suicide. The reward went to Sheriff Goodall, who may have split the money with Fox. (Kent County sheriff William Scoggin.)

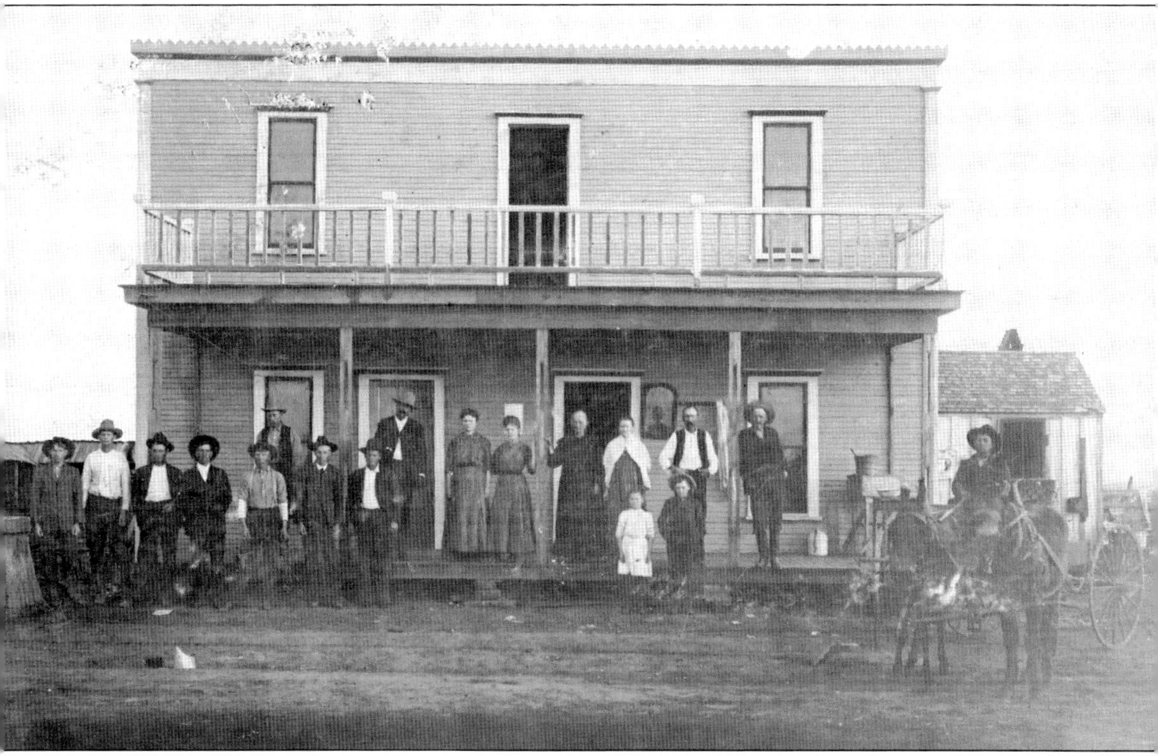

The Davidson family gathers in front of the Clairemont Hotel. William Maxwell Davidson is right of center, wearing a vest and a white shirt. The children in front of him are his daughter and son, Ellen and Creed. The woman in black at center is identified as grandma Geddi, and the woman in the light-colored shawl is grandma Davidson. The photograph at the bottom of page 77 shows a man appears to be sitting in midair—he is actually on the corner of the balcony at this hotel. (SCM.)

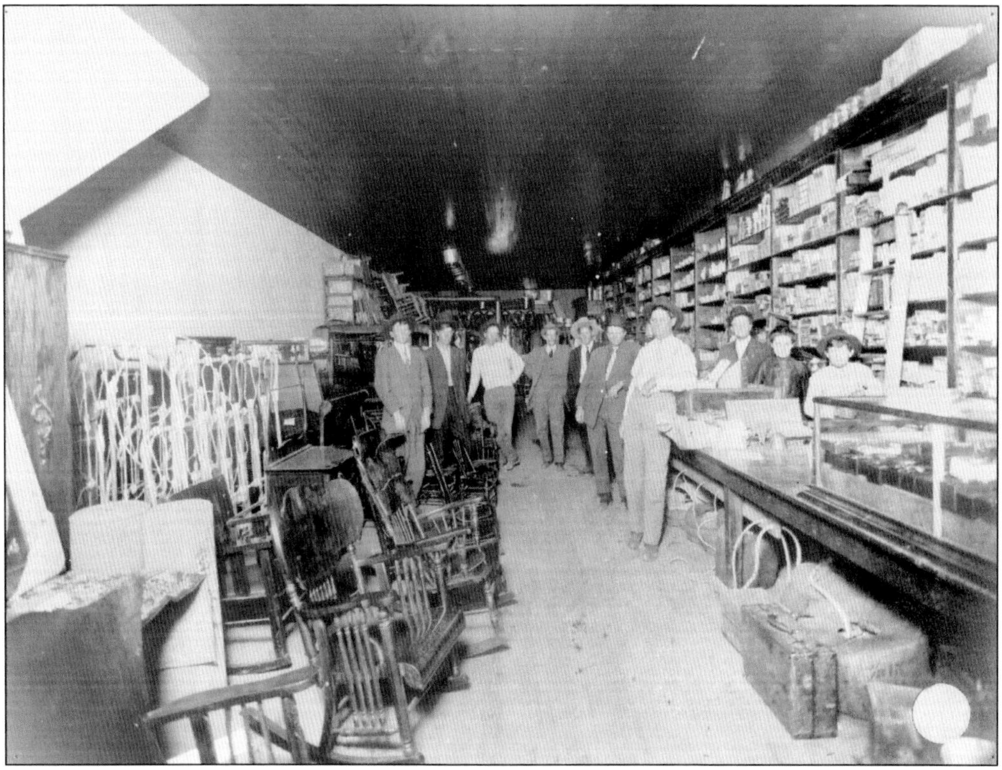

The Fluvanna community, originally called Light, was important to settlers of both Borden and Scurry Counties. This is a photograph of the first furniture and hardware store in Fluvanna. The owners were J.J. Belew and J.F. Dowdy, who also operated a local drugstore. Pictured here are, from left to right, ? Smith, Kirt Bradley, Edd Boles, an unidentified traveling salesman, Arch Odom, Edd Deer, Belew, Dowdy, Mrs. J.F. Dowdy, and Clarence Dowdy. (SCM.)

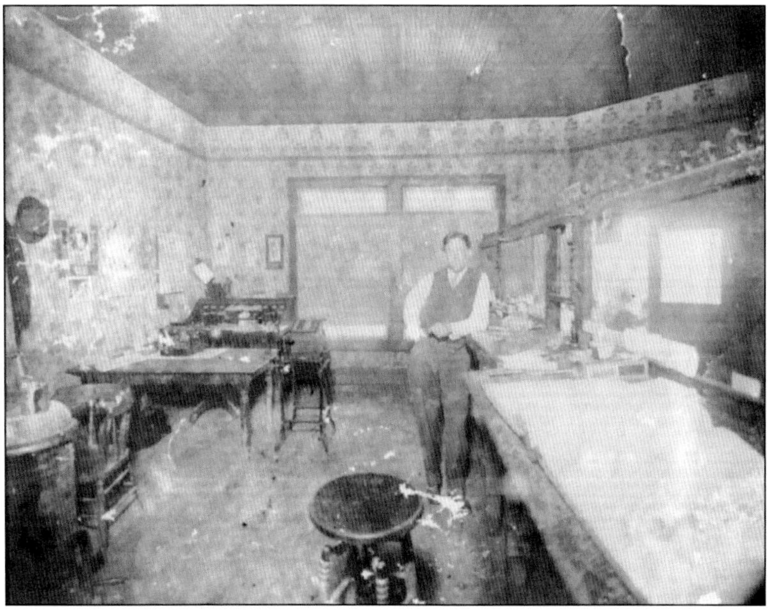

The first wooden building in Light was moved to the new town of Fluvanna in 1908. It was placed on the site where the first brick bank was later built. S.P. Smith is pictured here inside the wooden building shortly after it was moved.

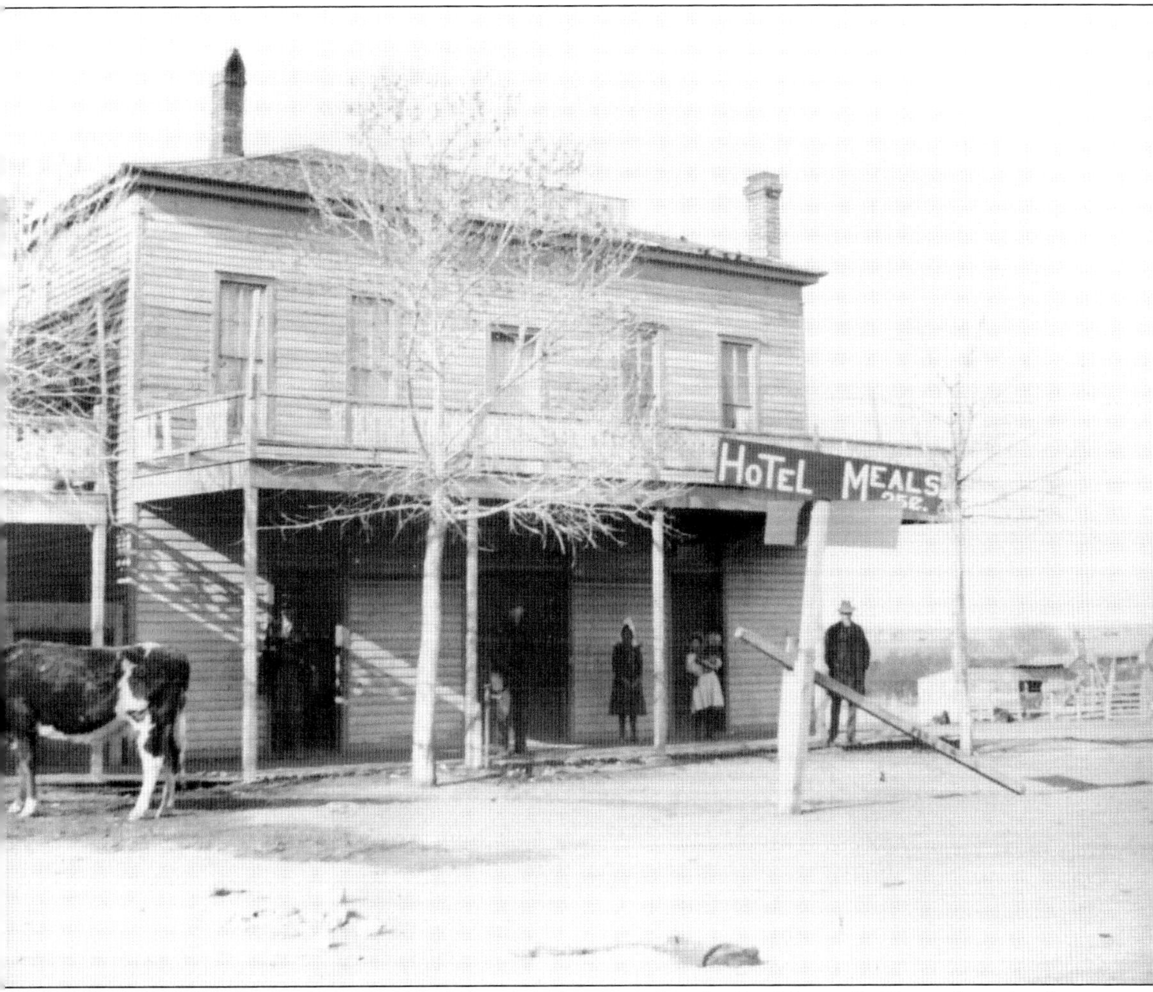

This photograph of the Belmont Hotel in Snyder was taken by Dr. Henry B. Kimmel in April 1898. The hotel was on the north side of the Snyder square in Scurry County. At one time, it was operated by the Lookwood family, who also ran a livery stable and wagon yard just west of the hotel. Enterprising pioneers often had several businesses, fulfilling needs within their communities. The sign reads "Hotel, Meals 25¢." (SCM.)

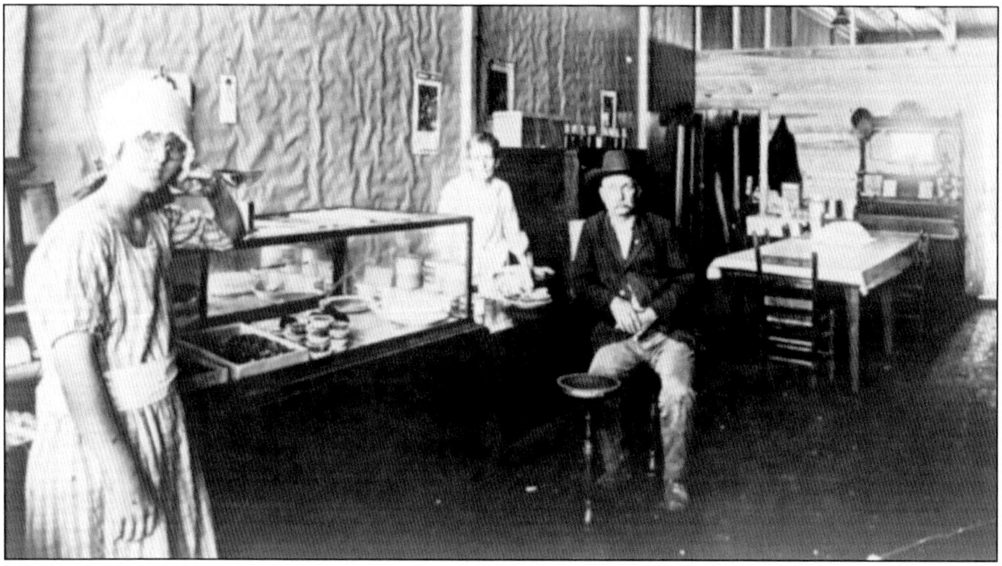

This is the Etheredge Rooming House in Hermleigh. Most hotels were small, family-run businesses. Pictured here are Alma Etheredge (center), J.B. Etheredge (right), and their daughter, Jelma.

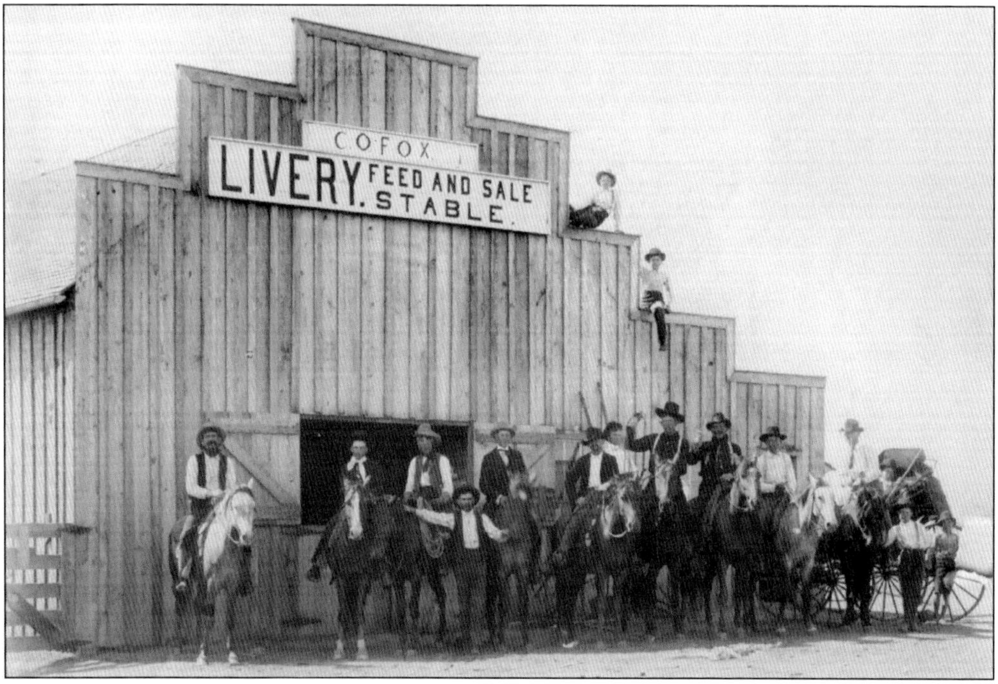

This livery stable in Clairemont, Kent County, was first owned by Jeff Hardin, brother of the famous gunfighter John Wesley Hardin. The room at right was a saloon, and Jeff was killed there in 1901 during a gunfight with John Snowden. Years later, Charles O. Fox purchased the livery from Hardin's widow. The men pictured here are, from left to right, John Sampson, Mace Hunter, Will Rogers, Fox, Gee McMeans, Jack Rogers, Maxie Williams, Willis Rogers, Dick Jay, Ed Underwood, Lee Byrd, and Dick Sampson (in buggy). The two boys standing at far right are unidentified. The boys on the roof are Gene Selmon (left) and Burley Sampson. (Don M. Jay Collection, SCM.)

Young Lena Mae "Maye" Greenfield went to the post office at Polar, in Kent County, to pick up the mail for her parents, who were farmers in the area. Polar has been a ghost town for many years. (SCM.)

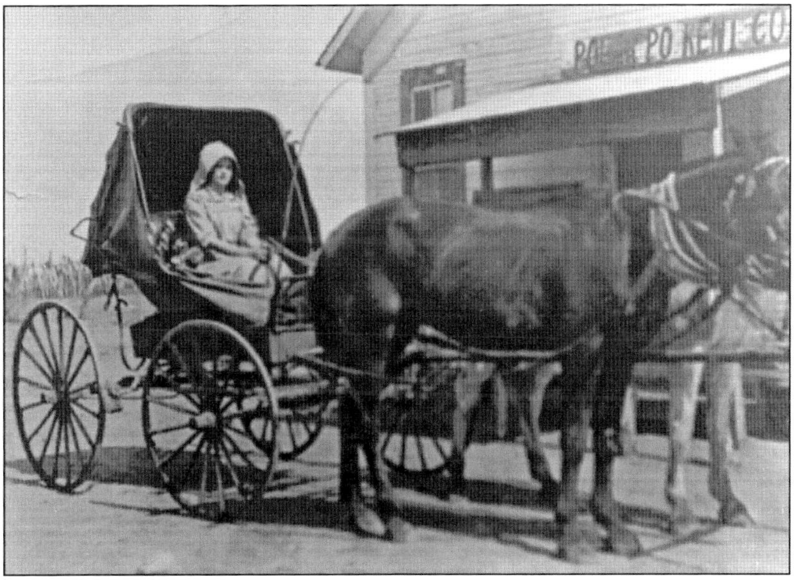

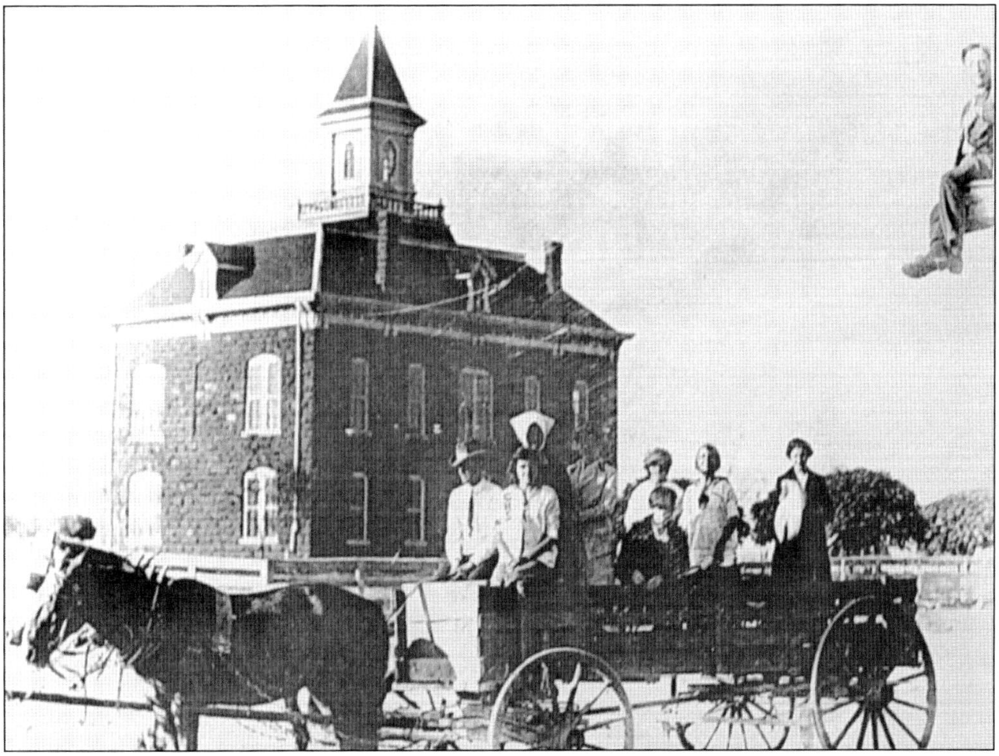

Clairemont was seat of Kent County until 1952, when someone made a proposal to move the seat to Jayton; there were not enough votes to make the change. After a three-year court battle, the move was officially approved. Someone, apparently fearful that the court might overturn the verdict, burned down the courthouse one windy night. The mystery arsonist was never brought to justice. The woman at far right in the wagon is Fannie Hardin Fox, and the man in the upper right corner of the photograph is sitting on the balcony of the Clairemont Hotel (pictured on page 73). (Don M. Jay Collection, SCM.)

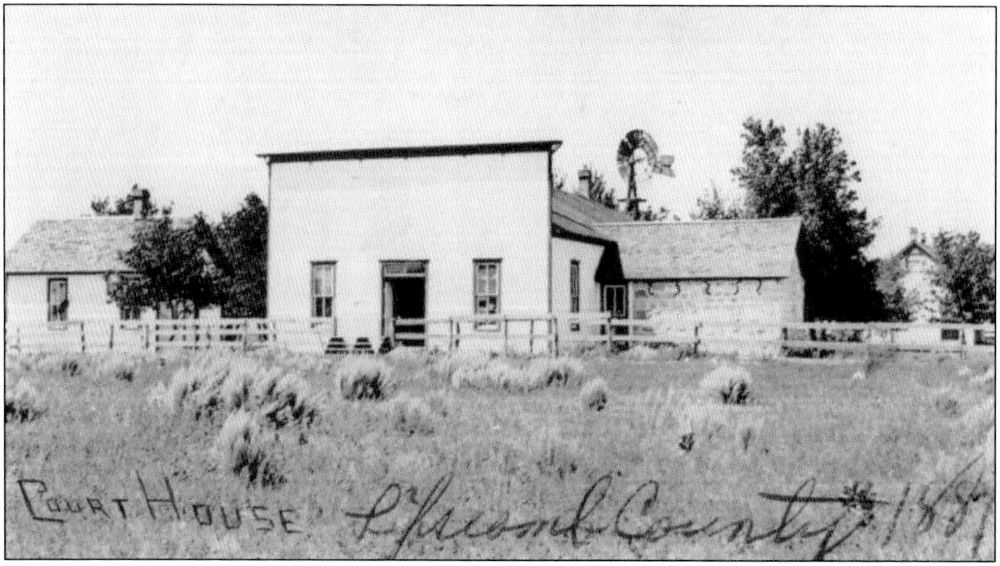

Lipscomb County is located in the northeast corner of the Texas Panhandle. This is the first courthouse of Lipscomb County, which was built in 1887. (Wolf Creek Heritage Museum.)

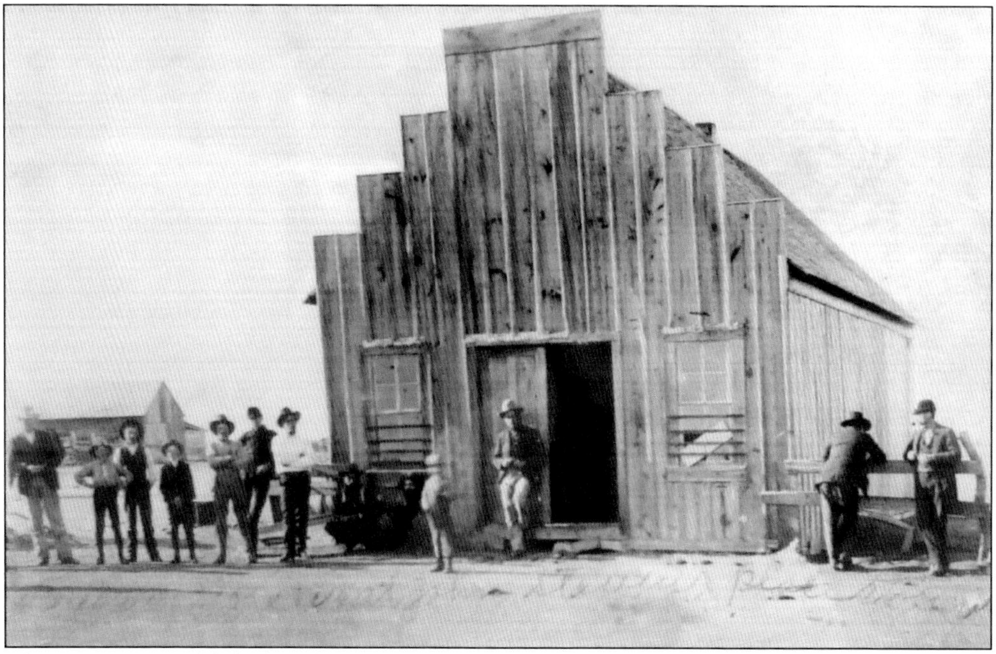

This store was established at the old Stephens homesite in the Treadway community of Borden County. (Borden County Museum.)

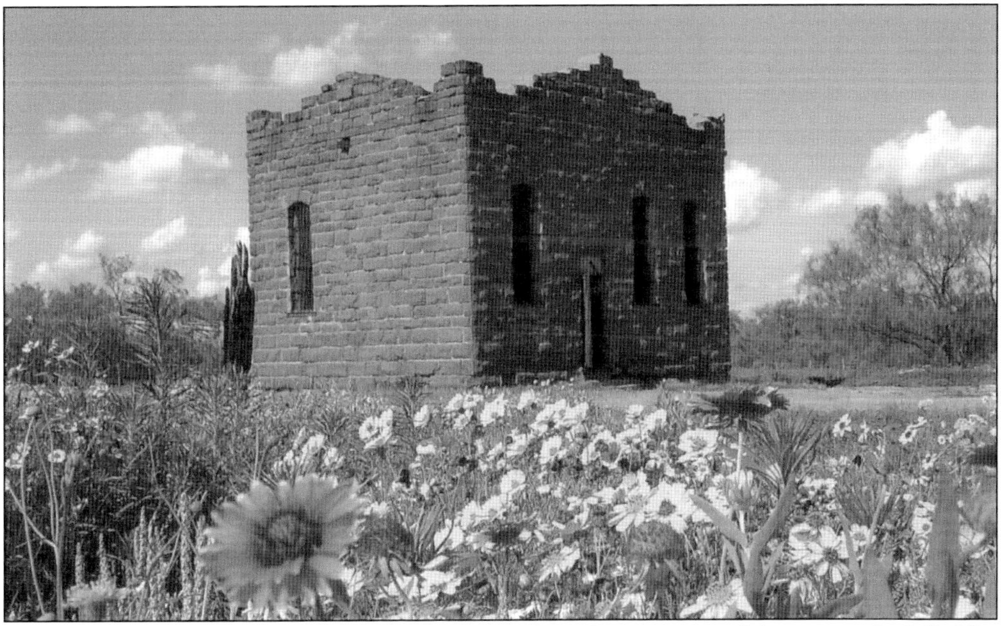

The Clairemont jail was constructed in 1895 of red sandstone quarried from a nearby hill. The jail was originally two stories, with the sheriff's quarters upstairs and cells for prisoners downstairs. The upper floor was removed in 1904. One prisoner who escaped from the jail hid in the cupola of the courthouse, where he watched the law hunt for him for two days and nights before hunger and thirst forced him to surrender. Although the jail was set to be preserved as a historic site, the facility is currently abandoned and in poor condition. (Photograph by Keith Pitner.)

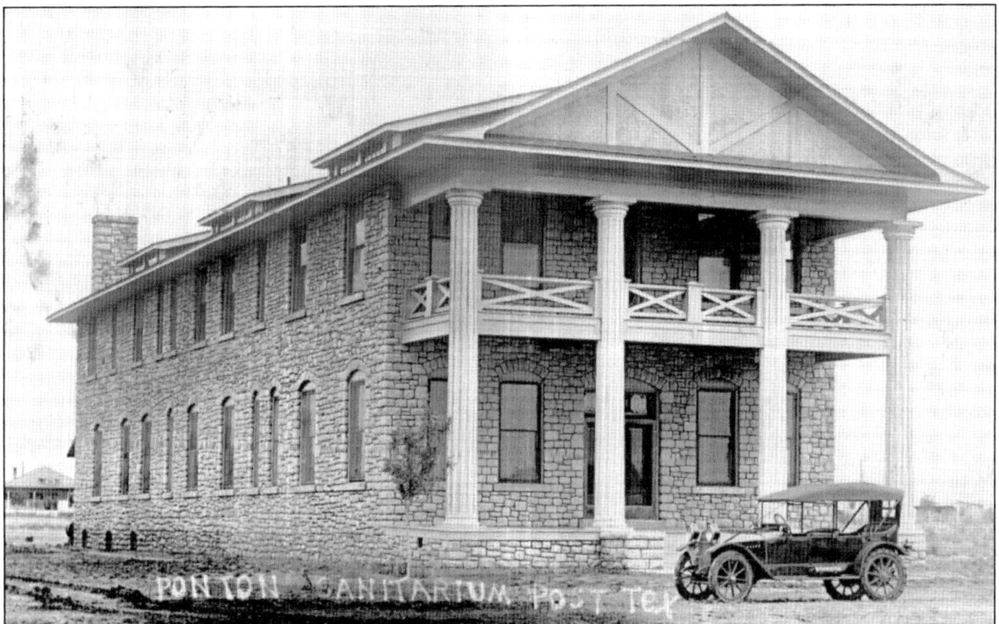

The old Post Sanitarium in Garza County was the first hospital in the area. The hospital was built by C.W. Post, the cereal millionaire. Dr. A.R. Ponton, the facility's physician, came to Post in 1910. This building now houses the Garza County Historical Museum. (SCM.)

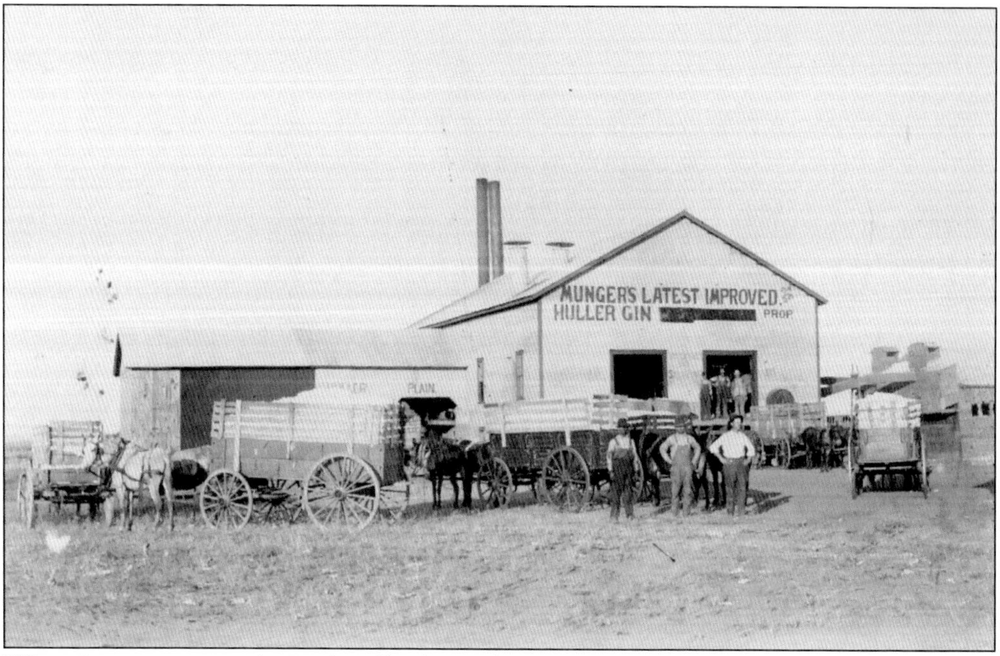

When farmers came to the Panhandle Plains, they soon discovered that cotton could be grown in this semi-arid region. The cotton was planted and cultivated by hand, and plows were usually drawn by mules. Sideboards were made for the wagons, and the loads were driven to the nearest gin. One early farmer named Lafoon wrote that he had to take his loads of cotton from Kent County south to Abilene, and that it took a week to make the trip there and back. Robert S. Munger, of Mexia, Limestone County, invented system ginning, which ended the labor-intensive plantation ginning. He used steam power and conveyor belts to make ginning cotton much easier. Individuals could not afford to buy his equipment, however, so farmers formed collectives, and Munger gins appeared throughout Texas. Diesel engines and electric power later replaced steam. (SCM.)

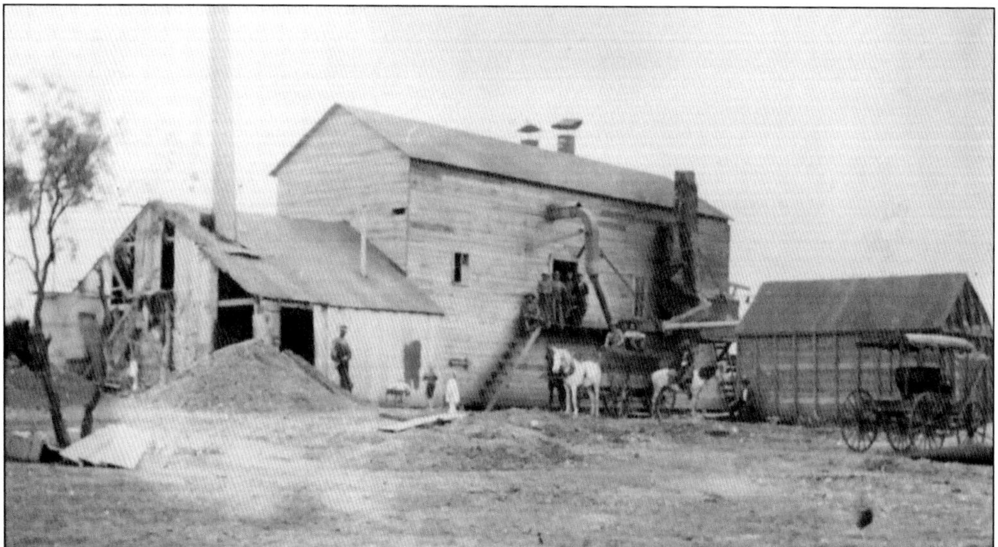

This is the Camp Springs cotton gin. The man at left, near the seed house, is "Grandpa" Joe Trice. W.V. Jones is sitting on the horse.

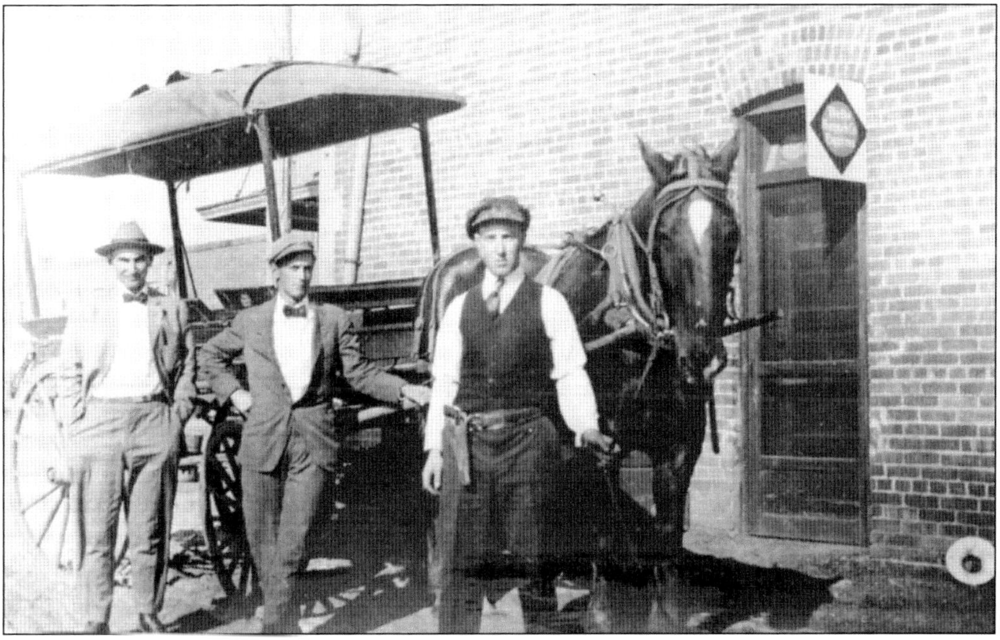

These three men pose in front of a horse-drawn Wells Fargo wagon, probably at the Amarillo Wells Fargo headquarters. The two men at left are unidentified. The man at right, wearing a pistol, was a Wells Fargo security agent named Carl Mountz. (Deaf Smith County Historical Museum.)

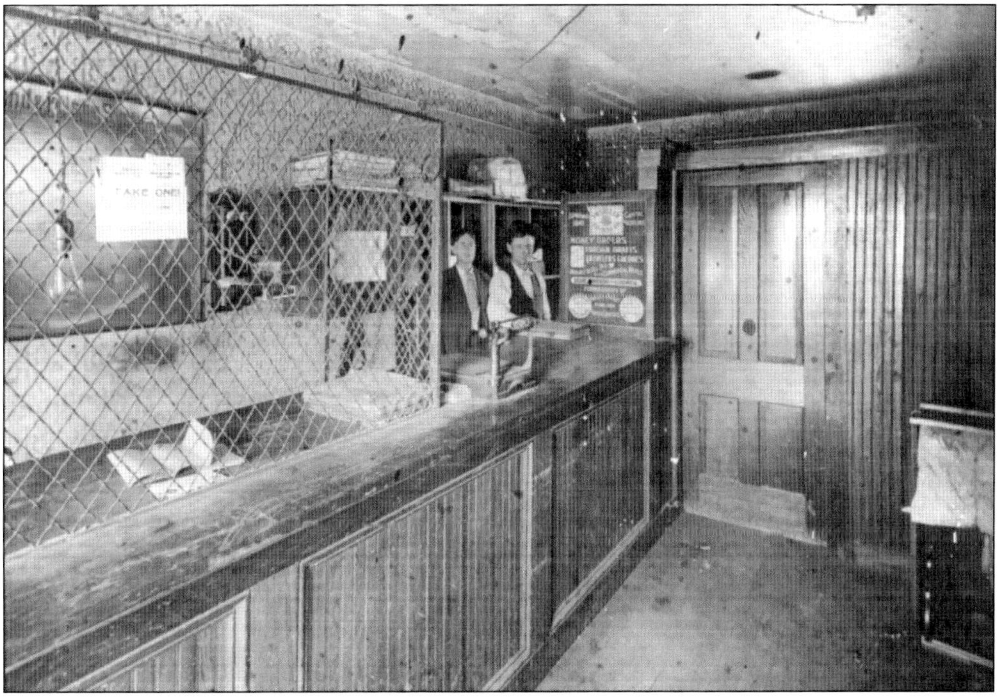

These men are posing at the American Express office at the Rock Island train station in Amarillo. The sign between the men and the door lists some of the services available, such as money orders, travelers' checks, and foreign drafts. The sign also mentions that American Express was established in 1841. (SCM.)

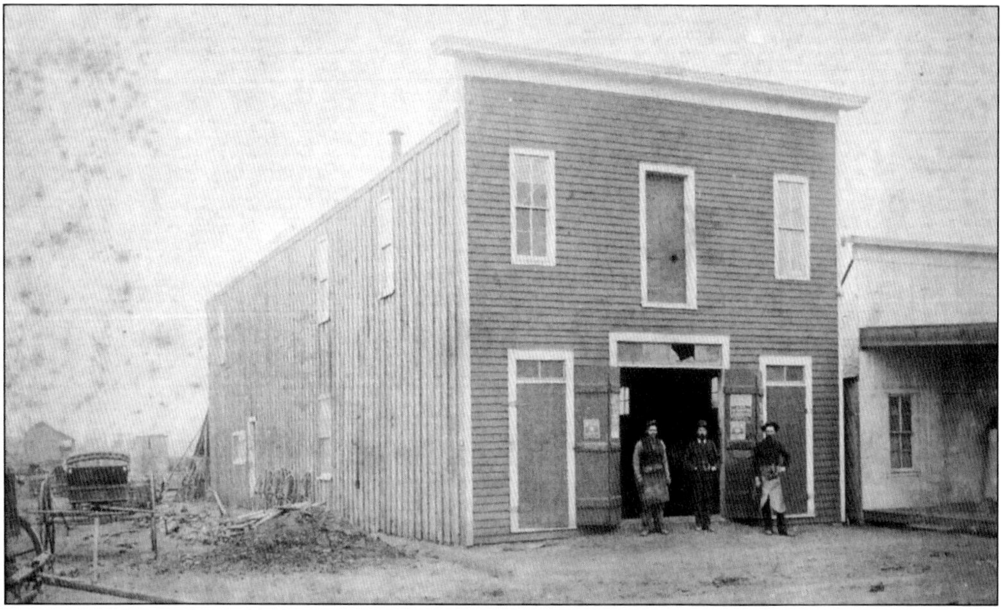

B.F. Camp (center) established a carriage shop in Colorado, Texas, in 1881. This photograph was taken in 1882. With the arrival of the railroad in 1881, property values soared. The lots were long but very narrow, and it appears Camp had two adjacent lots (as indicated by the carriage and woodpile next to his building). Around 1883, Camp sold his lots and building and moved west to the town of Big Spring, where he established another carriage shop. (Jane G. Wilson Adams.)

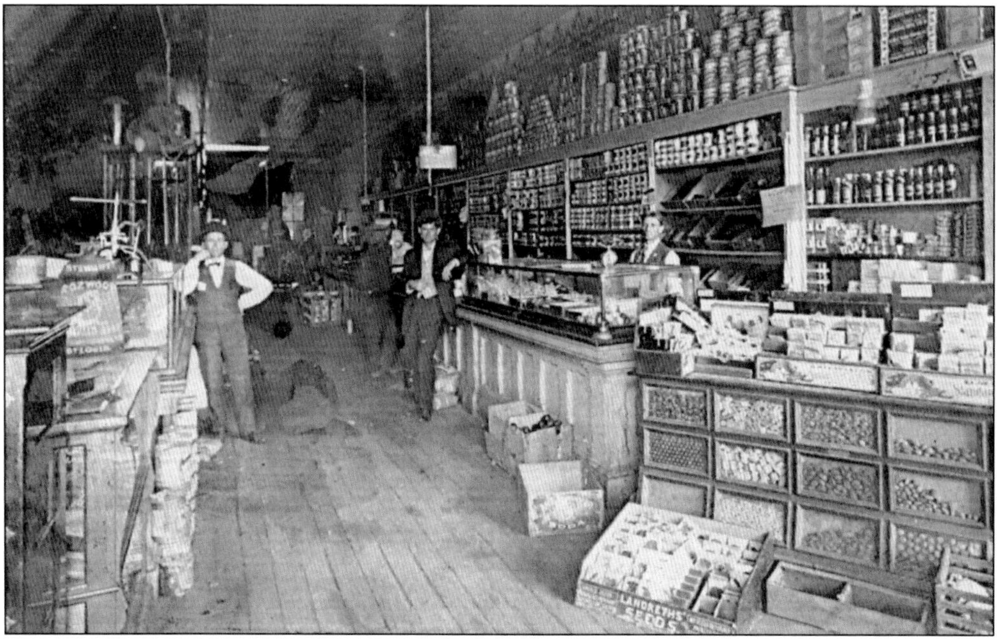

After the railroads came to Colorado in 1881, the trails to Kansas were closed, and the town of Colorado flourished and became known as the "Cowboy Capital of Texas" as its new railhead gave it precedence over Dodge and Abilene. Ranchers came from miles away to purchase supplies. This mercantile store belonged to William Lafayette Gross (center). (SCM.)

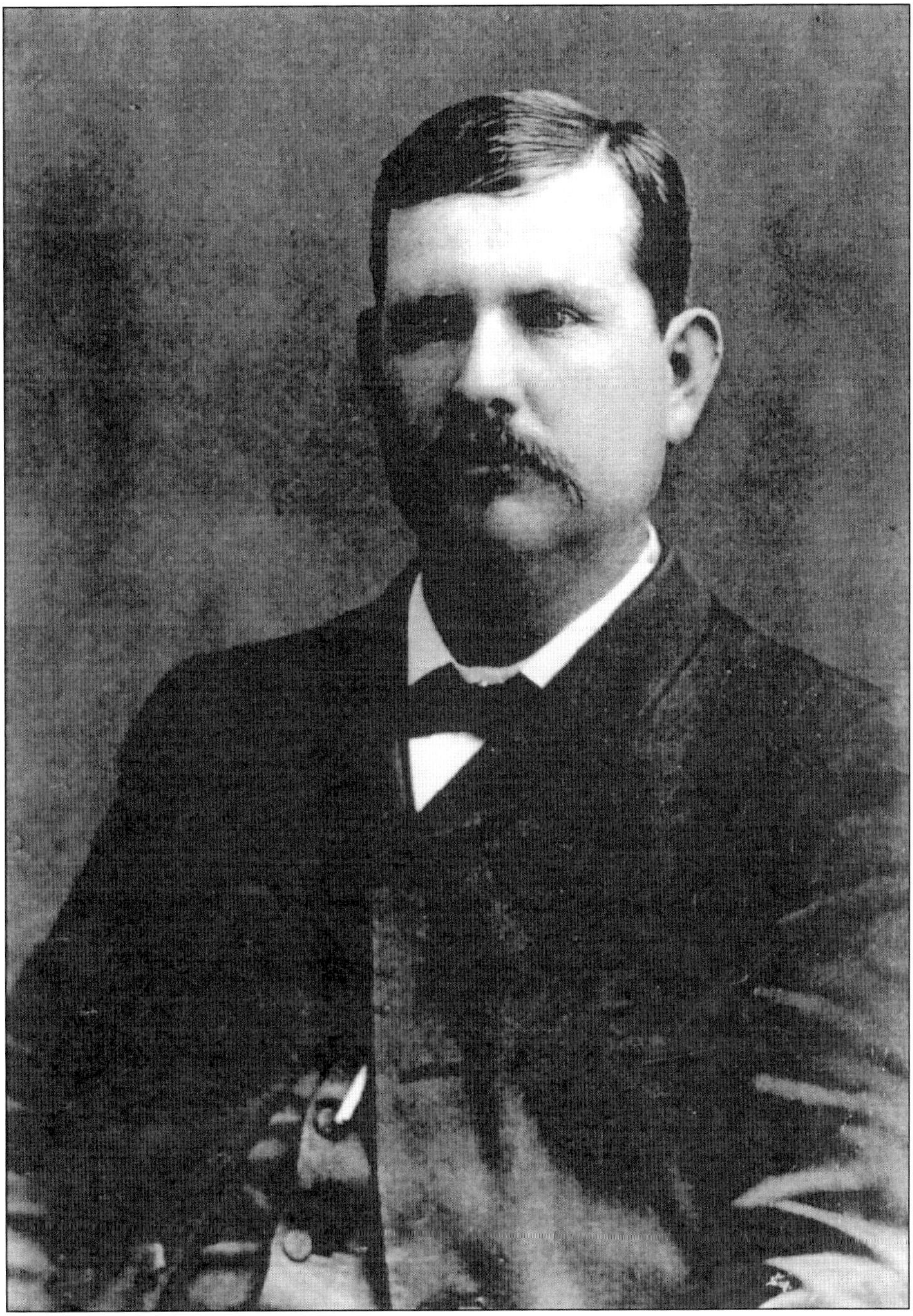

Texas Ranger Dick Ware was responsible for killing the outlaw Sam Bass in Round Rock, Texas, in 1878. Ware became sheriff of Mitchell County in 1881, winning the election by one vote. When he ran for a second term in 1892, he was defeated by one vote. Two friends in Borden County mounted their horses on election day and headed south with the intention to vote for Ware before the polls closed. It was a hot day, and the men stopped at Deep Creek to rest. They fell asleep, and by the time they awoke, the polls were closed. One vote would have tied the race, and the other would have won it for Ware. (Roland Graham.)

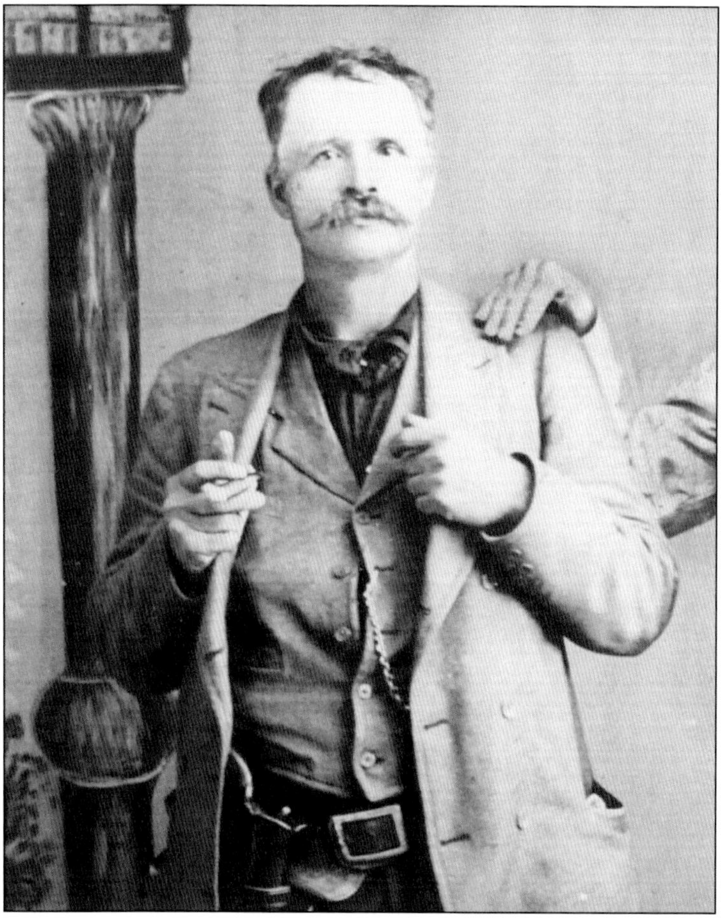

The first sheriff of Kent County was W.H. Butler. He was appointed in 1892, when the county was organized, and was elected in 1893. As the sheriff of a brand-new county, he had his work cut out for him—in the unlawful atmosphere of Clairemont, the town experienced at least one murder per week. Butler died in Bethel, New Mexico, in 1911. (Kent County sheriff William Scoggin.)

In the days before bridges were erected, travelers forded streams when possible. If this could not be done, they utilized ferries. This ferry operated on the Colorado River in the lower plains of Texas. (Don M. Jay collection, SCM.)

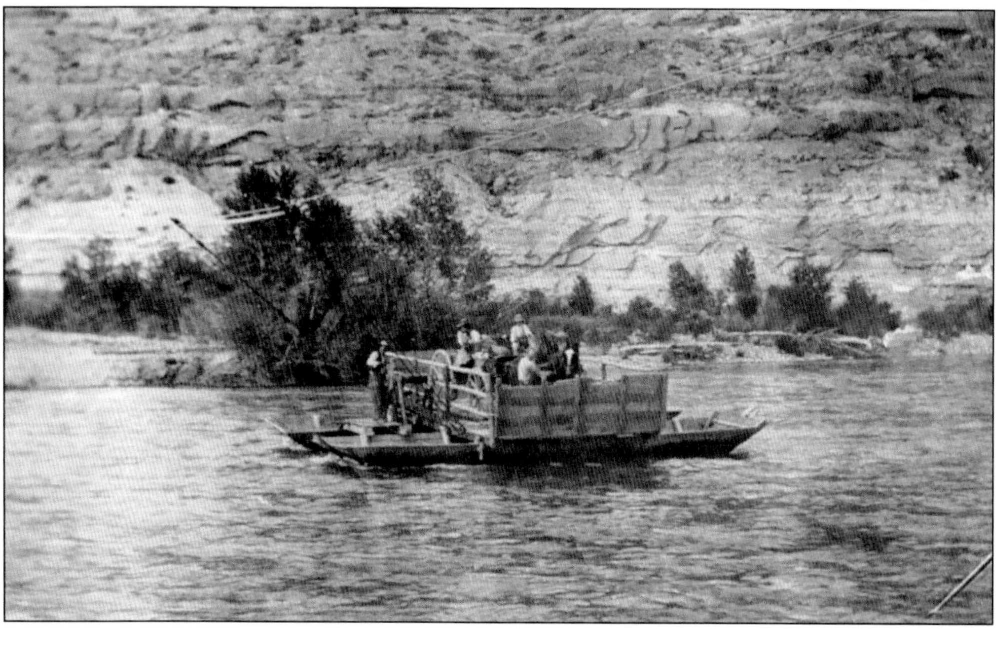

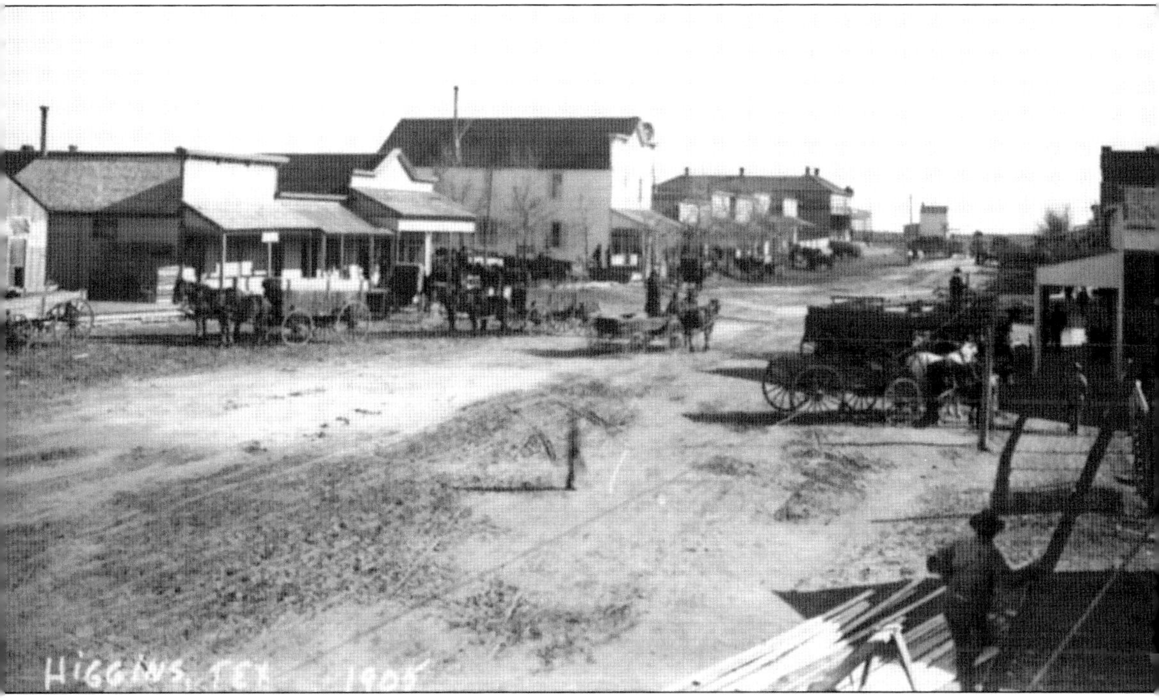

Higgins was established in 1886 in southeastern Lipscomb County. It is in the heart of the North Texas grasslands of the early cattle ranges. The area has been associated with Juan de Padilla, a Franciscan monk who came into the region with Francisco Vazquez de Coronado. This photograph was taken in 1905. (Wolf Creek Heritage Museum.)

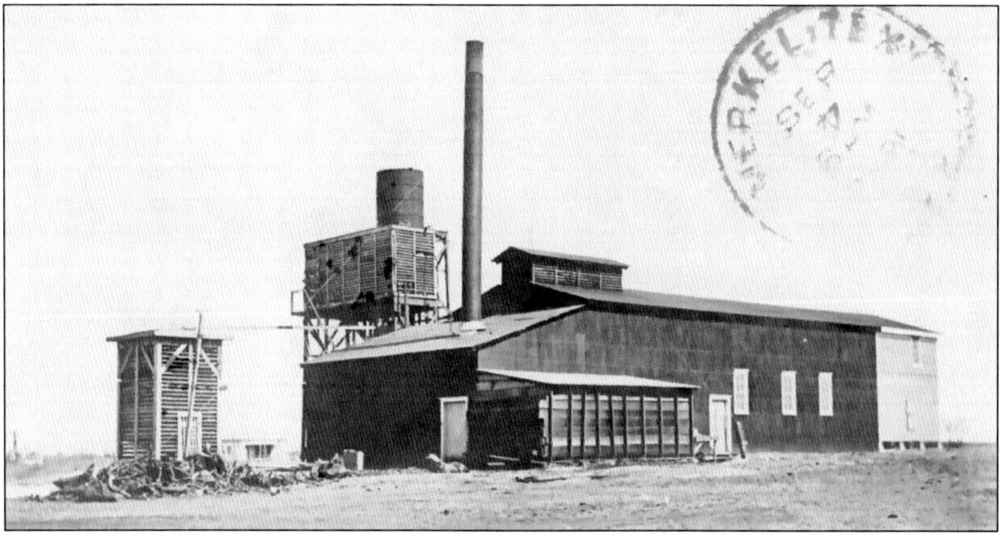

Keeping cool was a challenge during hot West Texas summers. Before electricity and refrigeration, residents picked up blocks of ice at an icehouse (like this one in Snyder) or had them delivered.

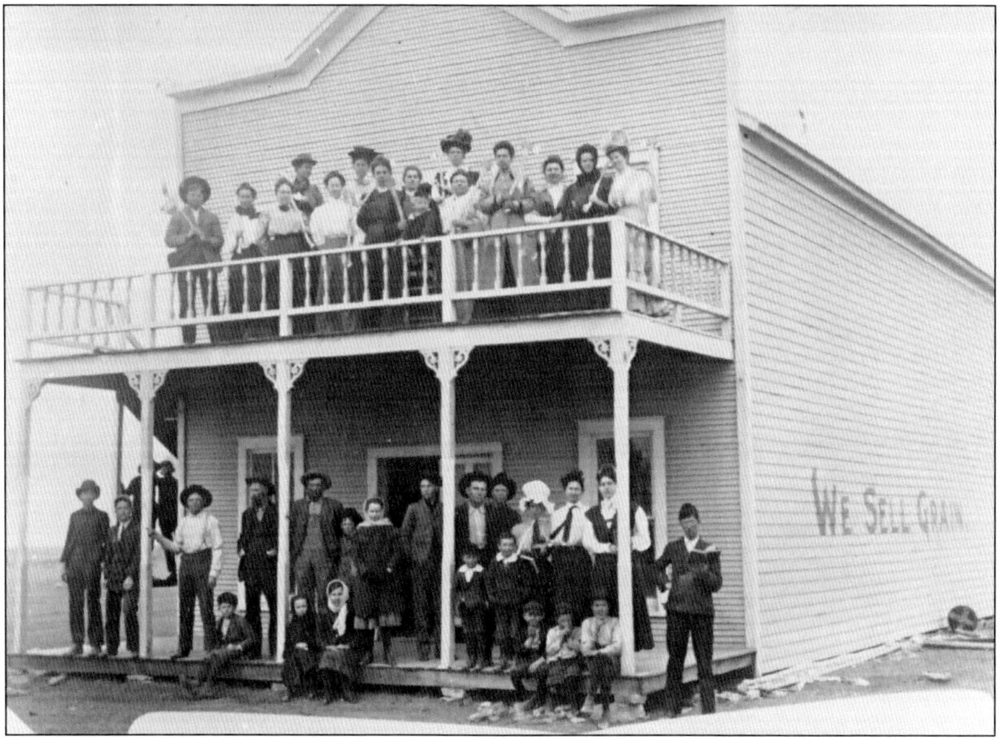

It seems strange that a region with so few trees would host a social organization called Woodmen of the World, but the group's presence is indicated by these Ira residents and their symbolic axes. Organizations such as the Masons and women's clubs played a major role in the lives of early settlers. Woodmen of the World, founded by Joseph Root, received its unusual name because Root had heard a sermon about pioneer woodsmen clearing land for their families. He intended to create a fraternal benefit society that would help its members achieve financial security—obviously a great benefit for early settlers who often risked everything by moving west. (SCM.)

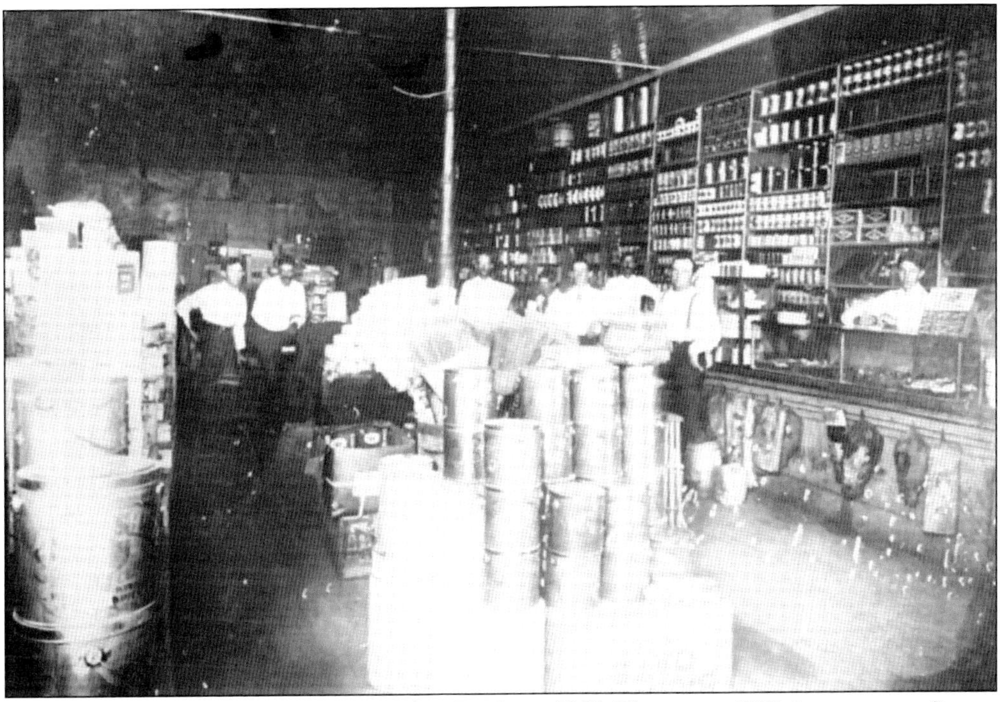

The Lee Brothers Grocery Store opened in Snyder in 1903. The owner, W.B. Lee, came to Scurry County from Comanche in 1902. He was formerly a racehorse jockey, but an injury led to him spending the rest of his life dependent on crutches. He married Etta Jones, whose parents ran the Jones Hotel, where Lee stayed when he arrived in town. Pictured here are, from left to right, W.B. Lee, Charley Burks, Woodsin Stimpson, Lee Boren, J.A. "Joe" Lee, and Marmy Looney. The stack of large tins in the foreground contain Silver Shield Coffee.

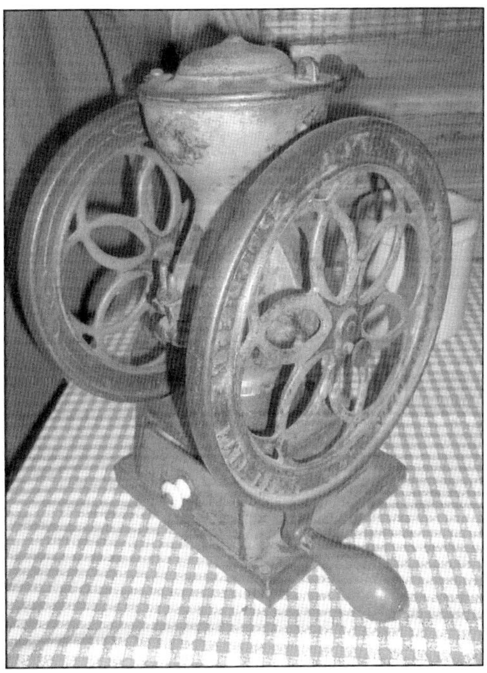

St. Louis was the coffee-roasting capital of the world in the 1800s, and coffee beans had to be imported from the Caribbean or South America. Pioneers drank large quantities of coffee; along with bacon, cornbread, and beans, it was a cowboy staple. This coffee grinder is now housed in the Scurry County Museum. Cowboys preferred their coffee strong, and one old adage says that the coffee is ready to drink if one can toss a horseshoe in the pot and have it stand straight up.

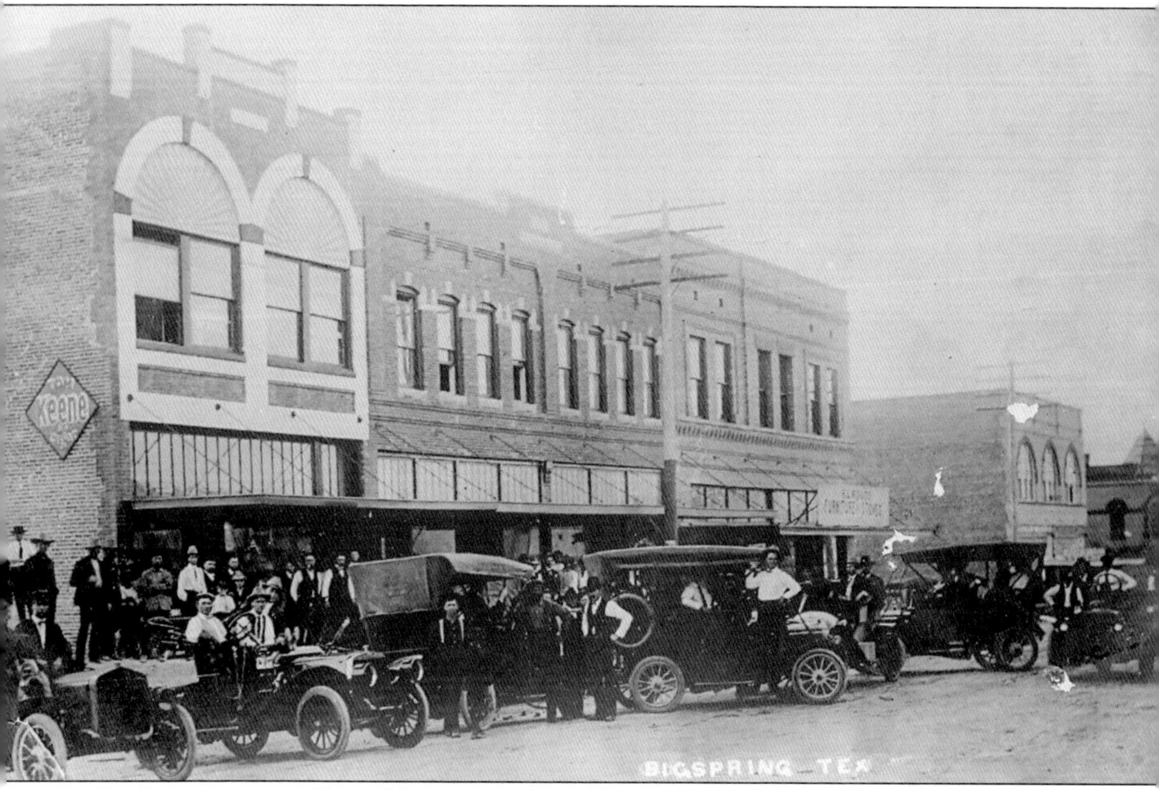

Big Spring, a town in Howard County, was named for a large spring discovered by early pioneers. The Texas and Pacific Railway came to the town in 1881, and this brought commerce to the area. Many ranchers from surrounding counties came to Big Spring to buy supplies. This photograph was taken in 1915, although many of the buildings were erected much earlier than that year. (SCM.)

Five

COMMUNITY

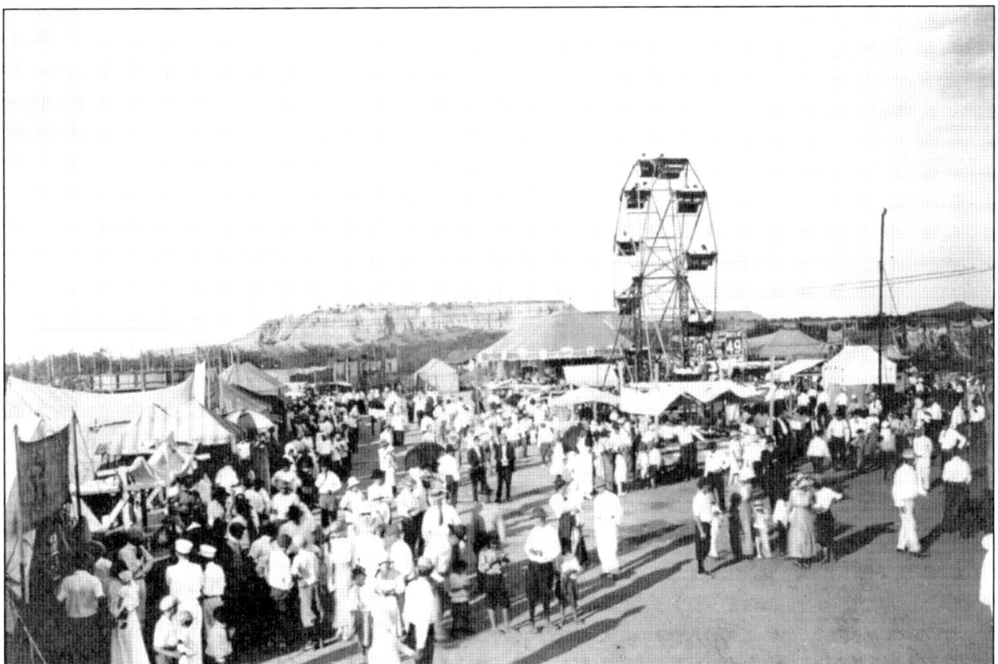

"Most of the people came in their covered wagons and camped on a small creek that ran along what is now 22nd or 23rd street. The men dug ditches along the creek to cook the meat; everyone was welcome to all they could eat. The celebration lasted three days. We had a dance every night. The Boston Bloomers, a girl's baseball team, came in on the train and played the Snyder men's team. A merry-go-round was there for the children. Mr. William Harrison and I brought in a big steer that belonged to Tom Morrison; kept it in a pen and charged 'ten cents a sight!'" Loyd Holley gave this description of the 1907 arrival of the railroad in Snyder, Texas, in a 1972 interview. This c. 1911 photograph—possibly taken near Post, Texas—shows a similar carnival near the Caprock. (SCM.)

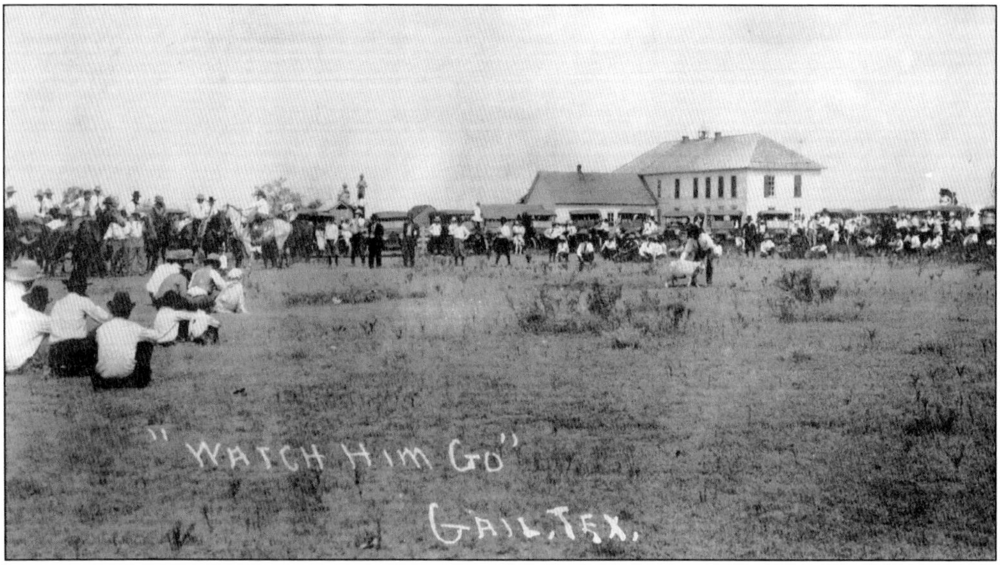

Cowboys often had extra energy for entertainment. This gathering at the old Gail school in Borden County was a goat-roping contest and probably part of a Fourth of July celebration. A large number of people came to the event. The handwritten words "Watch Him Go" on the photograph probably refer to the goat. (Borden County Historical Museum.)

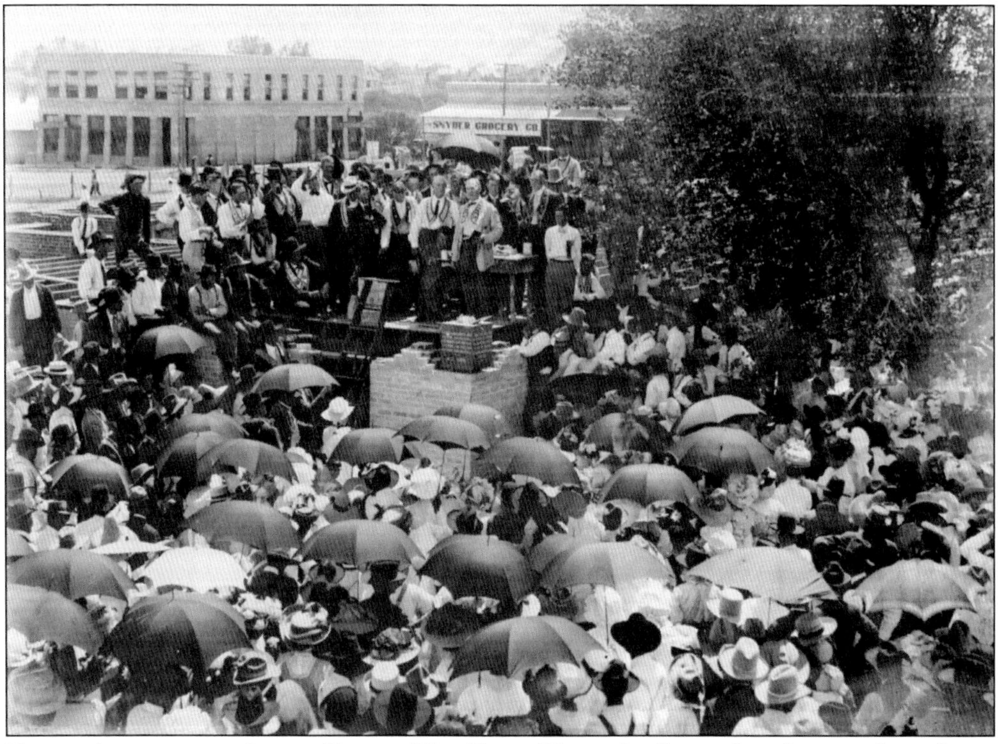

Too much rain was rarely a problem in West Texas. The umbrellas in this photograph are being used to ward off the sun. The crowd is gathered to watch the cornerstone being laid for the Scurry County Courthouse in 1909. Early settlers were proud to have brick buildings constructed in their towns; such an investment meant that the community was thriving.

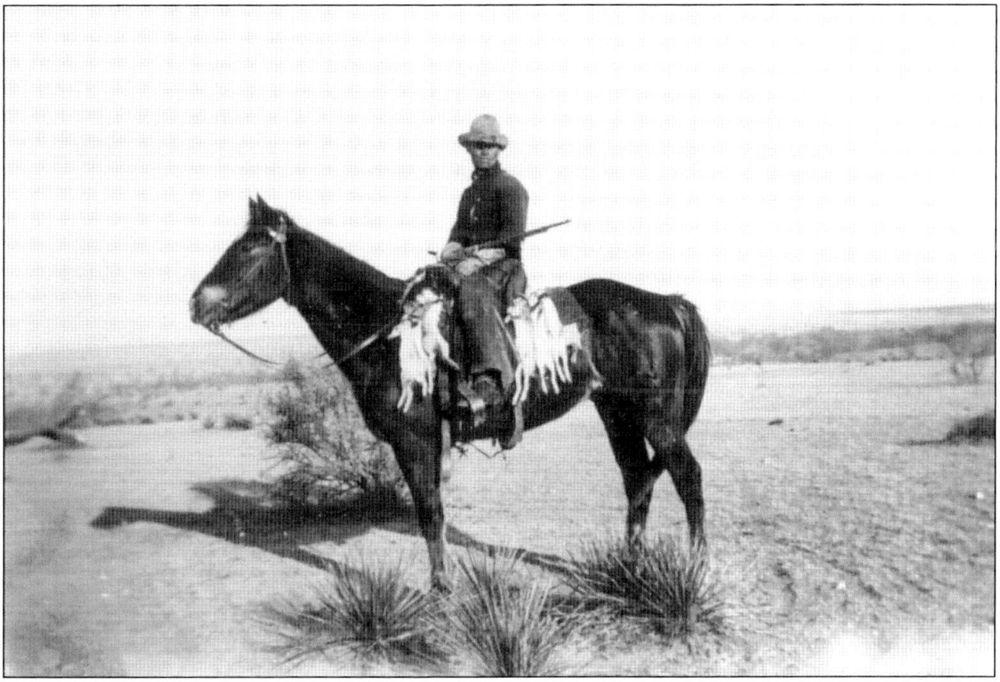

Rabbit drives were a phenomenon during the Great Depression. In Kansas, Nebraska, Colorado, Idaho, Oregon, and Texas, the population of jackrabbits was very high. In times of drought, rabbits could decimate farmers' crops. It was estimated that around 2,000 rabbits could eat as much grass as 35 to 40 head of cattle could. This photograph of Joe York was taken in Borden County around 1920. (Joe York Collection, SCM.)

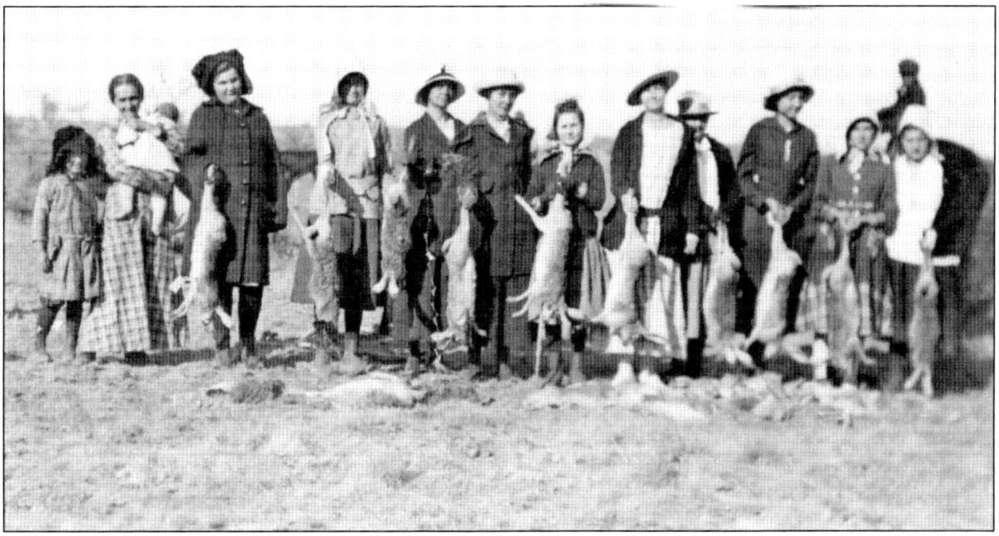

In preparation for rabbit drives, men and boys would construct fences. Then, either on foot or on horseback, they would drive the rabbits into the fences and kill them with wooden clubs. While this practice might seem violent or bloody to modern readers, rabbit drives were more than just necessity. They were also a form of entertainment often paired with cookouts, baseball games, or other Saturday events. Drives could yield anywhere from 500 to 1,200 rabbits. In some states, a bounty of 3¢ to 5¢ was placed on each pair of rabbit ears. (Joe York Collection, SCM.)

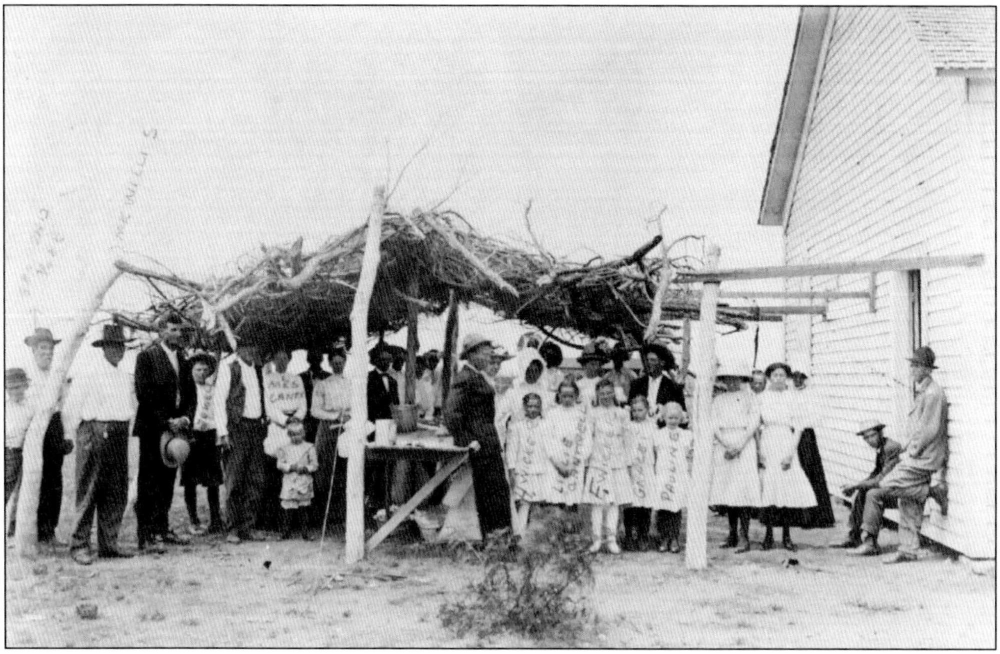

Church was an important activity for early settlers. Along with services, churches provided important opportunities for social interaction in a region where families often lived many miles apart. This c. 1909 image shows "dinner on the ground" after a morning service at a Durham church. Grandpa York is second from left, next to W.H. Willis. Sixth and seventh from left are Mr. and Mrs. A.J. Cantrell. Also pictured are a Wicker girl, Grace Cantrell, and Pauline Cantrell. The other parishioners are unidentified. (Borden County Historical Museum.)

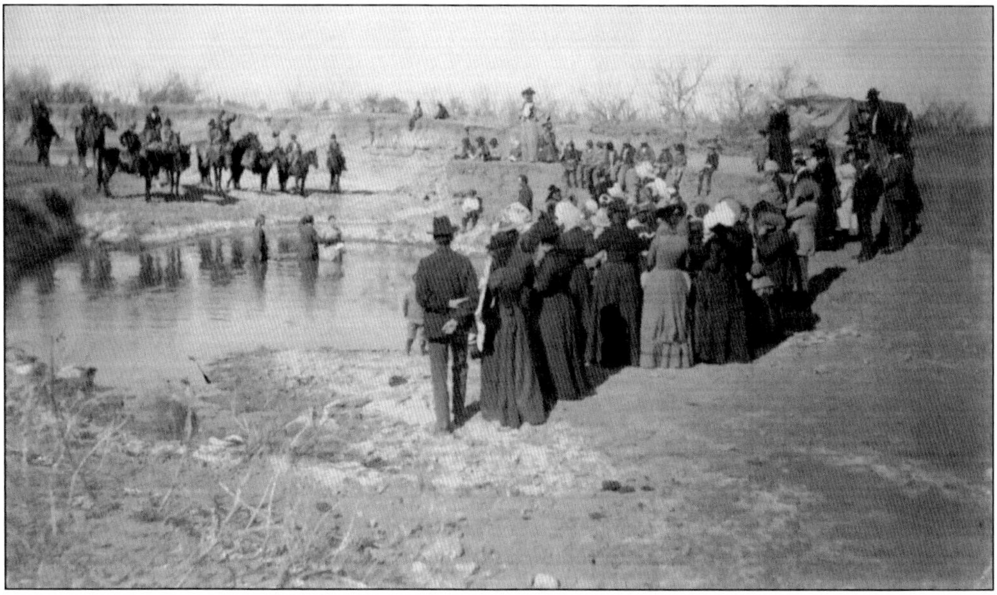

A stock tank is being used for baptisms in this c. 1900 photograph taken in Borden County. In all likelihood, the creek was dry at the time. When the railroads began to arrive on the plains, problems with water had already become apparent. Baptisms were an important church function, and people came from miles around to share the experience.

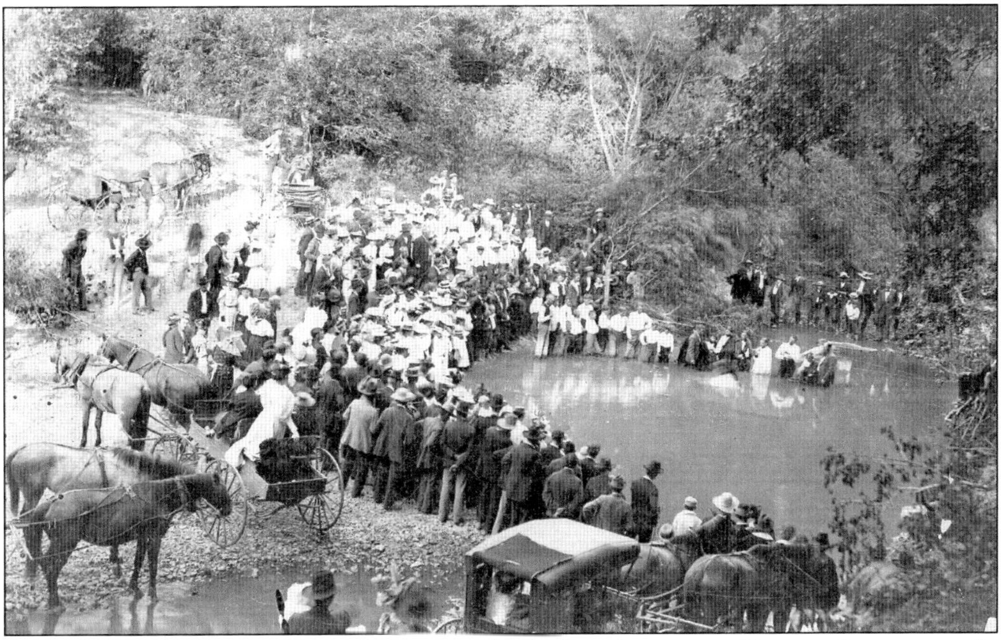

As much as religion was a unifying factor, it could also be a divisive one. Even small towns usually had churches of several different Protestant denominations, including Baptists, Methodists, and Presbyterians. German immigrants also brought Catholicism to the region. Records dating from the early 1900s describe births, deaths, and marriages, but they also record when new parishioners joined a church and, sometimes, why they left. Belonging to a specific church could give a person status within a community, but churches also placed certain expectations upon their members. The prohibition of alcohol was common, and some counties in West Texas remained "dry" until after 2000. (SCM.)

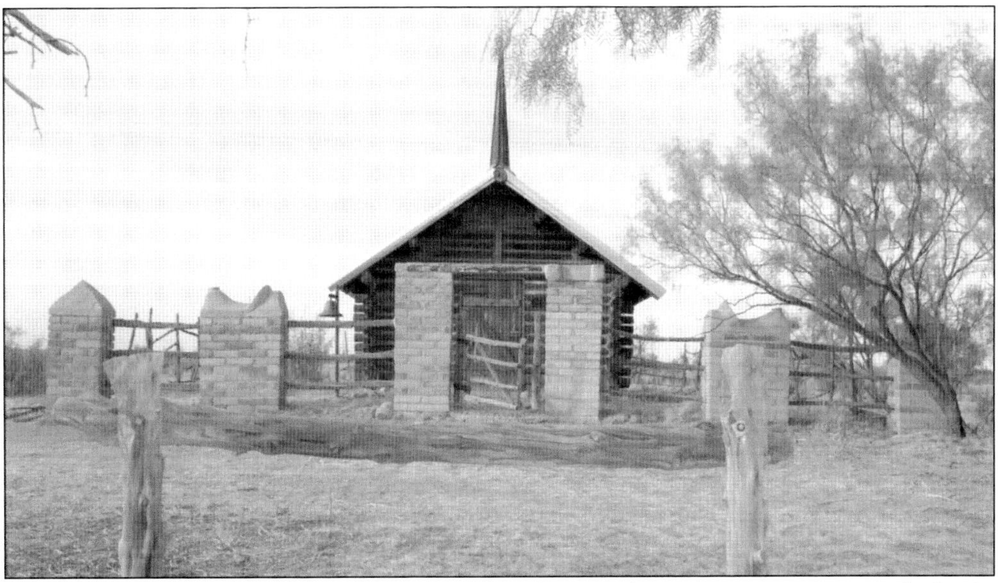

This cowboy church stands on the Riley Miller Ranch in southwest Garza County, near the banks of the Double Mountain Fork of the Brazos River. The building, erected in 1981 in memory of Miller's family, was constructed on a high hill overlooking a wild prairie.

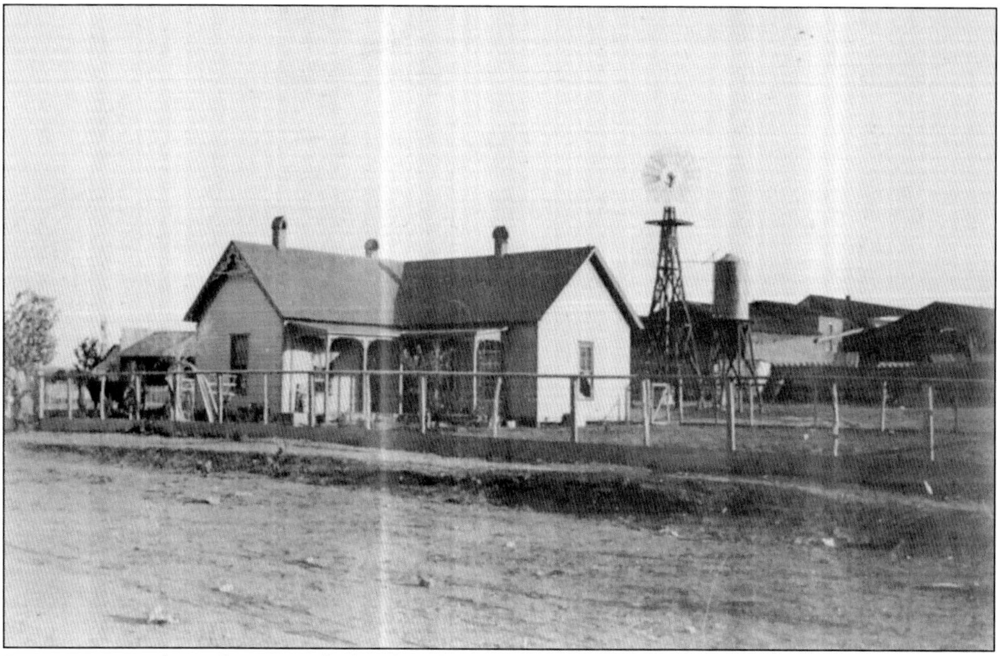

Since many early settlers initially lived in dugouts, a wooden house like this was something to be proud of. A water tank and windmill are visible behind the home, which was built by the Nation family. The back of the photograph says "Our first home" in elegant cursive. (SCM.)

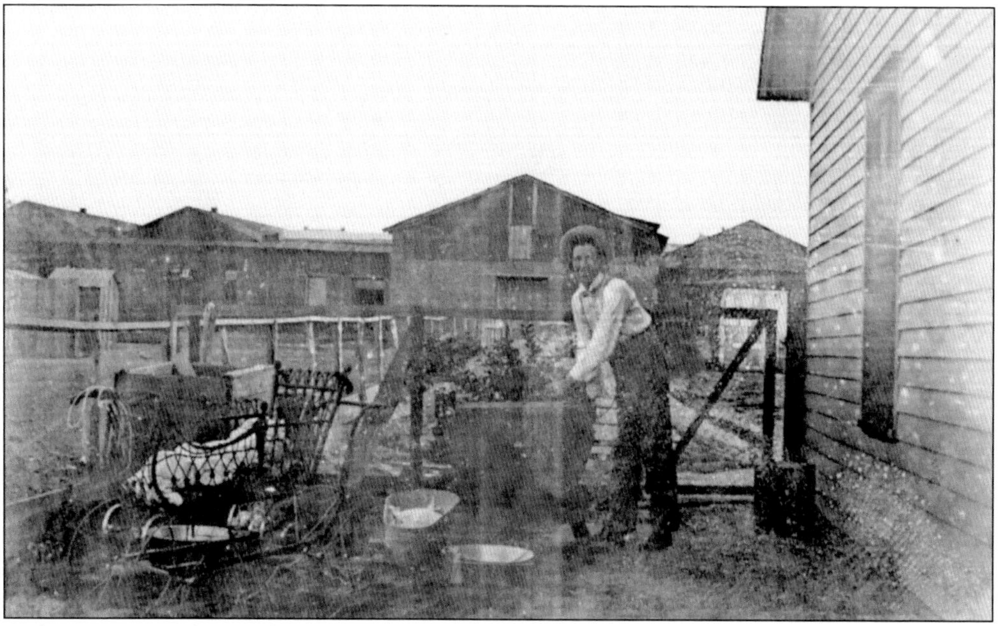

Viola Nation caught "Dad doing laundry" in this c. 1900 photograph taken behind the family's first home. The washing machine he is using was a new invention at the time. The presence of this convenience, and the fancy English pram, shows that the family was doing very well. Items like these were ordered through the mail from catalogs such as Sears and Montgomery Ward. Purchased items were shipped by train and then Wells Fargo Wagon to the remote corners of West Texas. (SCM.)

Laura Edmonson Stinson and Viola Nation Warren used photographs to chronicle their experiences growing up in Snyder and Ira. Here, the girls jump rope with some of their friends. Children were expected to entertain themselves, and if they were not studying or doing chores, they played outdoor games or made their own toys. Boys carved slingshots, and girls cut paper dolls from old catalogs or magazines. Marbles were also very popular with boys. Jump rope was almost exclusively a girls' pastime. (SCM.)

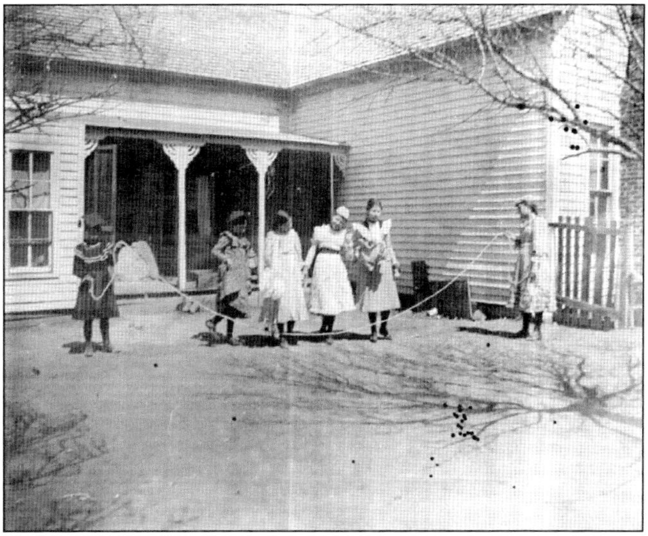

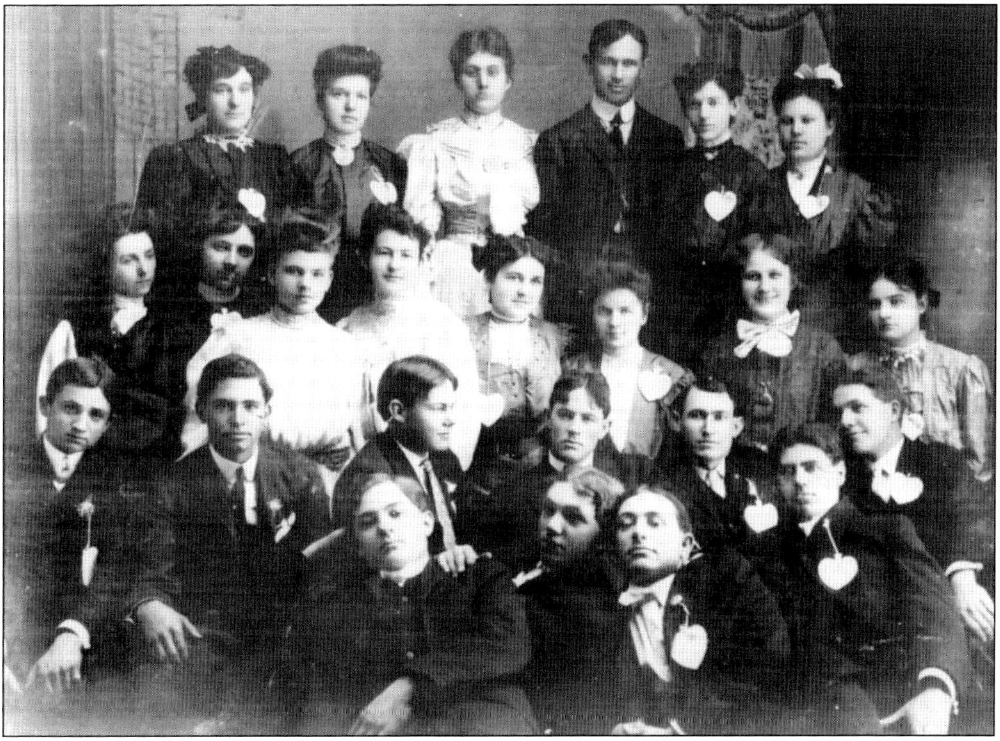

This group gathered in the early part of 1906 to honor a recently-married couple, Maggie and E.B. Barnes. She was the former Maggie Parkhouse, a music teacher who came to Snyder from Sherman. The party was given by Mrs. A.J. Grantham at her home on Avenue N and Twenty-fifth Street. Pictured here are, from left to right, (first row) Herman Nickolson, Cleveland Wood, and Billy Lee; (second row) Guy E. Paxton (Payton?), Emmett Johnson, Rue Nation (brother of Viola), Allen Warren (Viola's future husband), Walter Adamson, Hendrix Wood, and unidentified; (third row) Ione Scarborough, Maude Merrill, Ella Grantham, Jetty Rodgers, Laura Edmondson Stinson, Ida Ingle, Nina Cotton, and Nettie Knight; (fourth row) Minnie McMillan, Edna Grayum, Maggie Parkhouse Barnes, E.B. Barnes, Lois Gross, and Viola Nation Warren. (SCM.)

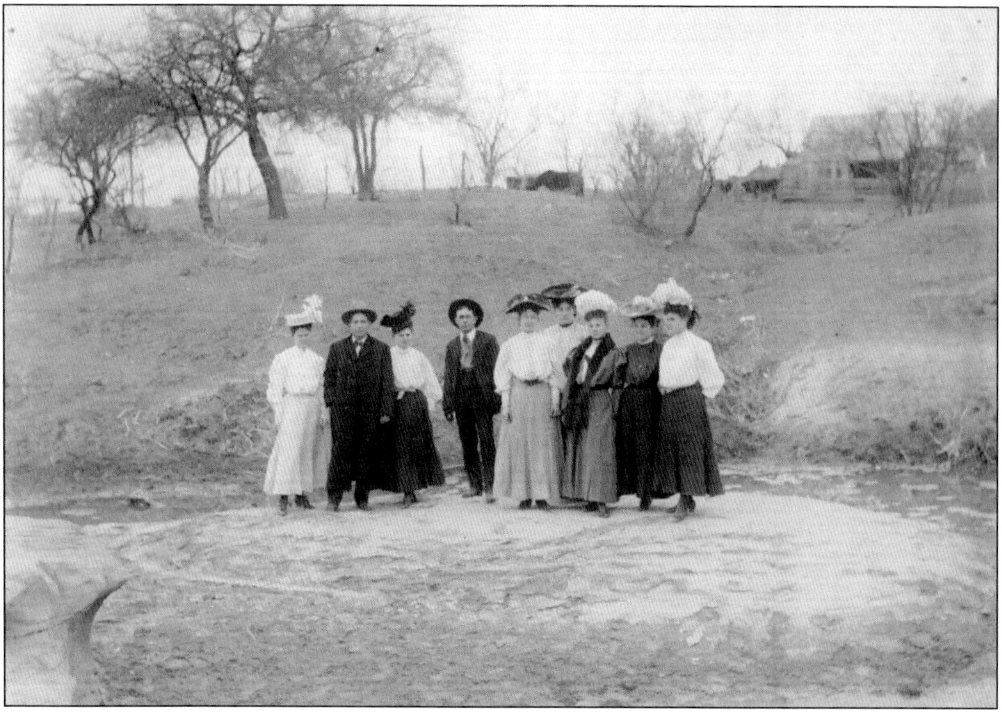

This group of men and women is standing in a dry water tank. Pictured here are, from left to right, unidentified, Hendrix Wood, Laura Edmondson Stinson, W.B. Lee, unidentified, Minny McMillan, Ella Grantham, unidentified, and Viola Nation Warren. (SCM.)

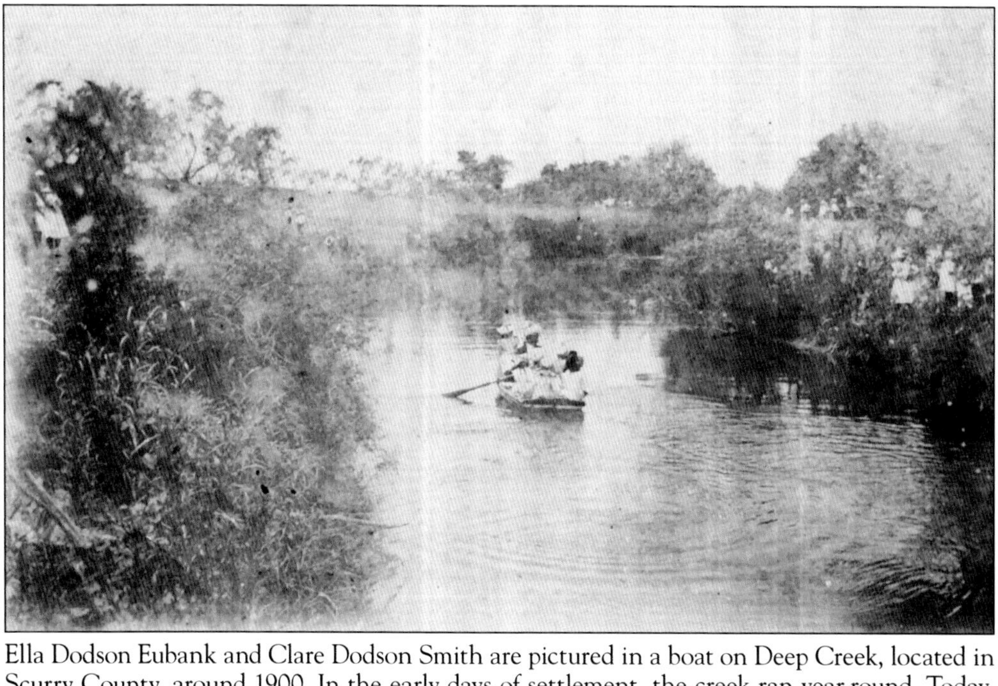

Ella Dodson Eubank and Clare Dodson Smith are pictured in a boat on Deep Creek, located in Scurry County, around 1900. In the early days of settlement, the creek ran year-round. Today, however, it is only seasonal and often dry. (SCM.)

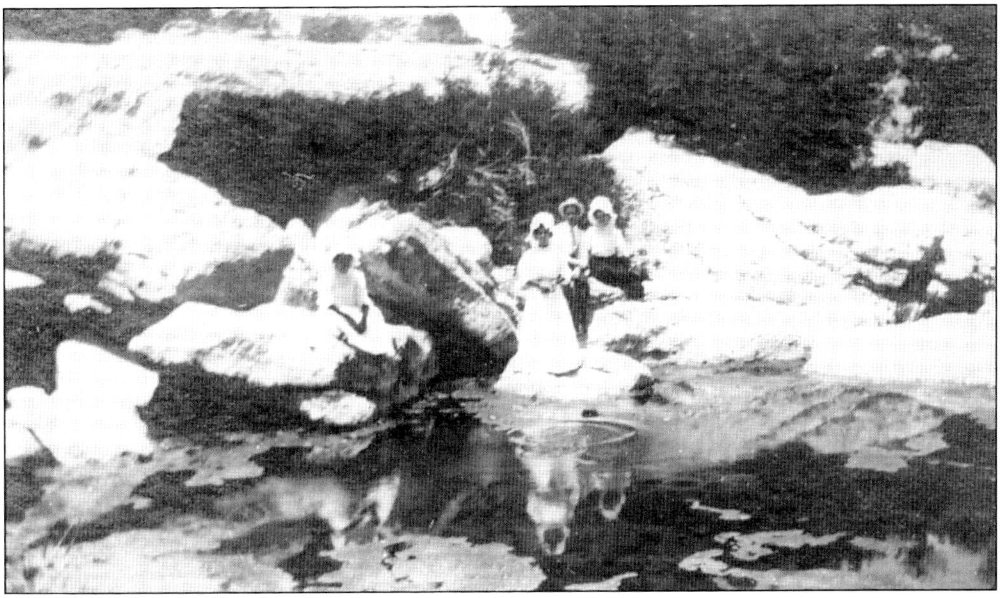

Like most of the water sources of the Panhandle Plains, Ennis Creek was often brackish. Two of the young women pictured here are probably Viola Nation Warren and Laura Edmondson Stinson. The young man is either Rue Nation or Allen Warren. Despite the fact that the water was not suitable for drinking, visiting a local creek for a picnic was a good way to cool off on a hot summer's day. (SCM.)

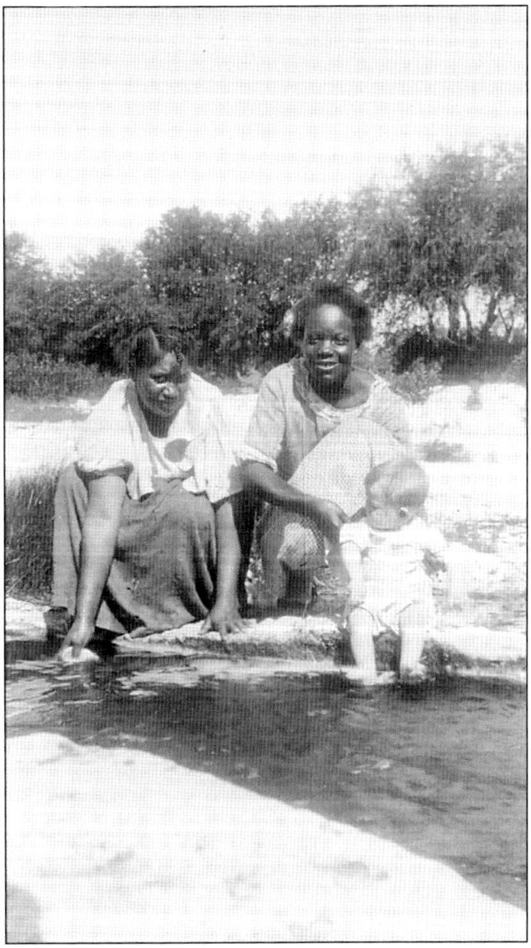

In the 1880s, having a photograph made could cost as much as $5—a week's pay for many workers. Most of the photographs that survive show the wives and children of wealthy white families. However, railroad, ranch, and cotton gin work also brought black and Hispanic settlers to the Panhandle Plains. While the men took dirty and dangerous jobs, their wives also worked—washing laundry, cooking, or caring for children. This photograph was taken around 1920, probably at Seven Wells in Mitchell County. (SCM.)

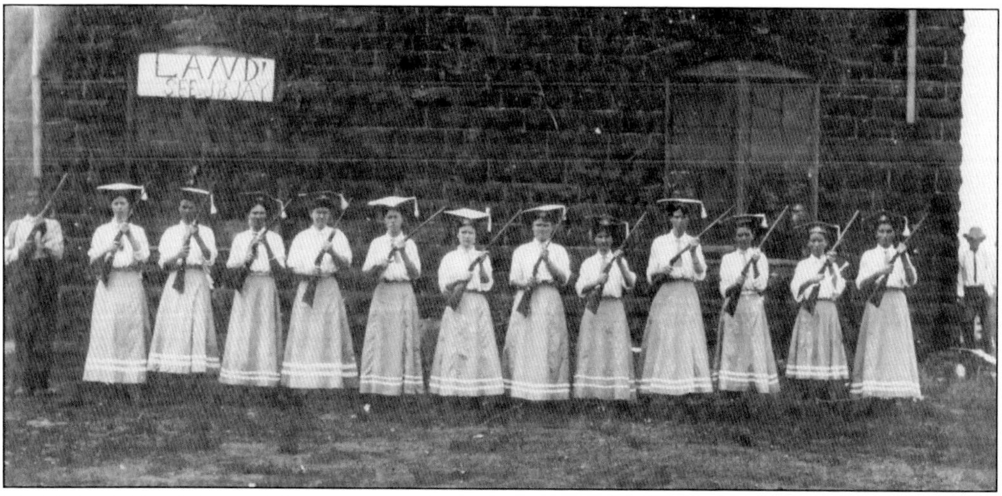

This ladies' rifle club posed for a photograph in front of the Kent County courthouse in Clairemont. The man at far left is probably their instructor. (Don M. Jay collection, SCM.)

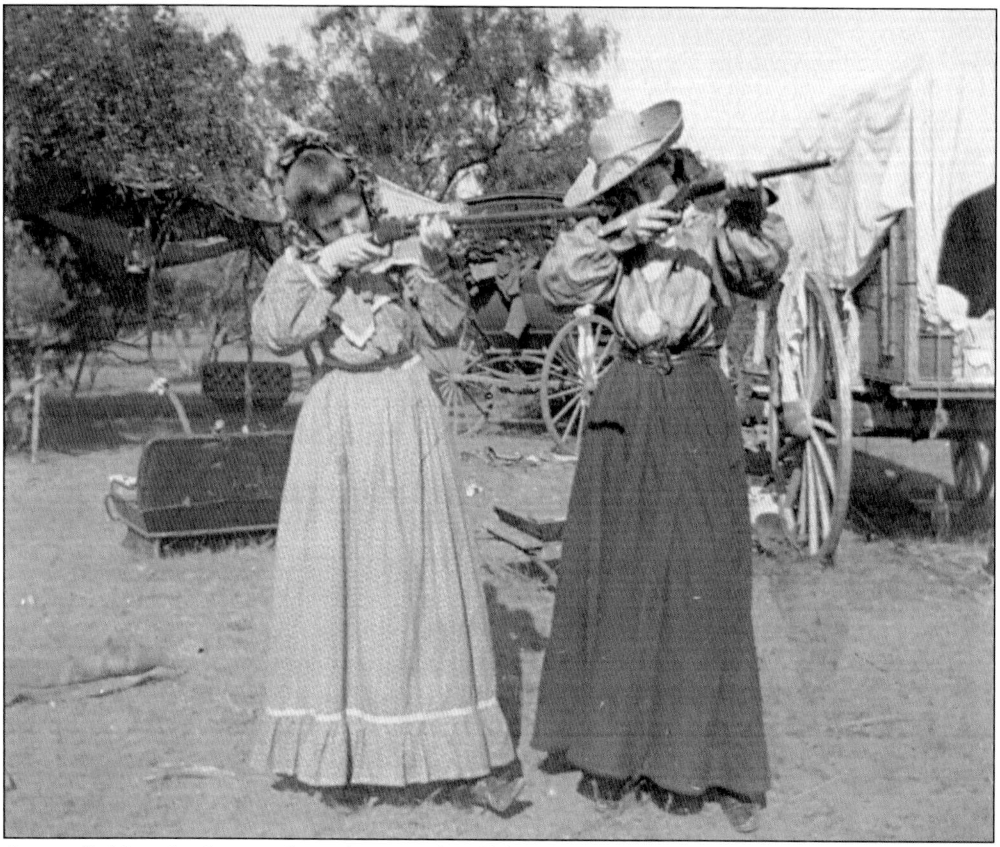

Annie Oakley, the famous sharpshooter of Buffalo Bill's Wild West show, inspired many women to practice shooting. Buffalo Bill's performers traveled all over Europe and put on shows for many famous people. Such a lifestyle must have seemed very exciting to these girls, who are practicing their aim while out on a picnic. They are believed to be Rose (left) and Lois, the daughters of William Lafayette Gross, who ran a grocery store in Colorado City. (SCM.)

Rancher Pete Scoggins once had a group of hopeful farmers set down on his land during a rather harsh winter. The families had no food and very little clothing. Sympathetic to their plight, Scoggins took them to Colorado City and let them purchase supplies on his bill. One elderly man confessed that he wished he still had his fiddle, which he had sold the year before to feed his family. Scoggins told him to pick a new one out and added it to his bill. The men seen in this tintype are relatives of the Beaver family of Fluvanna. Skill with a fiddle was prized as highly as skill with a gun.

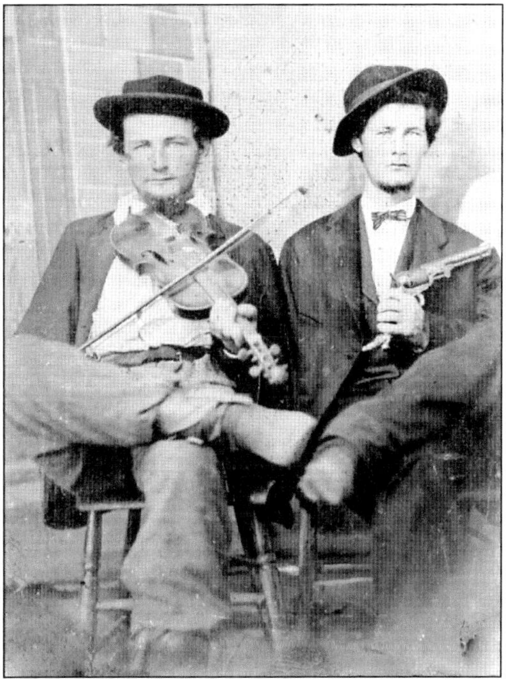

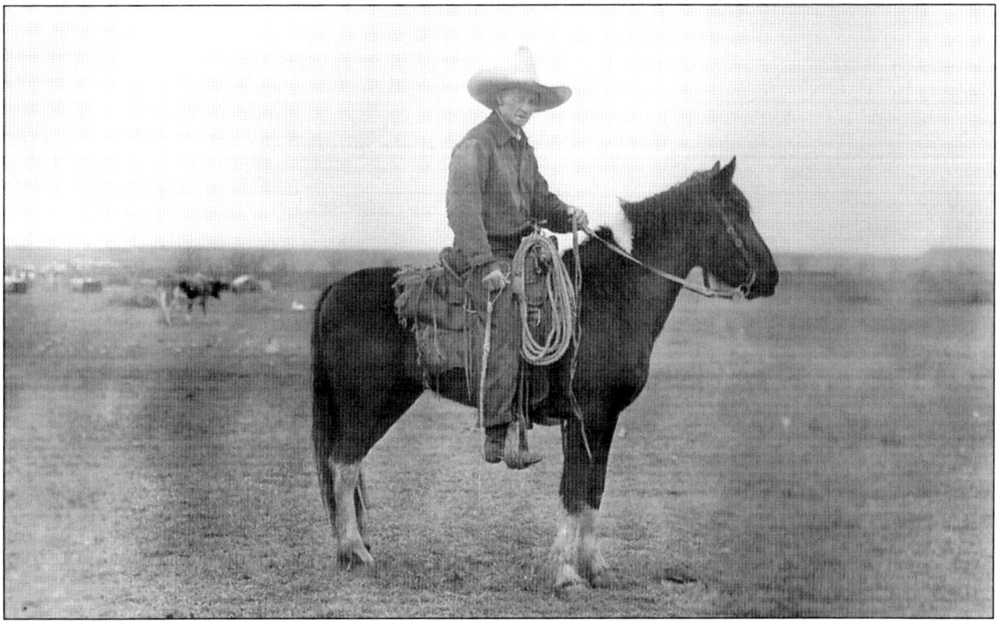

Cowboys often have a rough and tumble reputation in fiction, and, to some extent, this portrayal is true. However, one West Texas cowboy—"Uncle Dink" Logan—was a top-notch square dancer, which certainly made him popular with the ladies. Logan was a nephew of the Beal brothers, who started the Jumbo Ranch in Borden County. Logan helped Nick Beal drive 1,500 cattle into Northeast Borden in 1879. He also worked for the OS Ranch. Mrs. M.J. Nix Cannon recalls that Logan was "a good rider with a pretty horse, but I don't know whether I ever heard of his ability as a cowboy. I rated [cowboys] according to how good they danced, and Dink could dance real good." (SCM.)

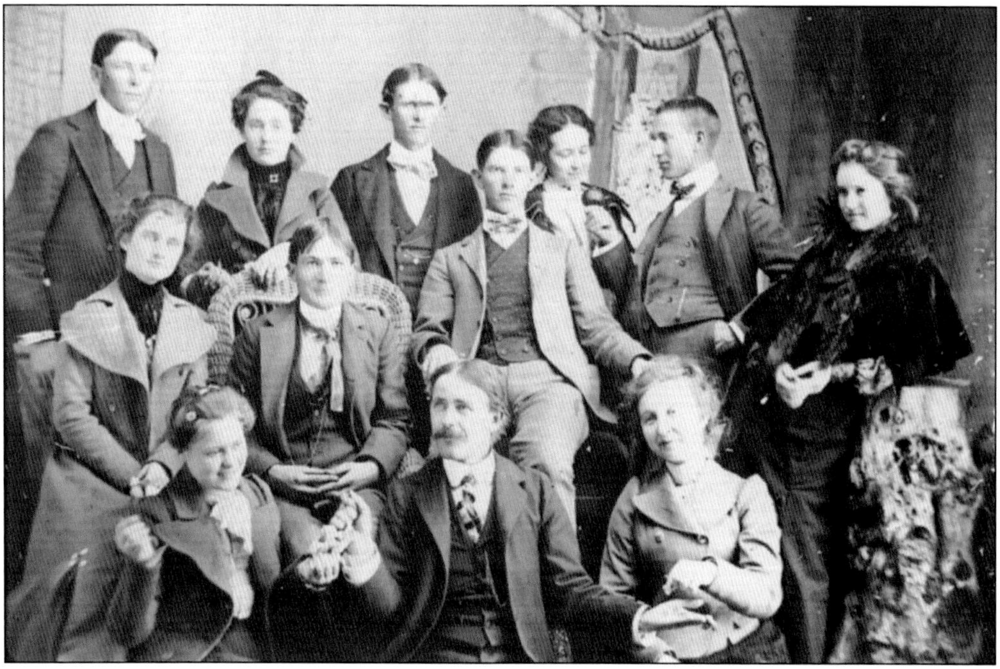

Speakers and preachers traveled from town to town, attracting attention everywhere they went. The expertise of this "Professor" Bowron is not known, but he clearly has the attention of most of the young people in this photograph. Pictured here are, from left to right, (first row) Clare Dodson, Professor Bowron, and an unidentified girl; (second row) Ida Godley, Sam Morris, J.I. Baze, and ? Lemons; (third row) Nick Alley, Ella Dodson, Homer Cotton, Tippy Person, and Orville Dodson.

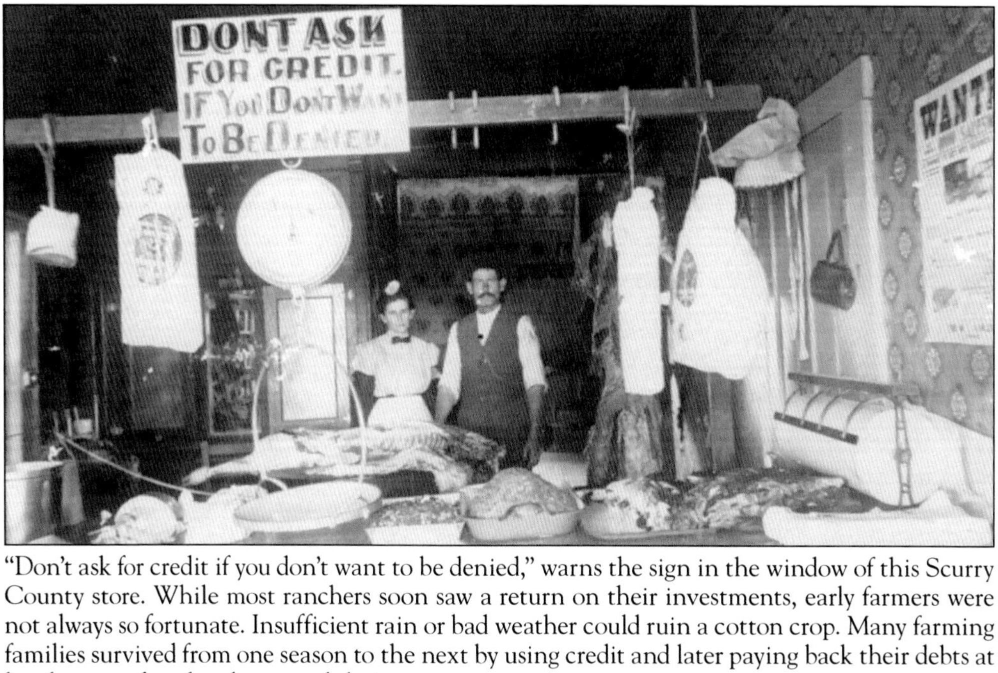

"Don't ask for credit if you don't want to be denied," warns the sign in the window of this Scurry County store. While most ranchers soon saw a return on their investments, early farmers were not always so fortunate. Insufficient rain or bad weather could ruin a cotton crop. Many farming families survived from one season to the next by using credit and later paying back their debts at local stores after they harvested their cotton.

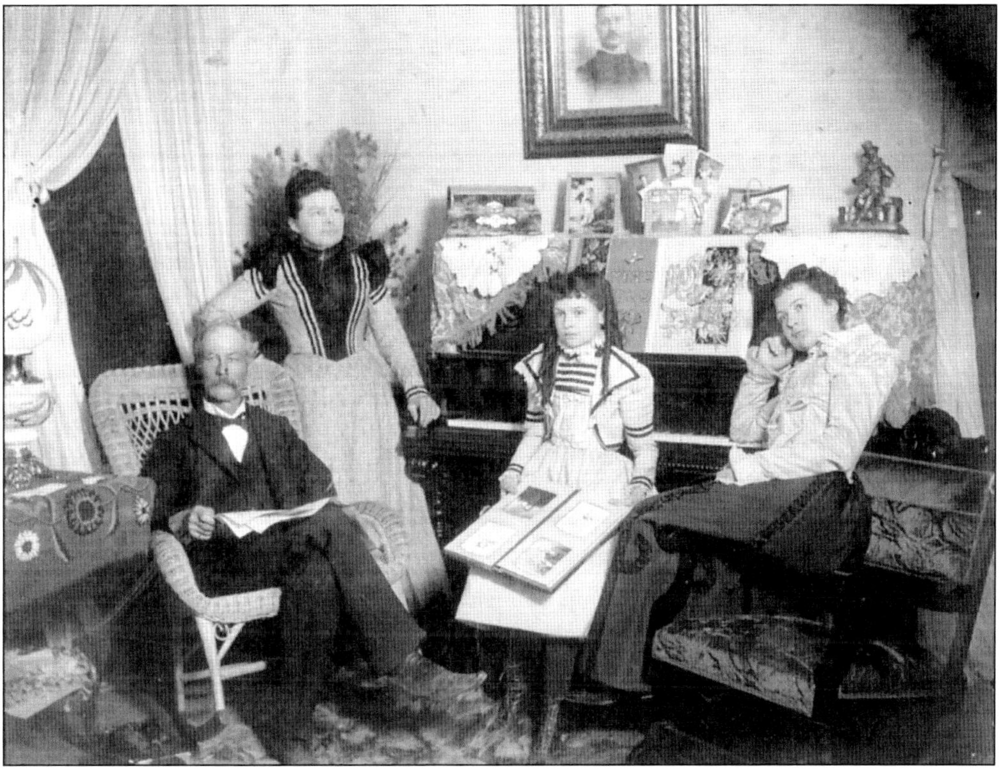

Dr. J.T. Jones moved his family from Arkansas to Fluvanna in the early 1900s. Injured in a cotton gin accident as a young man, he had only one arm. The photographer cleverly conceals what was surely a gruesome injury in this portrait of, from left to right, Dr. Jones; his wife, Mattie Francis; and their daughters, Stella Jones Beaver and Odyne Jones Mayhew. (SCM.)

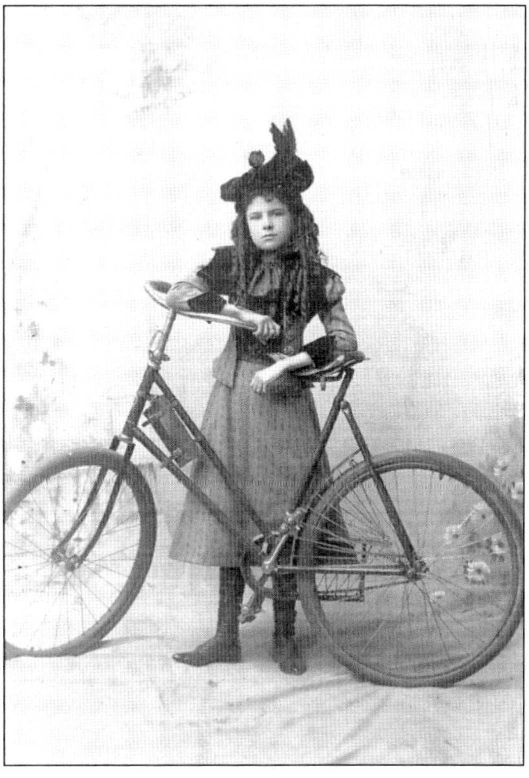

Since their father was a doctor (an uncle ran a pharmacy in Ezell, Texas) the two Jones girls were well-off and always had fashionable clothing. Young Odyne even had a bicycle, an invention that was gaining popularity with women in the early 20th century. Called a "freedom machine" by some, the growth of the bicycle's popularity helped lead to the abandonment of the corset as an essential part of a woman's wardrobe. (SCM.)

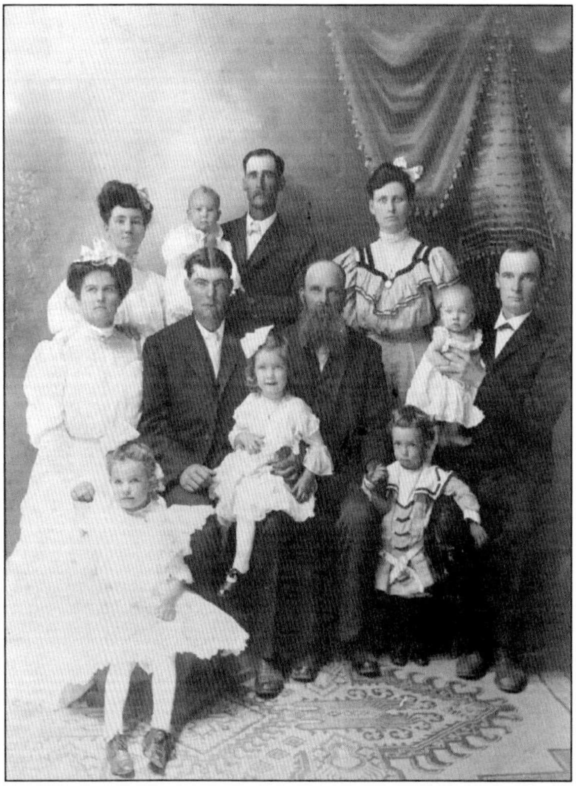

Settlers commonly had large families. This 1906 photograph shows the members of the Dorward family of Borden County. They are, in no particular order, Hattie, Ophelia Dorward Blackard, J.C., Minnie, Dave, Maurice, Cora, Rob, D. Dorward Sr., Catherine, Minnie, and Russell.

Porter King's Barber Shop, also known as "The Sanitary Barber Shop," operated in Snyder in the early 1900s. Porter King is standing beside the barber's chair at right. The man reclining in the front barber's chair is the father of C.L. Nobles. King had eight bathtubs in the back room for cowboys to use. The tubs were filled using water tanks on top of his building. King sent his clients' laundry to Fort Worth via the Roscoe, Snyder & Pacific Railroad, through Roscoe, and then on the Texas and Pacific Railway. (SCM.)

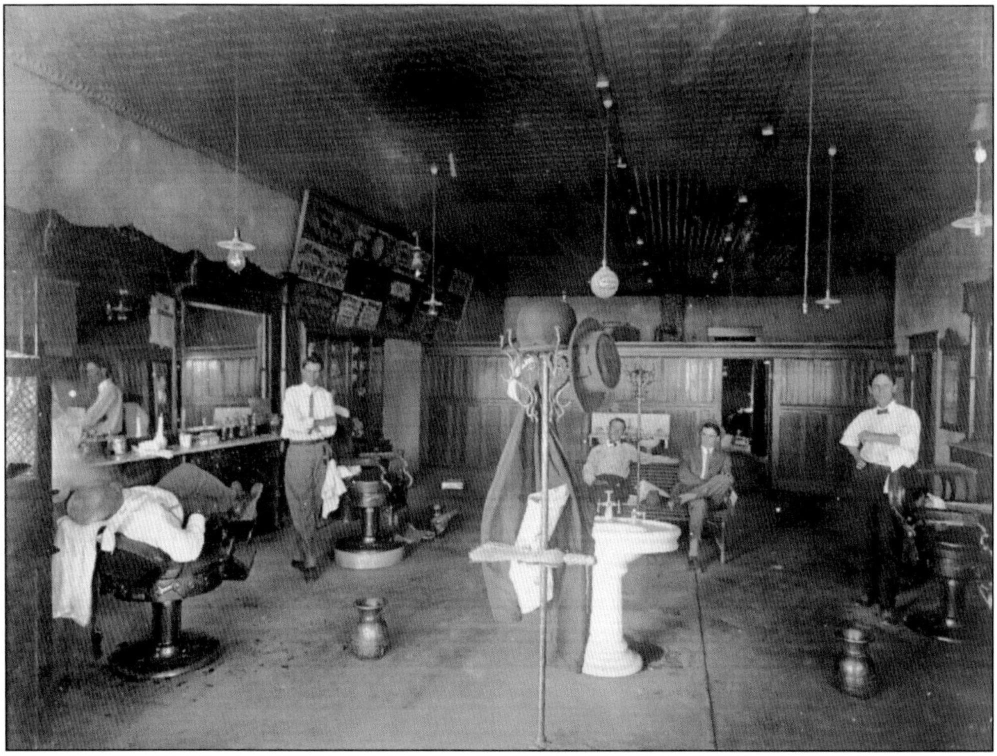

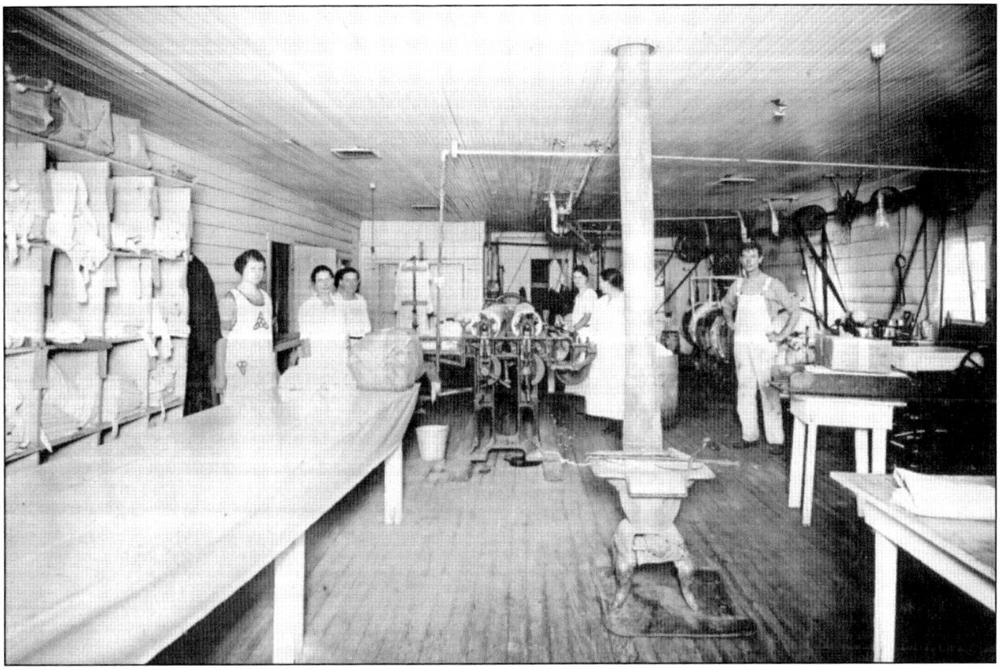

There were no laundries in Snyder until 1918, which probably resulted in a lot of smelly cowboys. La Rue Laundry provided jobs for six employees in the early 1920s. This photograph shows four barrel washing machines (at right) and a wood-burning stove. Businesses like this usually had large water tanks on the roof and their own windmills. (SCM.)

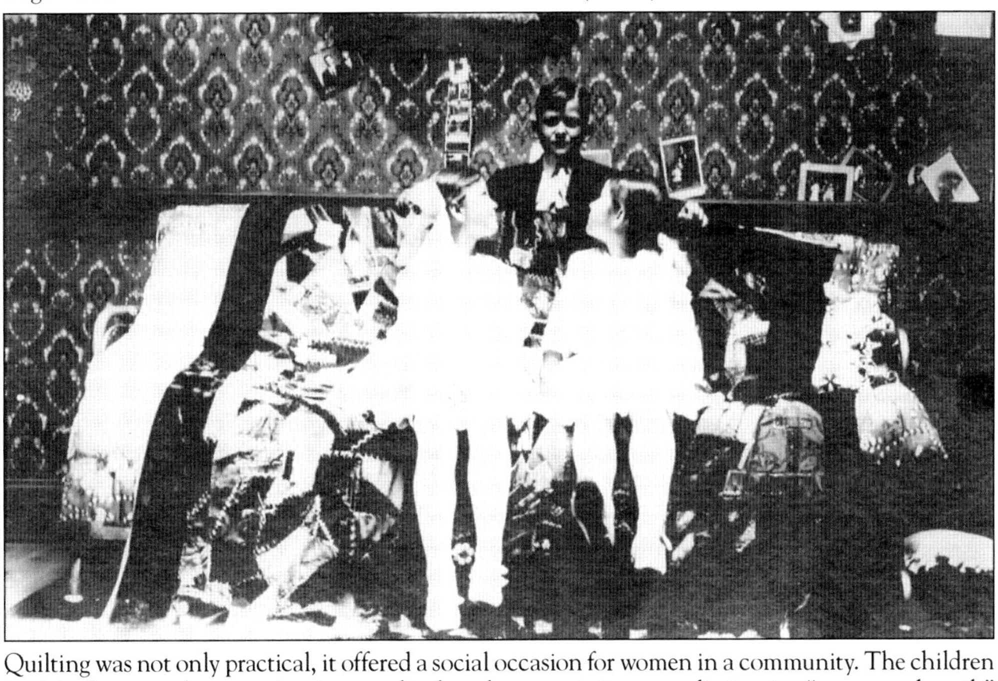

Quilting was not only practical, it offered a social occasion for women in a community. The children in this photograph are posing in a studio, but they are sitting on a distinctive "crazy patch quilt" made from scraps of fabric and clothing. This kind of quilt was very popular in the early 1900s, but since they were used in the home, they are rarely seen in studio photographs.

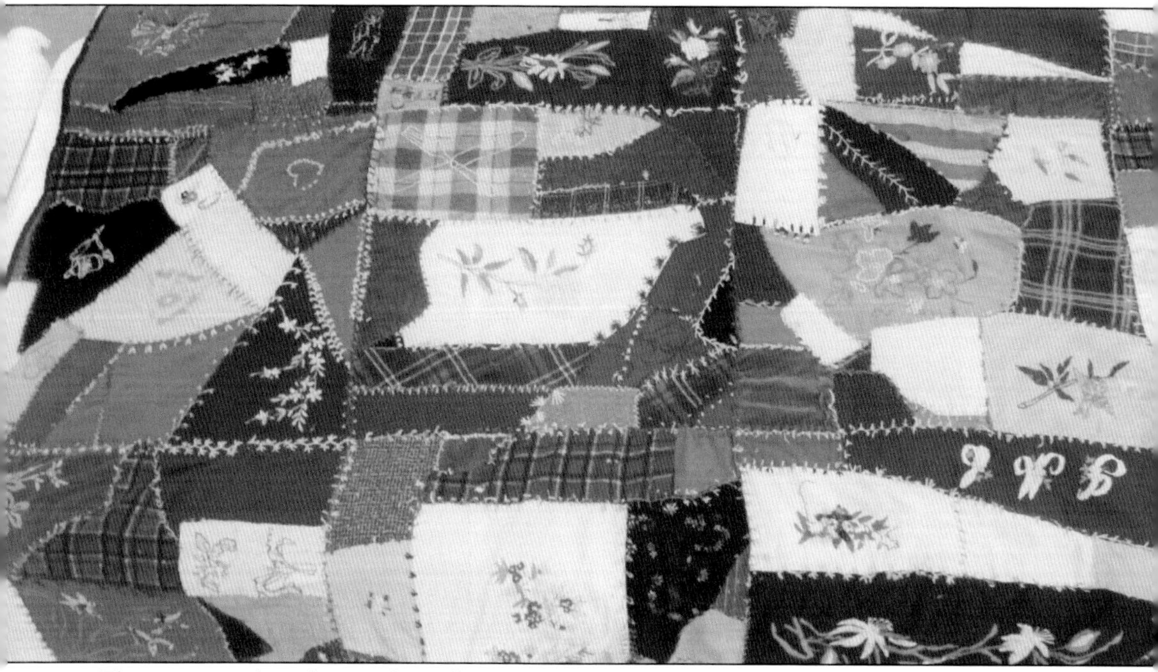

This crazy patch quilt is in the collection of the Scurry County Museum. It was made by Alice Spell Caffey in 1902 and contains pieces of dresses worn by three generations of Caffey women, including a portion of Ida Floy Wills Caffey's green wedding dress. Ida Floy was born on August 8, 1880, in Riley, Kansas, and married William Spell Caffey on December 15, 1899, at Comanche, Texas. William was born on February 5, 1870. The couple had 10 children, all but 2 of whom were born at Hermleigh, where the family farmed beginning in 1903. Few early settlers wrote of their experiences, but some quilts, like this one, tell the secret stories of the first women on the Panhandle Plains.

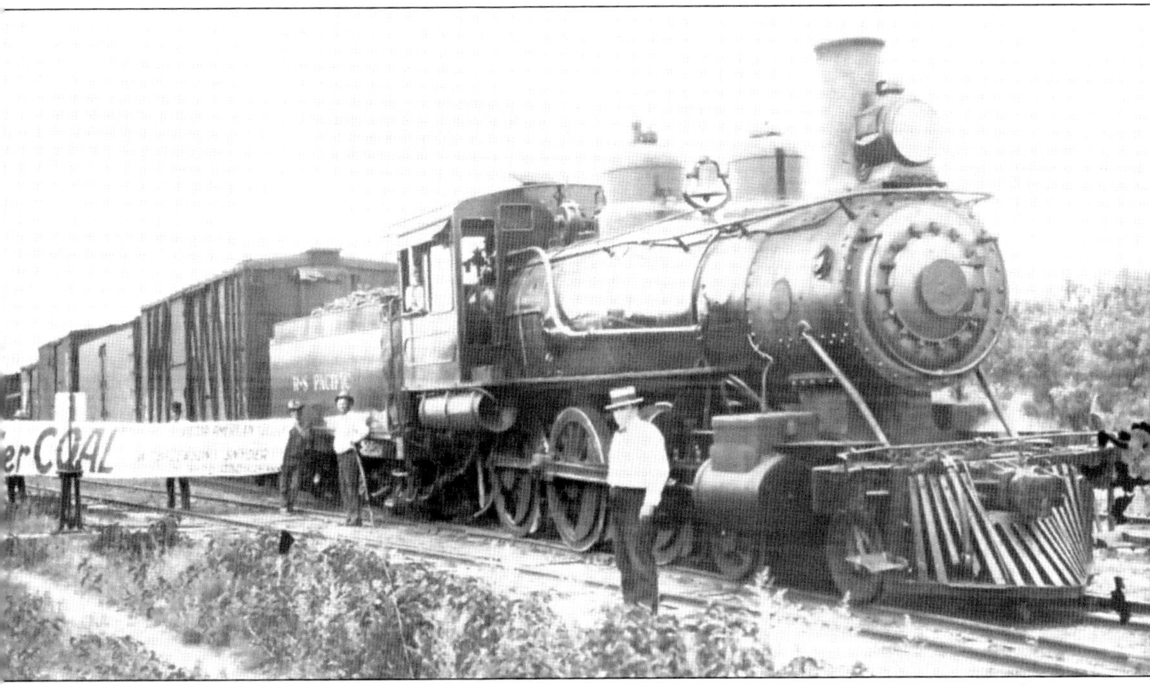

Life on the Panhandle Plains did not agree with all newcomers. In 1916, a young man arrived in Snyder and asked for a job with the railroad. While working, he complained of the sandstorm that was blowing. While the young man was out of the office, the old-timers ran outside, scooped up a bucket full of sand, and poured it on the newcomer's desk. When he saw all that dirt, he immediately decided that Snyder was not the place for him and left town before nightfall. In this photograph, A.C. Preuitt, one of the old-timers responsible for the prank, stands in the foreground. Behind him is a train full of coal destined for the coal yard of W.T. Baze. (SCM.)

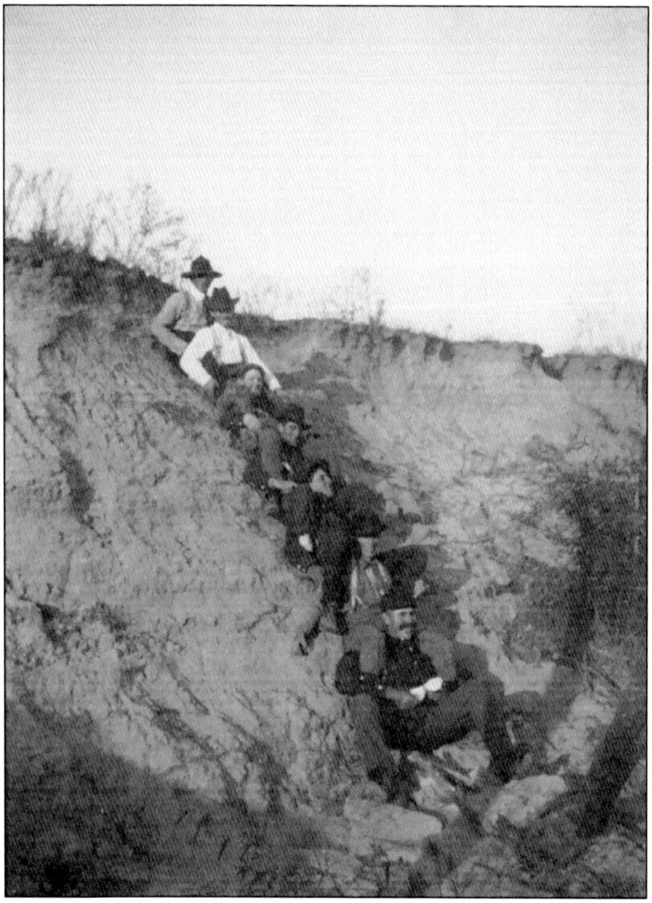

This railroad survey crew started working on a line in Memphis, Tennessee, and stopped in a ravine near Irving, Texas, to display a bit of humor for this c. 1902 photograph. (Irving Public Library.)

Florence Middleton Leftwich, of Scurry County, was the first passenger to arrive in Snyder via the Santa Fe Railroad. As she described it: "We visited a friend who was a conductor, and it so happened that the very next day he was going to Sweetwater. He said we were welcome to ride, but if we were killed we couldn't collect any insurance." The Leftwichs rode the train anyway and were let off at the Santa Fe depot in Snyder on June 15, 1911. The depot, designed by architect Louis Curtiss, still stands today, and Preservation Texas placed it on their 2011 list of Texas' most endangered historic places. (SCM.)

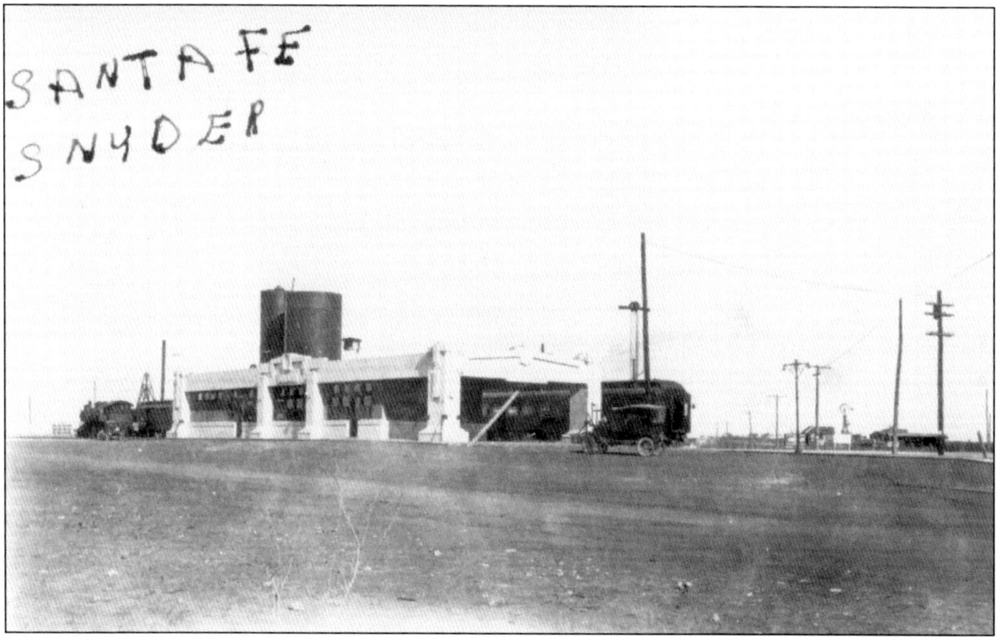

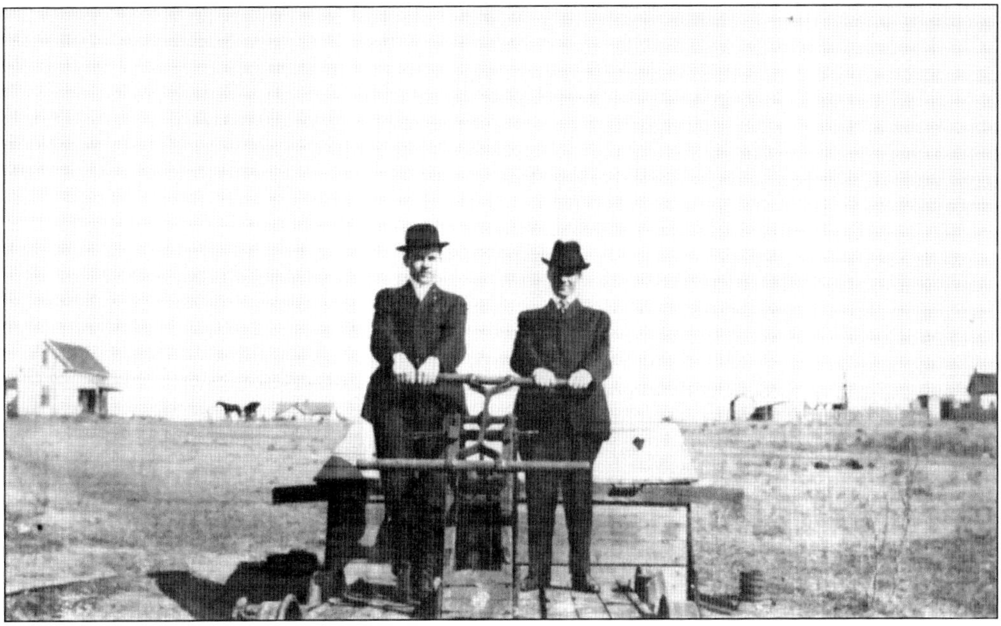

Railroad employees used handcars like this one to inspect sections of track. Handcars were useful because they could be lifted off the rails if a train needed to pass and then put back on.

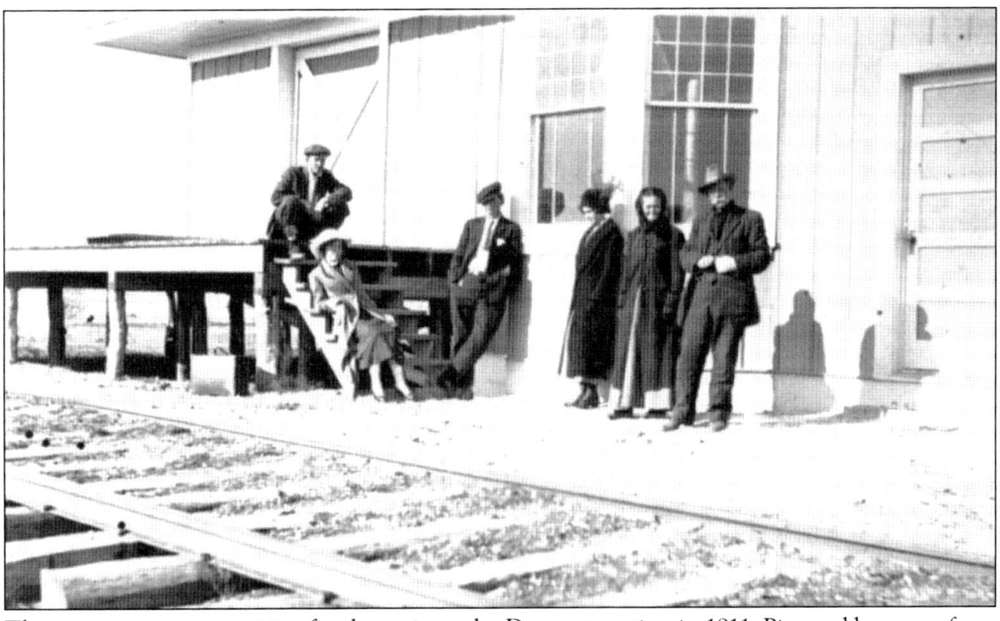

These passengers are waiting for the train at the Dermott station in 1911. Pictured here are, from left to right, H.O. Greenfield, Maye Greenfield, Everett Seribur, Bertha Greenfield, Mrs. H.C. Greenfield, and H.C. Greenfield.

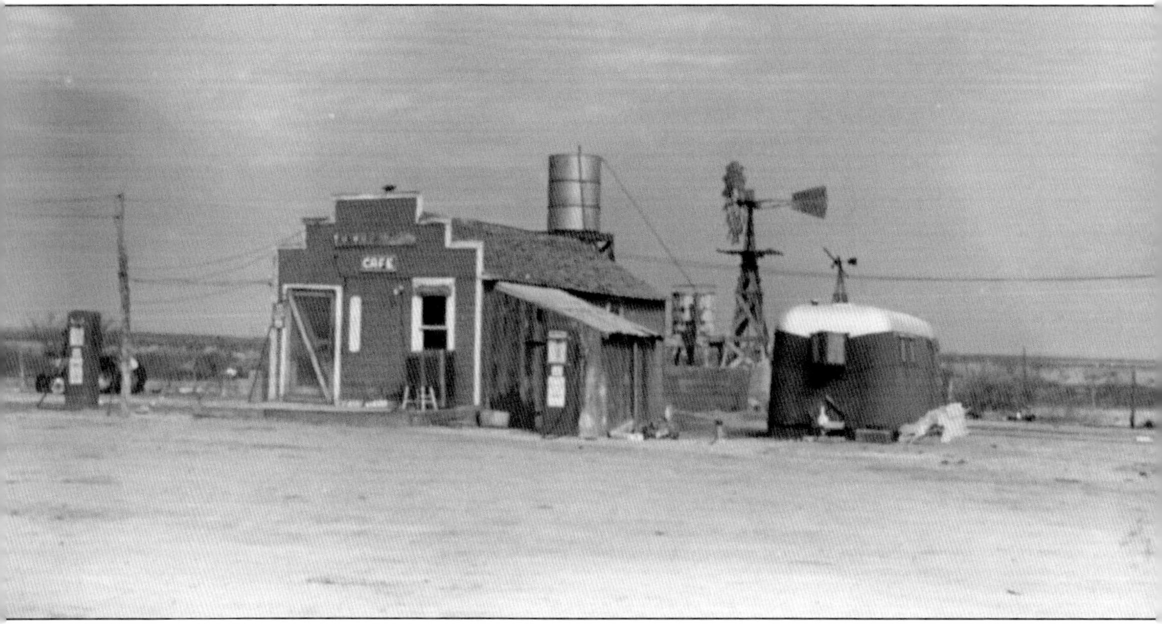

The popularization of the automobile changed the Panhandle Plains as significantly as the introduction of the windmill. While the windmill allowed towns to flourish, the automobile closed the distance between places. Isolated communities began to die off as even the region's most remote farmers and ranchers were able to "drive into town." This is the last business still running in the Knapp community. If it looks reminiscent of the image on page 51, that is because it is the same box-and-strip building—pictured here more than 60 years later. The post office and store, which provided an essential link to the outside world in 1890, had become a service station by the early 1940s—a remote outpost with a single gasoline pump. In 1968, Knapp received a historic marker. (SCM.)

Six

Changing Times

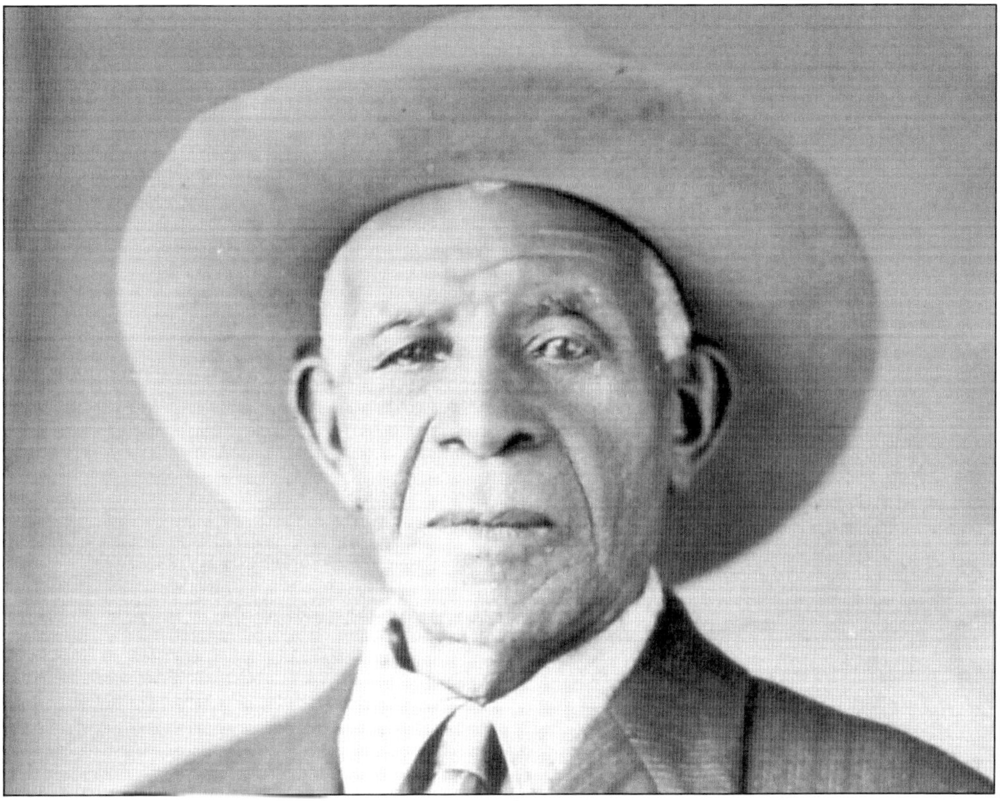

Of all the men and women who braved the Panhandle Plains, perhaps none of them embody the pioneering spirit of the region as well as Daniel Webster "80 John" Wallace. Wallace was born into slavery on September 15, 1860, to William and Mary Barber Wallace. He went on trail drives for C.C. Slaughter and other ranchers. He had not learned to read or write as a child, so, at the age of 25, he attended school for two winters. Wallace married Laura Dee Owens and joined Clay Mann's "80" brand outfit. Because another black cowboy was named John, Mann nicknamed Wallace "80 John." Wallace took most of his monthly salary in cattle and purchased land. He drilled oil on his property and, at the time of his death on March 28, 1939, he had amassed a fortune. His descendants remain on the land today, and a state historical marker in Loraine commemorates his life.

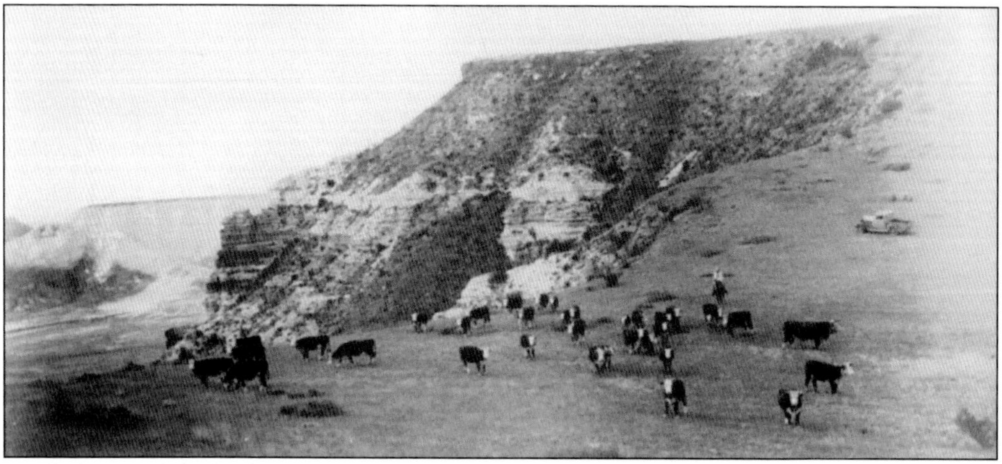

Cattle frequently had to be moved to fresh ranges and water to ward off die-ups. This herd belonged to W.D. Mitchell and his sons. Note the truck on the hill at right. Improvements in automotive suspension and tires allowed trucks to increasingly fill the roles of wagons and horses. By 1940, virtually every rancher owned a truck. Today's ranchers use horses, ATVs, or trucks to move cattle from one pasture to the next. (Cattle Raisers Museum.)

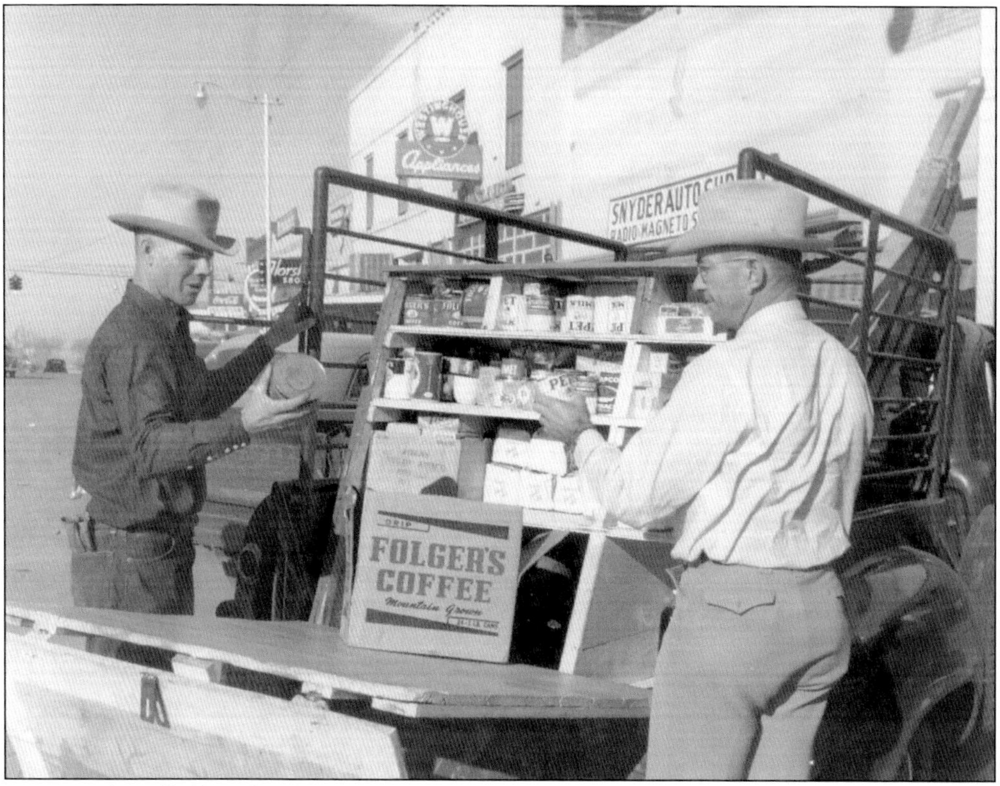

Ben Weathers (left) and Nolan Von Roeder load up a chuck box on the east side of the Snyder square in this photograph, which was probably taken in the late 1950s. Long after pickup trucks replaced horse-drawn chuck wagons, the tradition continued of having "cornbread and beans" suppers out on the plains. Coffee, another cowboy necessity, continued to be one of the key items stocked in every chuck box.

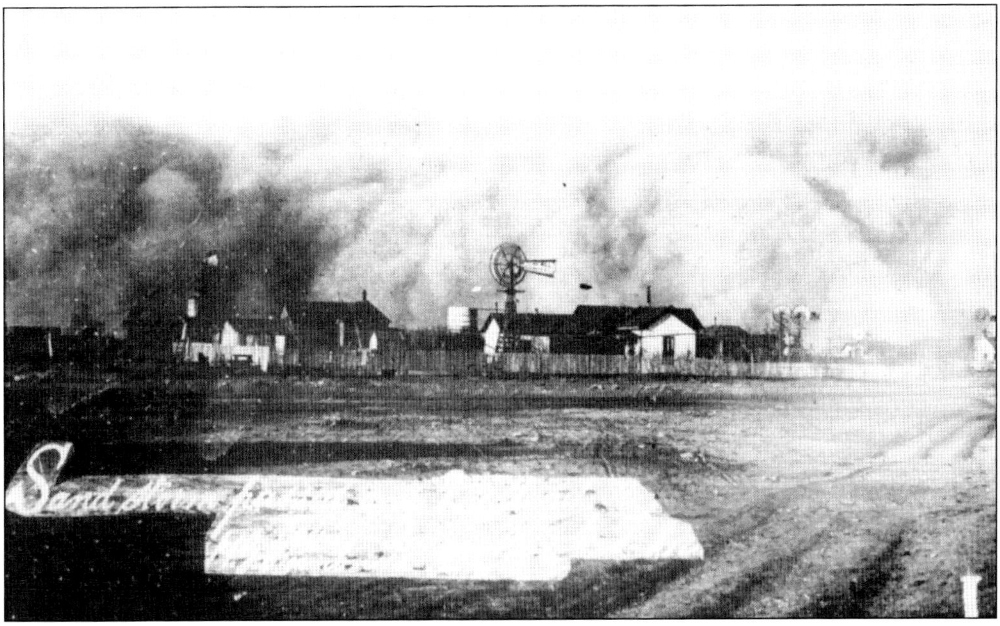

A huge dust storm tears across Midland in this photograph taken at 6:00 p.m. on February 20, 1894. A persistent fact of life on the Panhandle Plains, dust storms can be devastating to cotton crops. With sustained winds of up to 30 miles per hour and gusts regularly hitting 45 miles per hour, such storms are also a danger to modern drivers. Between Lubbock and Amarillo, wind speeds have been recorded of up to 70 miles per hour.

Although rain was always welcome in the arid region, too much water could pose a serious danger. In this 1924 photograph, M.E. Rosser watches Deep Creek rise from outside his home in Snyder, Texas. The Scurry County jail is in the background. Because of the usual lack of rain, the ground is unable to quickly absorb water. The 1936–1937 flood in Snyder caused nearly $500,000 in damage. (SCM.)

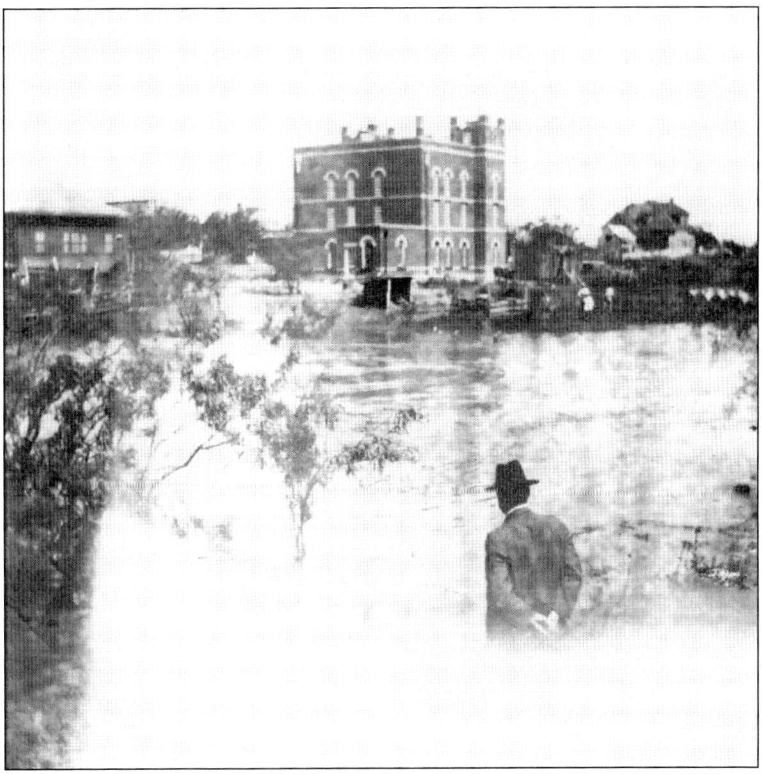

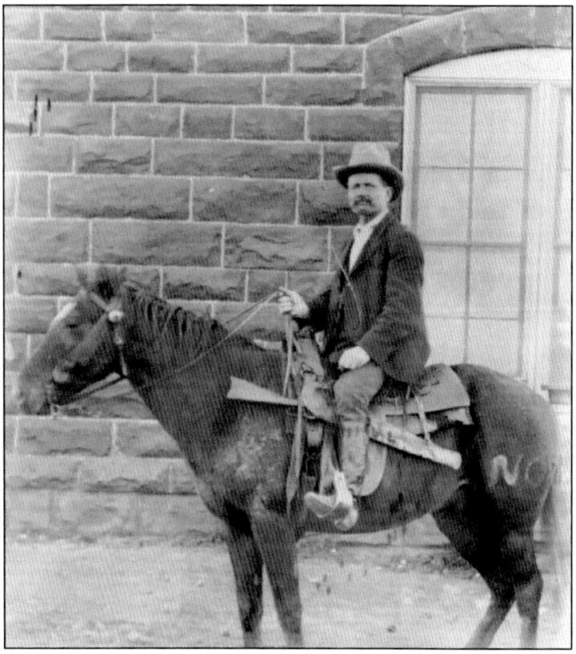

Norman N. Rodgers made his first trail drive at age 12. He was a fighter of Indians, a frontier Texas Ranger, and a sheriff of Kent County. He lived through changes from the old to the new. Rodgers made his final mark as a rancher south of Justiceburg in Garza County. (Kent County sheriff William Scoggin.)

Nonnie Rodgers, a granddaughter of Norman Rodgers, grew up on the family ranch. When Norman died, his son stayed on the ranch and raised his family. Nonnie married John Ward, son of Dr. John Ward of Snyder. She is now deceased, but John remains on the ranch. (SCM.)

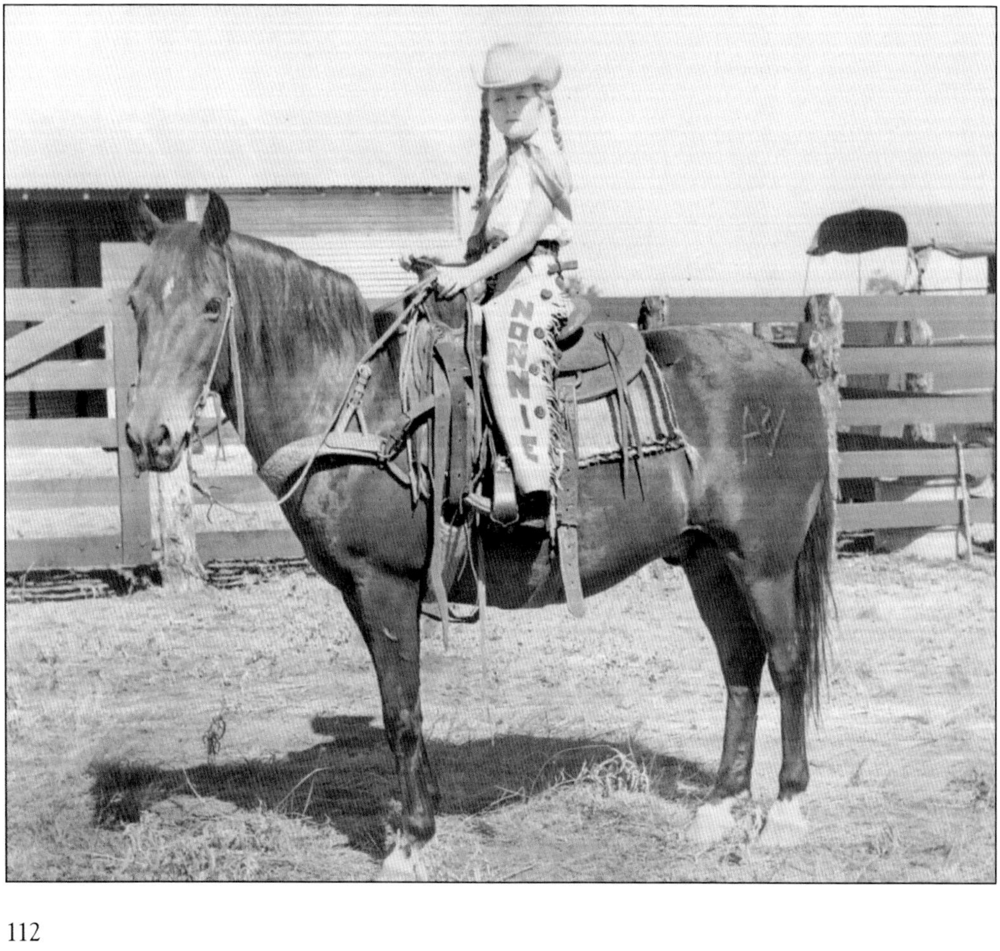

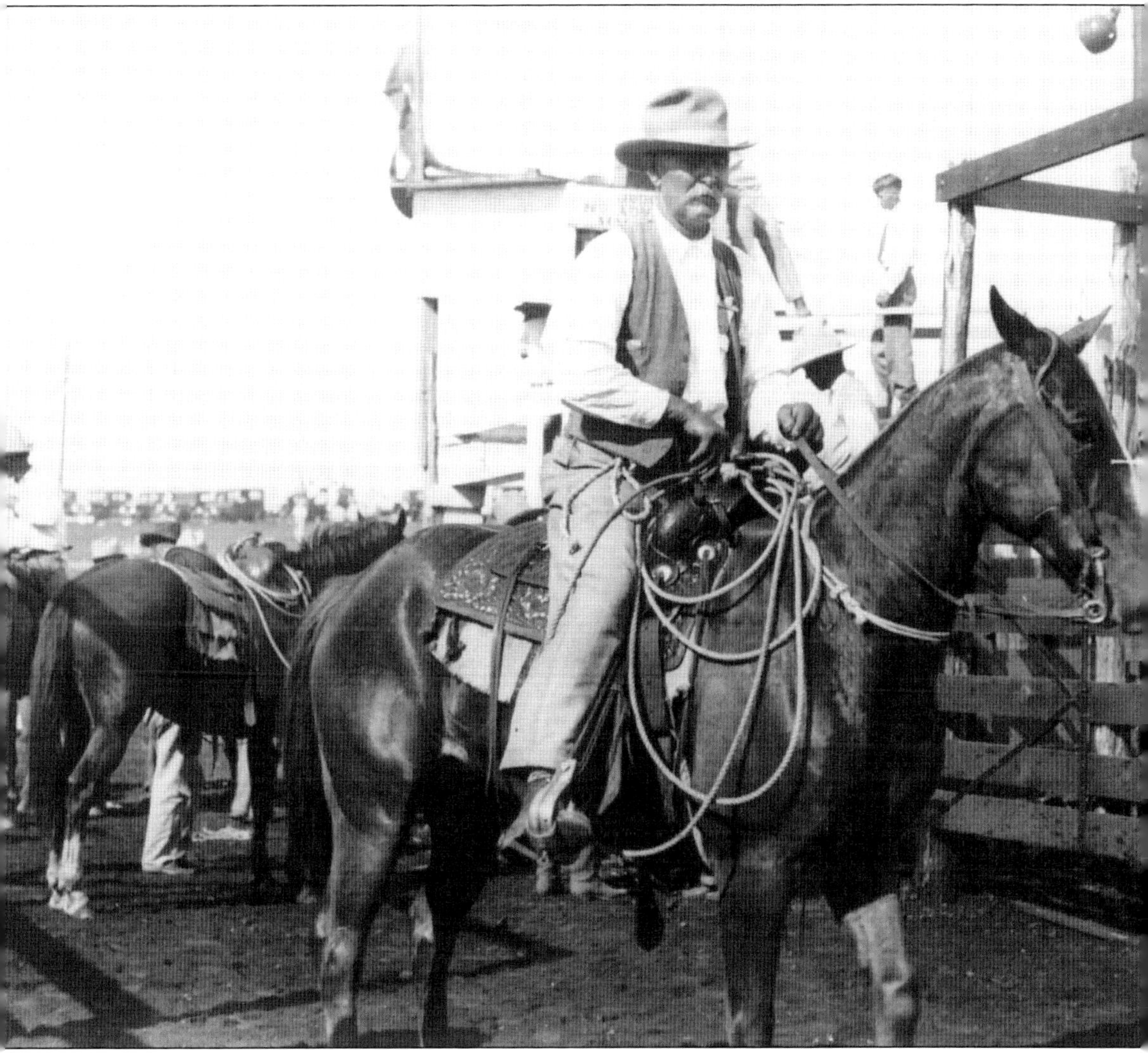

R.A. "Uncle Bob" Weatherby, one of the last "early day" cowboys living in West Texas, experienced his first cattle drive when his family moved to Brown County in 1878. At the time, he was only six years old. By age 10, he was riding the Chisholm Trail. Weatherby later became an independent cattleman who ranched between Roby and Rotan. A charter member of the Texas Cowboy Reunion, he helped organize the event in 1931. Weatherby won a saddle that year and was named top cowboy at the age of 59. He passed away in 1959.

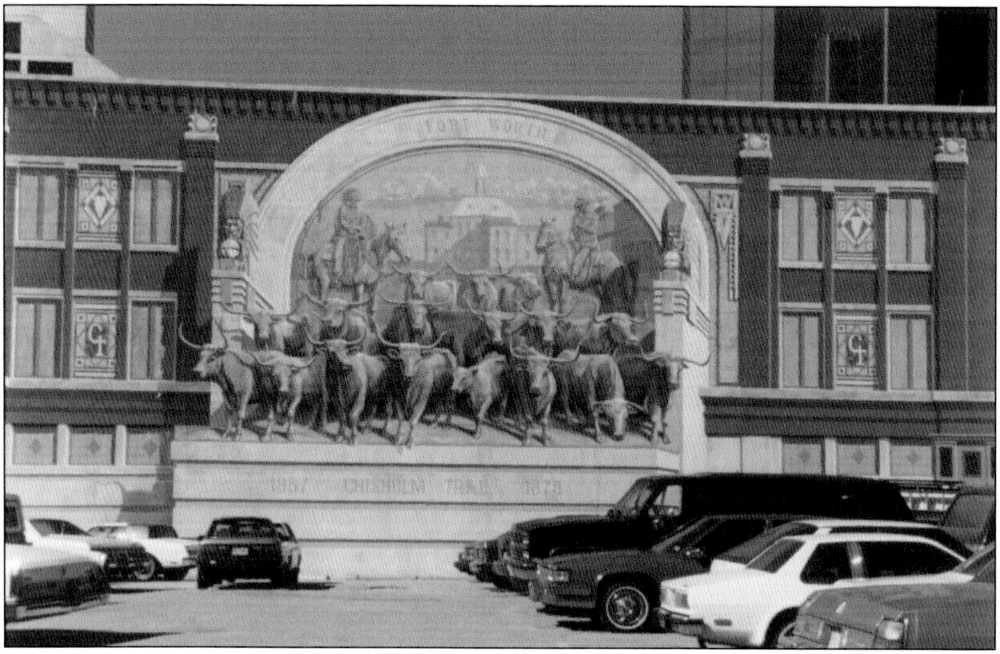

After the Civil War, Texas cowboys used the Chisholm Trail to drive cattle to Kansas railheads. Jesse Chisholm marked the trail from his southern trading post in Indian Territory, north of the Red River, to his northern trading post near Kansas City. The Texas cowboys entered his trail at Red River, crossing in Montague County, Texas. The Kansas railhead was the lifeblood for the Texas cattlemen, who brought their cattle to the rails. The cattlemen then sold the cattle, which were then freighted to markets. This memorial is on the side of the Cattle Raisers Museum in Fort Worth. (Cattle Raisers Museum.)

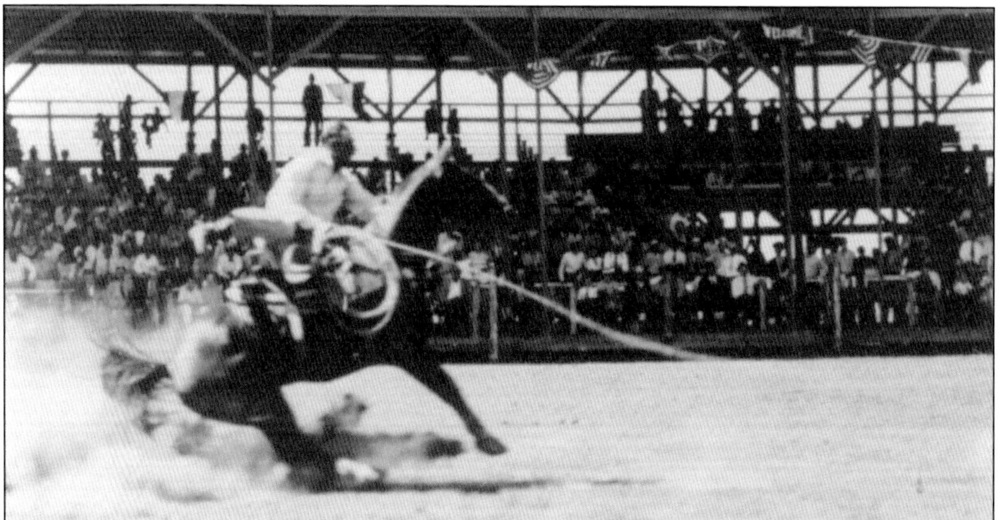

In this image, Joe York competes in a roping event on his horse, Old Glory. He paid $200 for the horse after borrowing the money from Snyder National Bank. The first show he took Old Glory to was in Midland, and he cleared $187 despite not taking first place. The promoter who wrote out the checks was Spence Joels, who later went to England with Will Rogers. Joels congratulated York, who was, by all accounts, a very skilled cowboy. (Joe York Collection, SCM.)

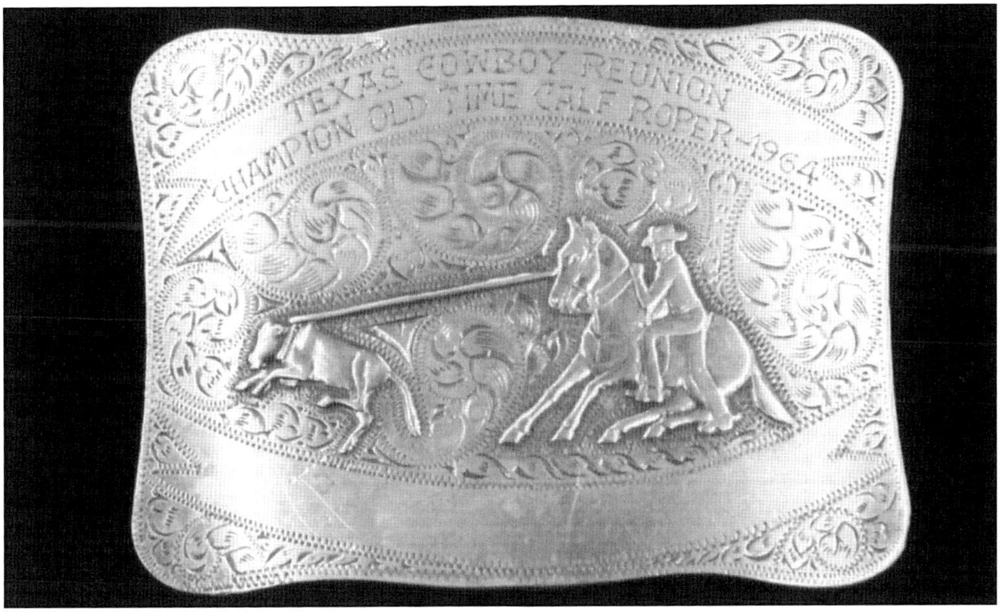

This belt buckle was awarded to Joe York in 1964 for being the "Old Time Calf Roper" champion at the Texas Cowboy Reunion rodeo. This was one of many buckles won by York. The competitors in this event had to be at least 65 years old to enter.

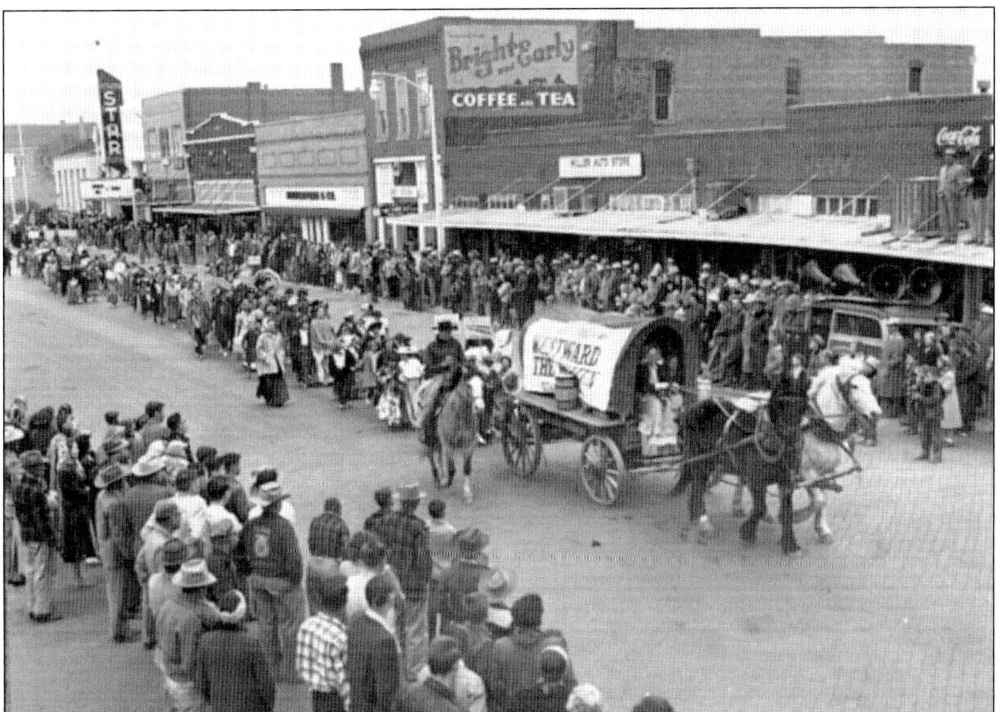

In this photograph, the city of Hereford is honoring the pioneer women who came west with their men. Two horses are pulling a covered wagon bearing an advertisement for the 1951 movie *Westward the Women*. A long line of women dressed in clothing from pioneer days follows the wagon. (Deaf Smith County Library.)

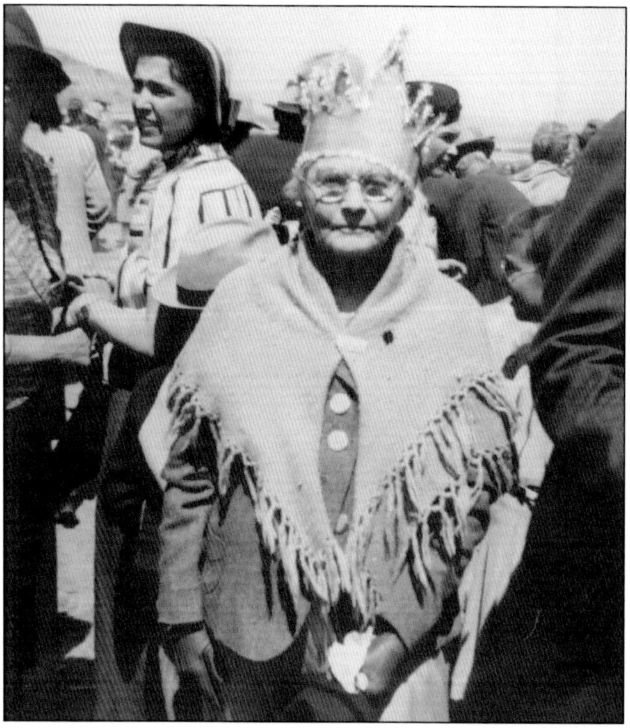

Catherine "Kate" Weatherby was crowned Queen of Borden County at the celebration of the 50th anniversary of the county in 1941. She married Joseph S. York on September 23, 1883, in Brown County. She and her husband were ranchers. At the time of this celebration, she was the county's oldest living settler. (SCM.)

Cowboys often did not use just one branding iron. In this case, eight irons are in the fire. When an iron was pulled from the hot coals, the cowboy ran to the calf, burned the brand on its hip, and had to return the cooled iron to the fire to reheat. With spares, a cowboy always had a hot iron. This c. 1951 photograph was taken by Joe Dave Scott on the Rodgers ranch. (SCM.)

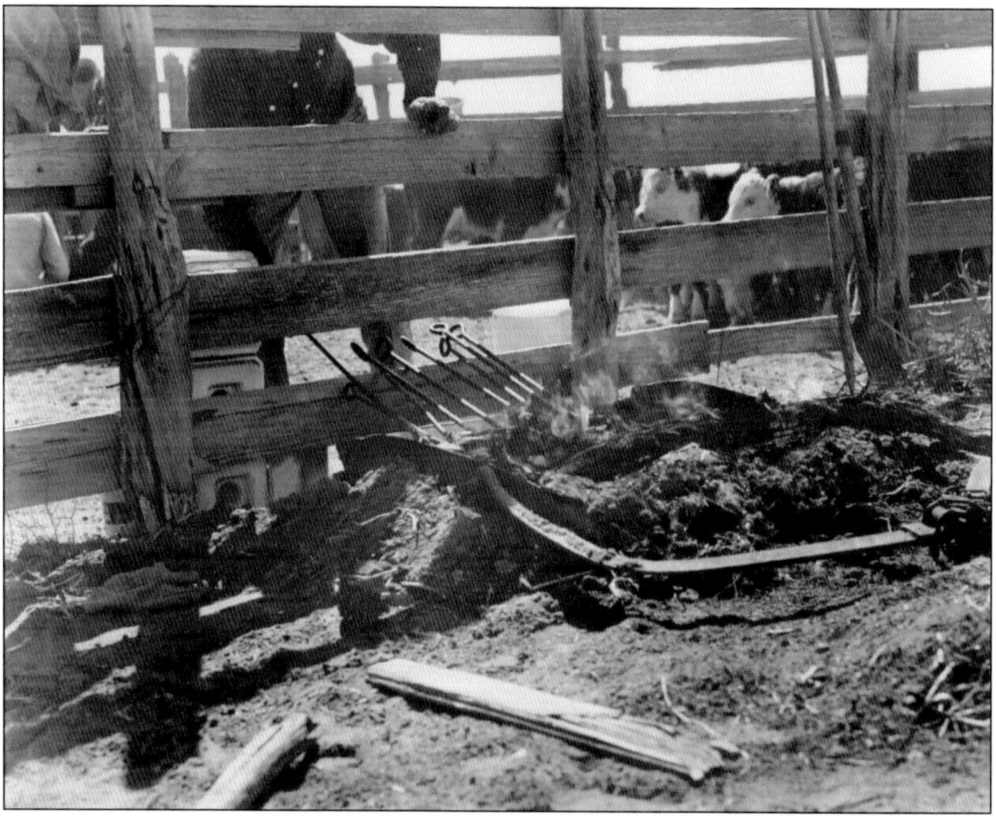

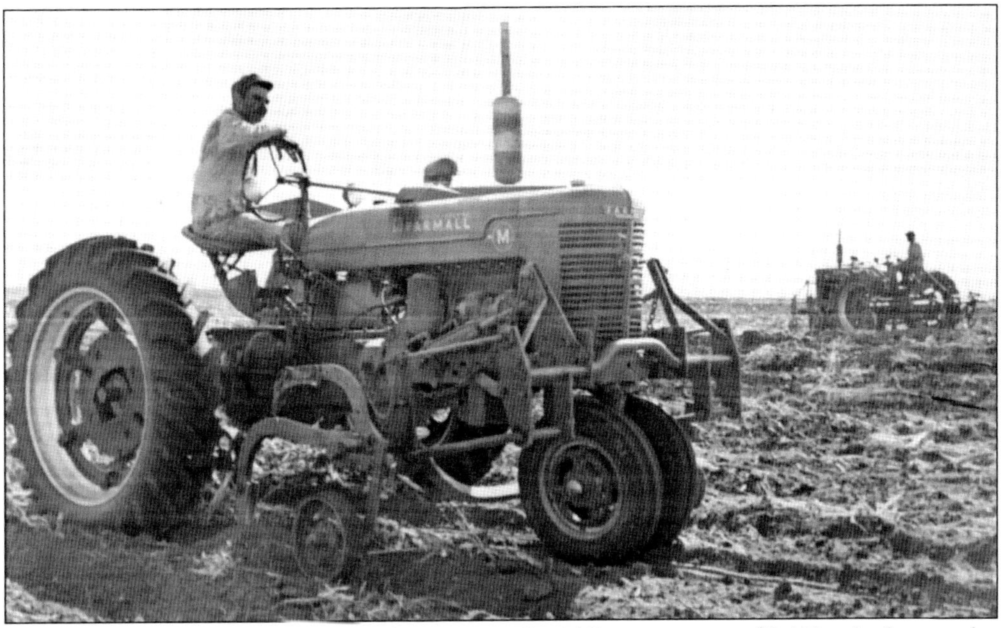

The tractor in this c. 1952 photograph is a Farmall M. The tractor cost $2,400, which was a lot of money. At the time, an average annual income was only about $3,400. Large farm equipment was often shared between neighbors, and most farmers became skilled mechanics.

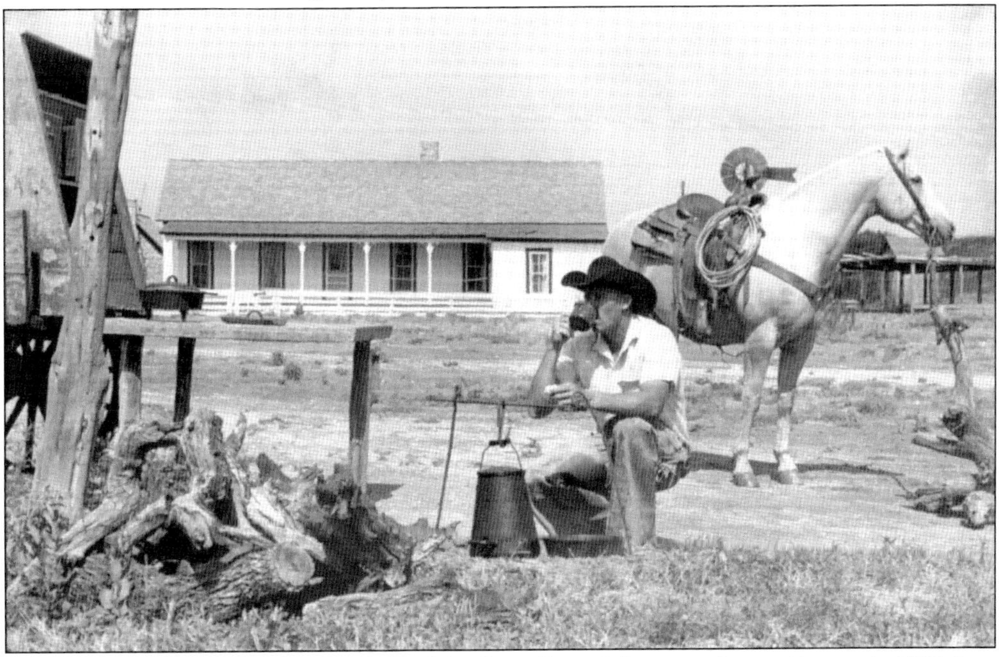

J.K. Smith built the original stone room of the Harrell ranch house in Scurry County in 1883. Lon Smith added additional rooms of box-and-strip construction between 1899 and 1913. The house was later purchased by Myrtle and Faye Harrell, who restored the house and moved it from Scurry County to the National Ranching Heritage Center in Lubbock, Texas, in 1972. This cowboy is recreating a range scene complete with a chuck wagon and a coffee pot on the fire. His horse is waiting for his master to mount up. (SCM.)

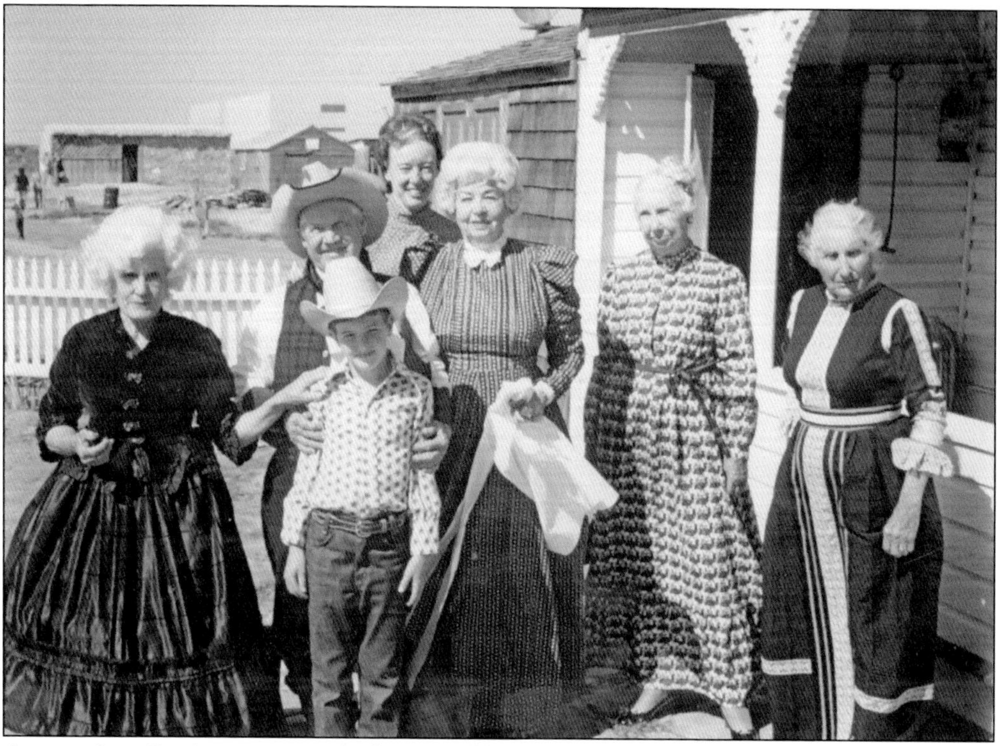

A group from Snyder poses outside the Harrell house at the National Ranching Heritage Center during the 1975 Ranch Day activities. From left to right are Elizabeth Connell, Whit Parks (standing in front of Bill Hart), Aline Parks, Edith McKanna, Myrtle Harrell, and Faye Harrell. The Harrell sisters (Myrtle and Faye) restored the house and donated it to the museum. This photograph was taken by G.A. Parks Jr. (Paula Parks Fulford.)

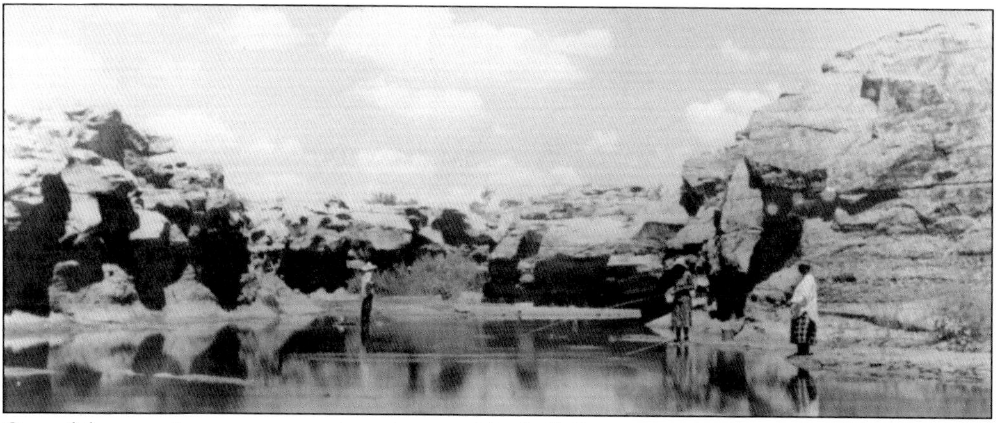

One of the most important watering places in Mitchell County was at the junction of North and South Champion Creeks. The site was visited by Native Americans for thousands of years and was named Seven Wells by early settlers, because the spring basins closely resembled man-made wells. In 1880, the Texas & Pacific Railroad reached the Colorado River, seven miles northwest of Seven Wells. The town of Colorado became the "Dodge City of the Southwest" and the "Mother City of West Texas." However, because much of the water in the area was brackish, many families continued to haul water from Seven Wells at a cost of 50¢ per barrel. Seven Wells is pictured here around 1920. (Paula Parks Fulford; Aline Parks Collection.)

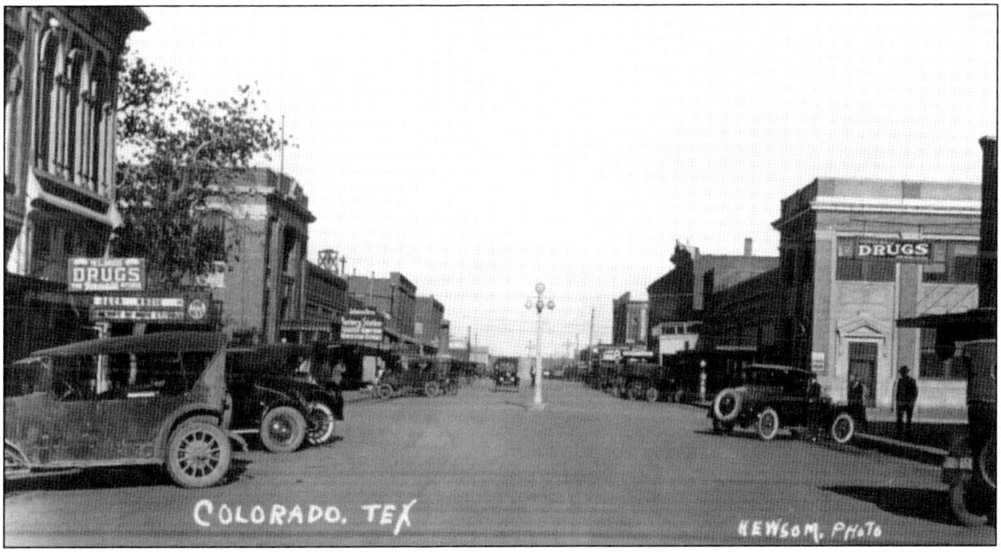

The town of Colorado (later Colorado City) stole the title of "Cowboy Capital" from Abilene and Dodge City, Kansas, when the railroads came to the Texas plains in 1881. At one time, Colorado City had 28 saloons and 4 variety theaters. The town reached the height of its fame during the 1880s and 1890s as the largest town between Fort Worth and El Paso. It had more millionaires than any other town in Texas and more saloons than any town in the West. This 1920s photograph shows the downtown Colorado area much cleaner and quieter than it was in its heyday.

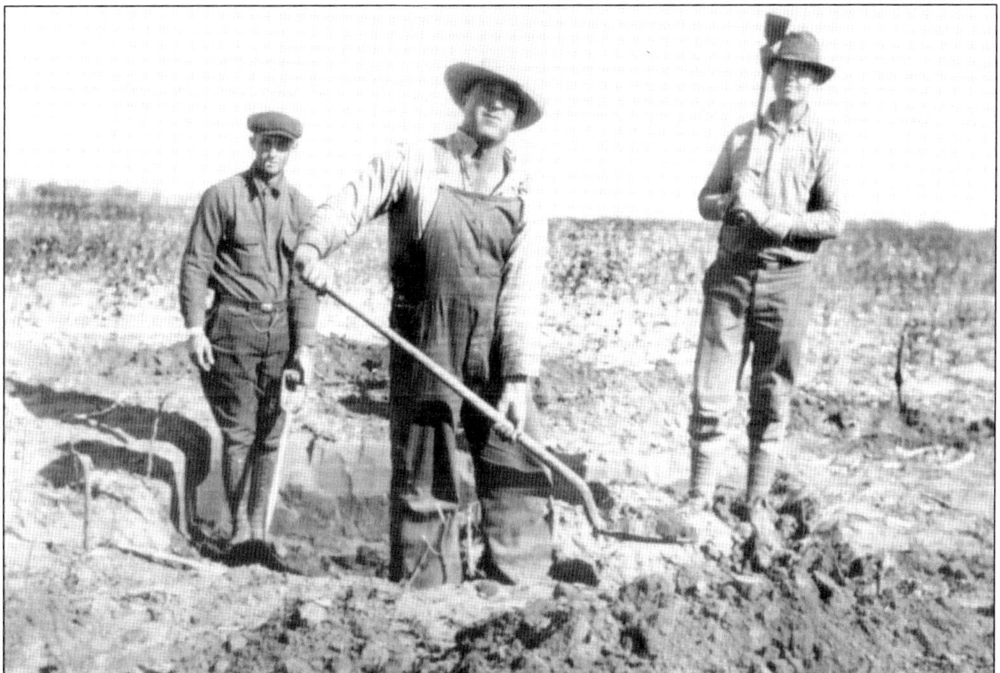

These men are digging the discovery well of the Sharon Ridge oil field, J.J. Moore No. 1. This was the first oil well in Scurry County and began production in 1924. The man in the center is Pat Moore. Completed to 3,575 feet in the San Andreas formation, the well yielded over 500,000 barrels of oil. (Paula Parks Fulford; Aline Parks Collection.)

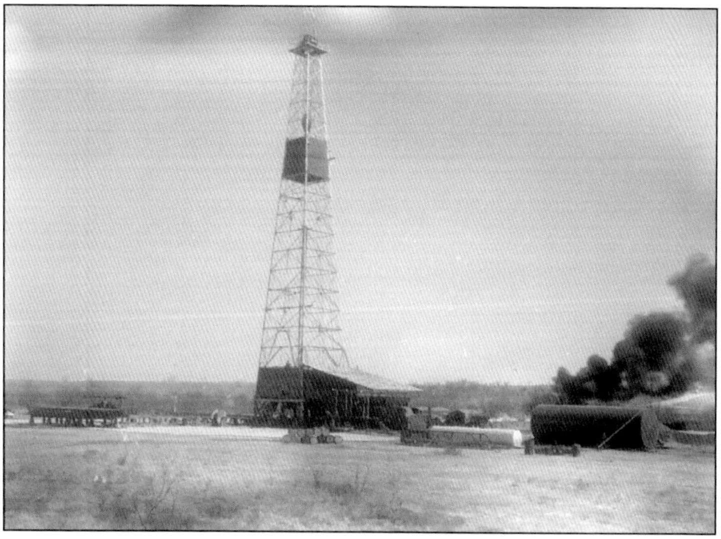

Rancher "Pie" Fuller's father purchased the LP Ranch from the Pruitt family. He invested in oil when the Kelly-Snyder field was discovered in 1949. Like many of his neighbors in northern Scurry County, he made more money from his wells than he had ever made in the cattle business. This c. 1951 photograph shows one of the wells on the Fuller lease. (Del Hirst Collection, SCM.)

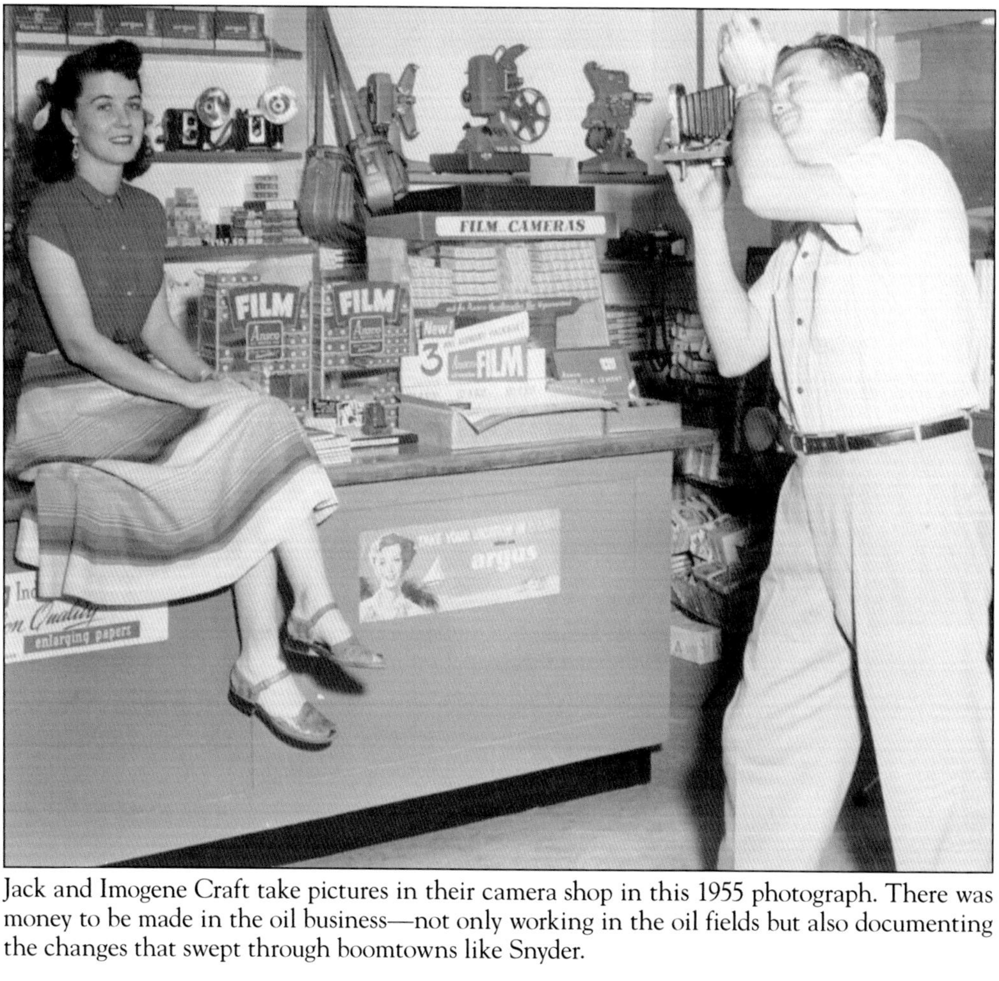

Jack and Imogene Craft take pictures in their camera shop in this 1955 photograph. There was money to be made in the oil business—not only working in the oil fields but also documenting the changes that swept through boomtowns like Snyder.

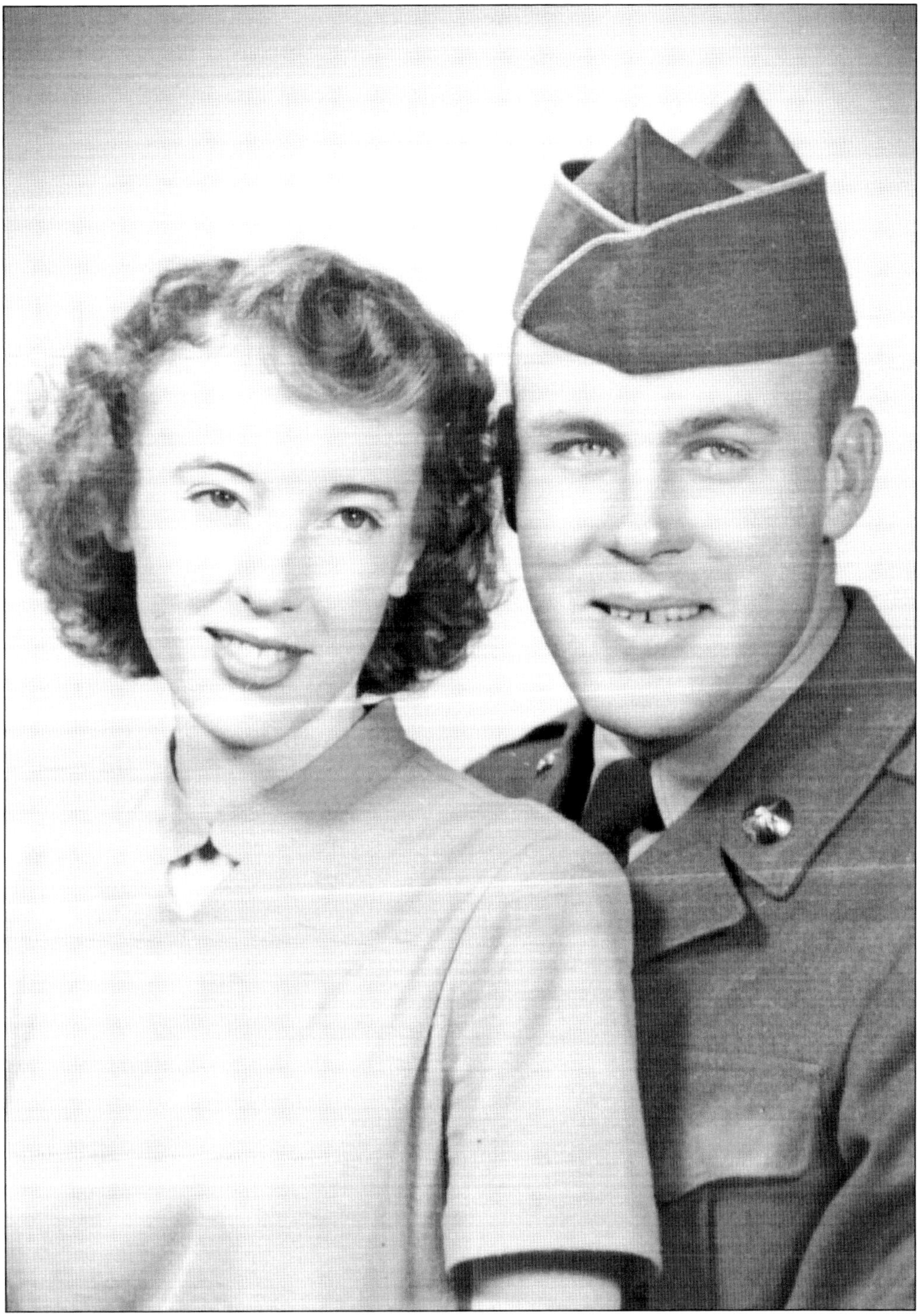

Aline Parks moved to Snyder during the oil boom to take a job as a journalist with the *Snyder Daily News*. She met and married her husband, G.A. Parks Jr., the son of a local ranching family, and eventually became one of the area's most prolific and dedicated historians. Aline Parks passed away in 2013. (Paula Parks Fulford; Aline Parks Collection.)

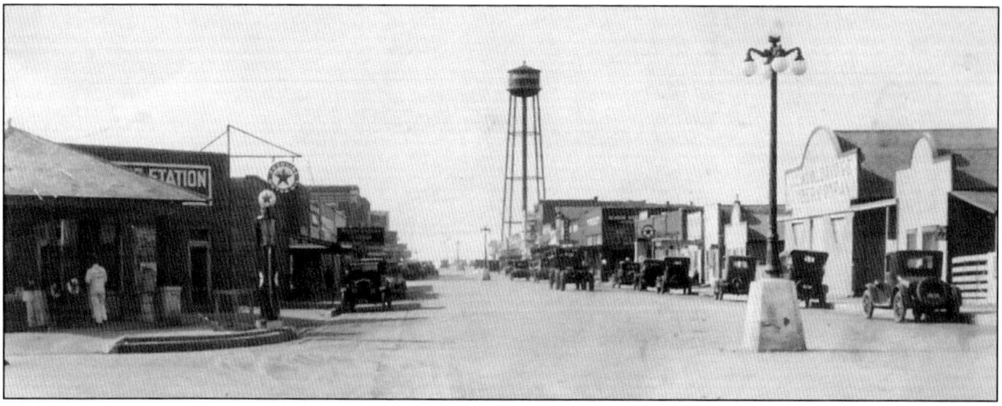

Bill Carlile came to Texas from Franklin County, Arkansas, after World War II to operate cotton gins owned by his brother Chester's father-in-law, Elmer Gage. Chester moved to Shamrock, while Bill came to Circle Back, near Sudan, every fall to run one of the Gage gins. He had to travel through Shamrock on his way home, and he always stopped to visit Chester and to rest overnight. Like many small towns of the Panhandle Plains, Shamrock, located between Oklahoma City and Amarillo, continued to be an important "pit stop" for travelers; the numerous gas stations in this 1920 photograph attest to that fact.

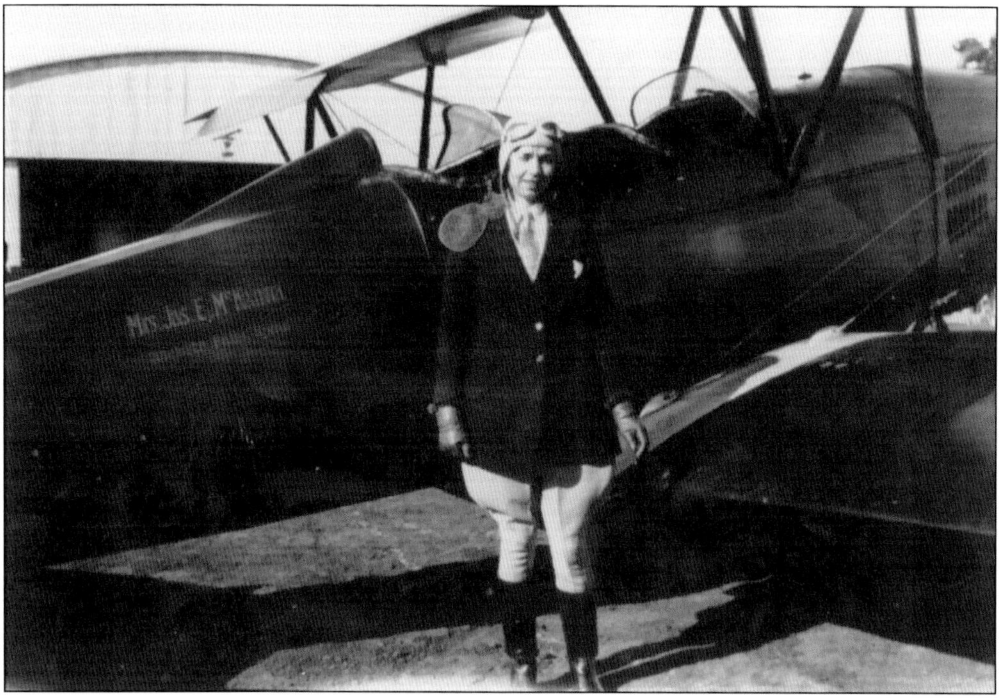

Edith Whatley McKanna and her husband, James Everett McKanna, owned many oil-producing properties throughout Texas. When James passed away in 1932, in his early 30s, Edith continued to run his business. The McKannas were extremely wealthy. They traveled first-class on steamships across the Atlantic and stayed in the most exclusive hotels. Edith had many famous friends. She was a member of the 99 club (the first 100 women to have a pilot's license) along with Amelia Earhart. She appeared in *Vogue* magazine and was regularly mentioned in the society pages of newspapers, including those in Dallas, Wichita Falls, and Kansas City, as well as the *New York Times*. (Paula Parks Fulford; Aline Parks Collection.)

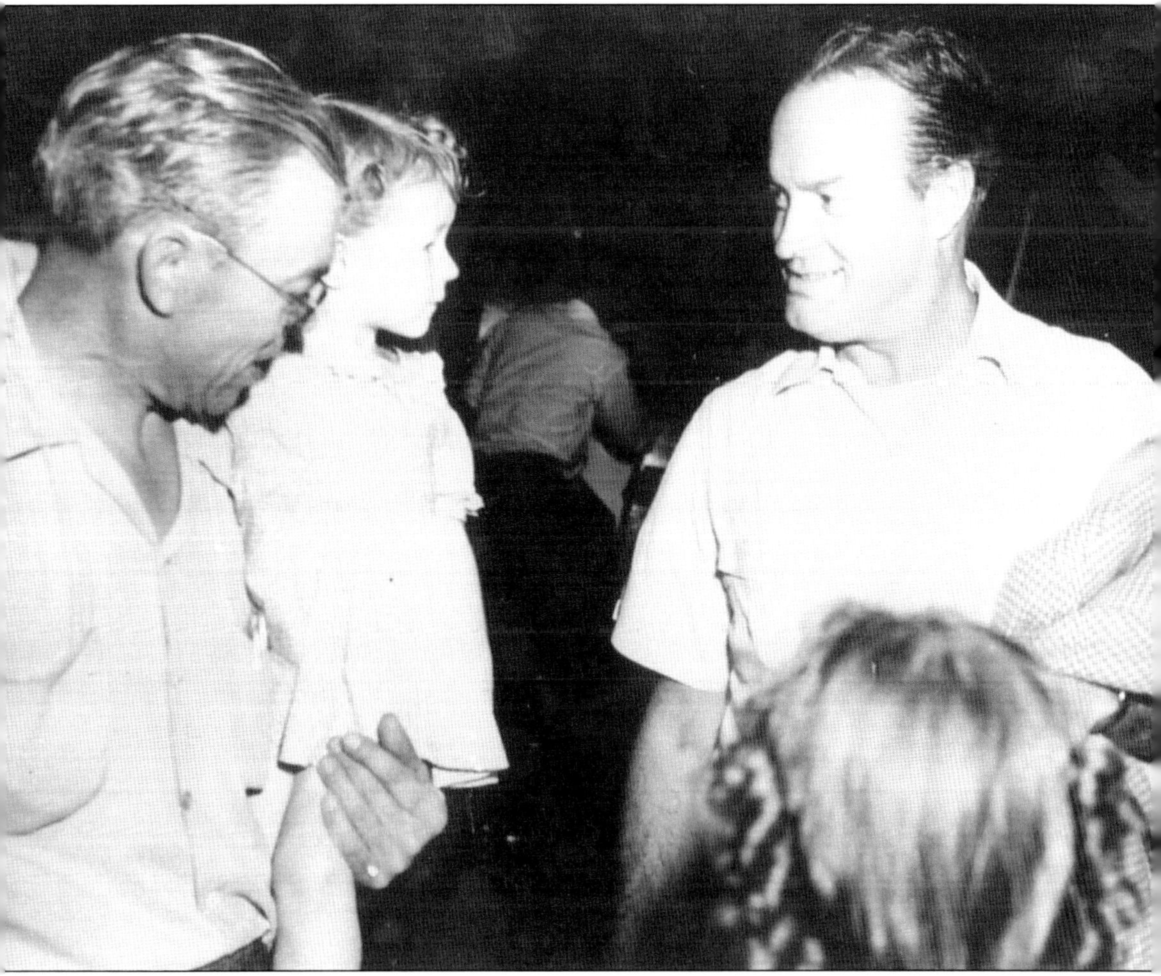

Oil brought famous individuals to West Texas, including popular actor and comedian Bob Hope (right). J.D. Scott (left) holds up Jan Johnson to meet Hope on one of his visits to Snyder, possibly in 1952. (Joe Dave Scott Collection, SCM.)

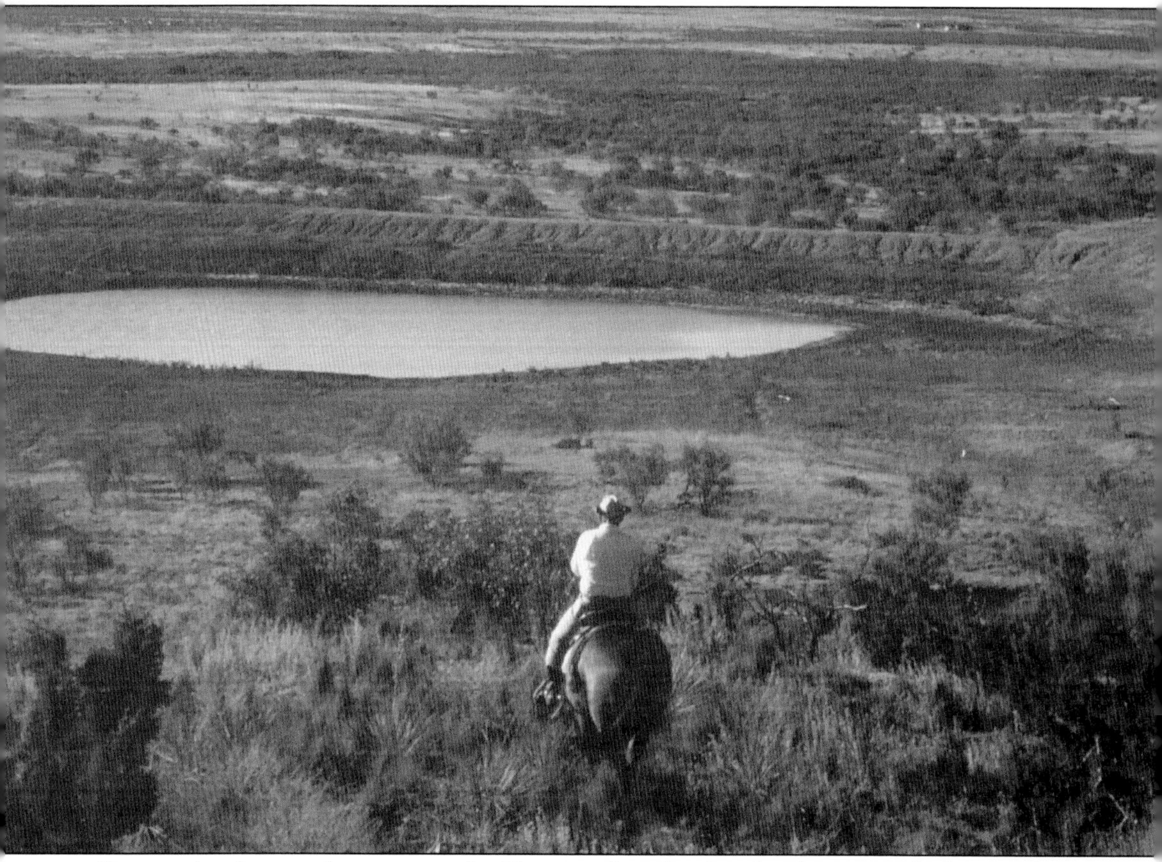

Despite the changes that came to the Texas panhandle after the discovery of oil, some things remain exactly the same. Here, Joe York surveys the Pruitt ranch on the border of Scurry and Kent Counties. T. Dudley Cramer took this photograph in 1971. Cramer, who was also a historian, had the foresight to photograph several of the oldest ranches of the Texas panhandle in the early 1970s, when some of the original houses, barns, and other buildings were still standing. (SCM.)

As oil production made water even more of a necessity, it became vital to create reservoirs to feed growing communities. This photograph shows R.A. Schooling (left), J.B. Thomas (center), and Bob Piver of Big Spring at the ground-breaking ceremony for Lake J.B. Thomas. On November 16, 1950, voters in Big Spring and Odessa approved bond issues that permitted the water district to sell bonds to finance its first lake, J.B. Thomas, which sits on the border of Borden and Scurry Counties. The money also provided for a well field and pipelines to move the water. Schooling was appointed to the Colorado River Municipal Water District in 1951. The lake proved to be an overly ambitious project. It never exceeded its 1992 level of 37 percent capacity and, as of 2013, it was at less than 3 percent capacity. (Del Hirst Collection, SCM.)

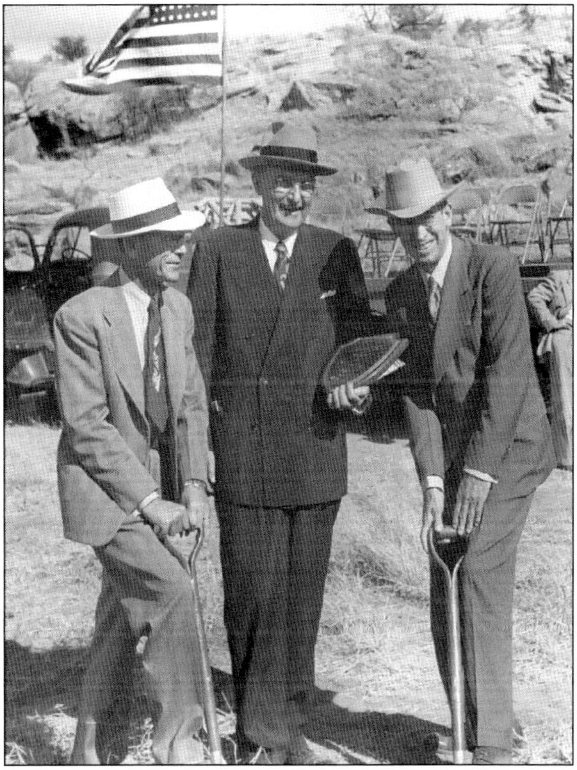

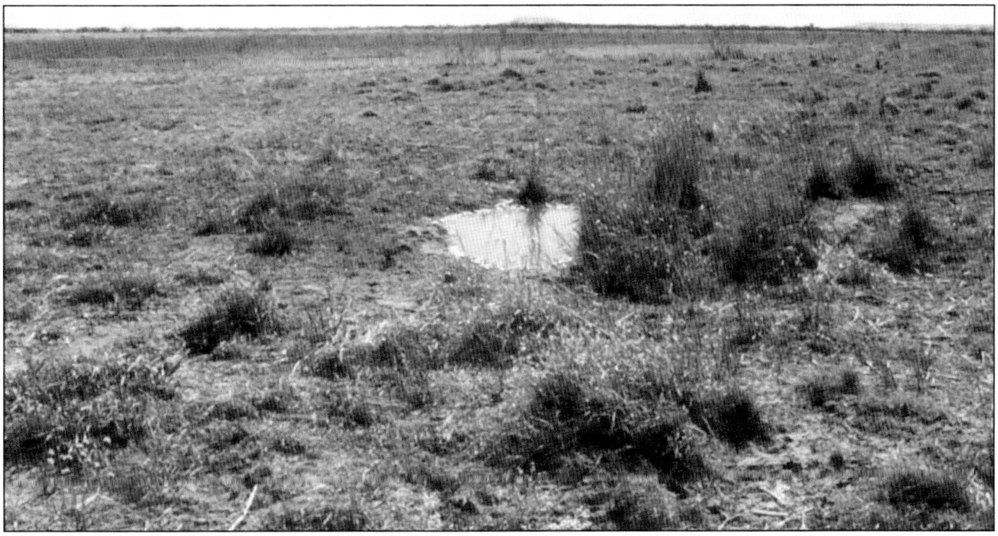

The Ogallala Aquifer lies underneath four states and provides 97 percent of all water for the Texas Panhandle Plains. About 27 percent of the irrigated land in the United States overlies this aquifer system. Before settlement, the aquifer was naturally replenished by water seeping into the ground after heavy rains, but oil production and irrigation now empty the aquifer at an alarming rate. As the amount of water decreases, the difficulty of accessing this resource becomes greater. In some areas, the groundwater already has high levels of fluoride, arsenic, or nitrate. In other areas, it has been contaminated by abandoned oil fields. Various sources suggest that the remaining water will not last more than 50 years.

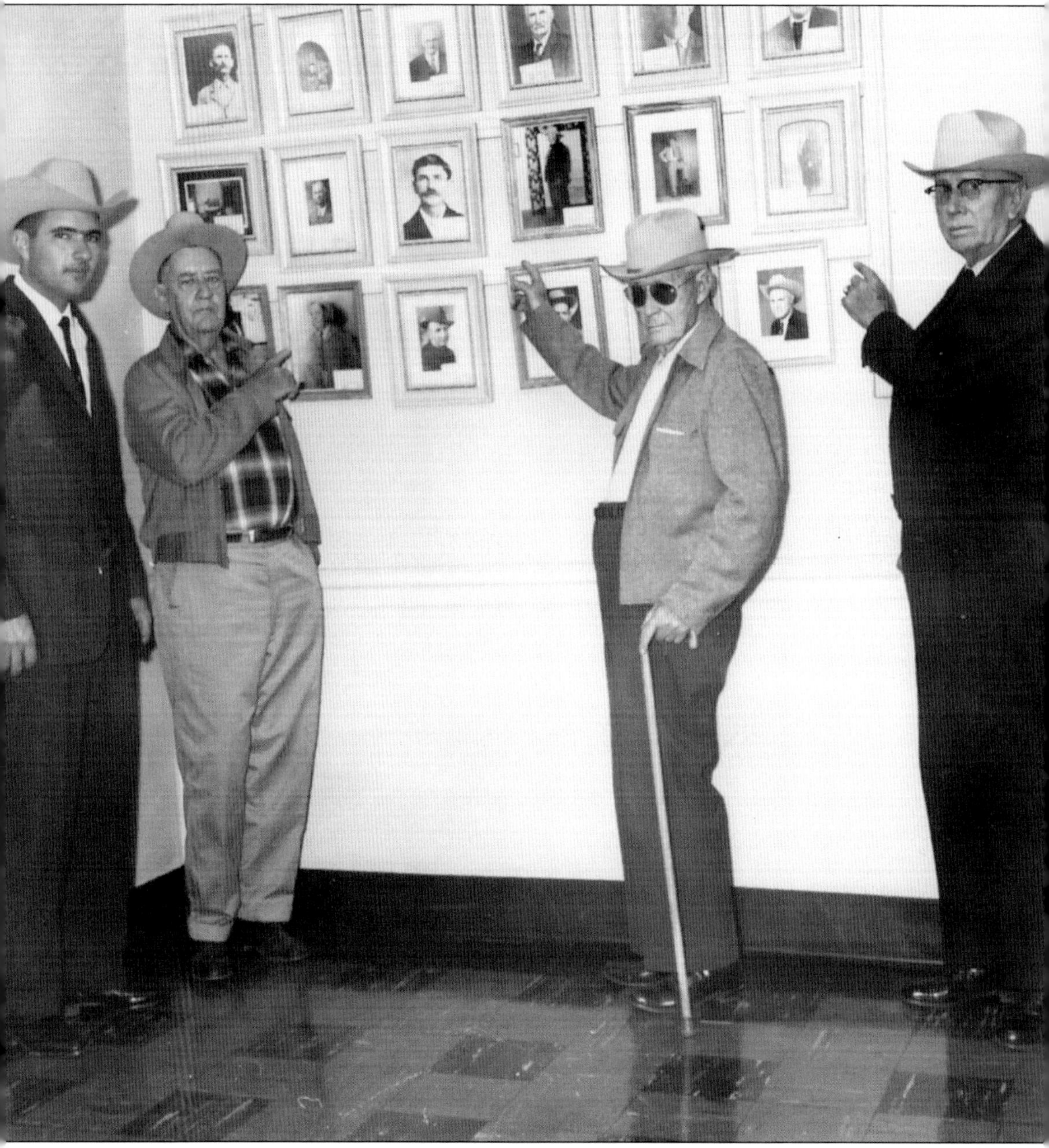

Three past sheriffs of Scurry County pose with Sheriff Keith Collier in 1965. Pictured here are, from left to right, Collier, Tom DeShazo (1944), Frank Brownfield (1927–1932), and Clyde Thomas (1937–1938). The office of city marshal and, later, sheriff, in many Panhandle towns is an important part of the community's heritage. Like Texas Rangers, Texas sheriffs usually wear Western-style hats, a nod to the lawmen of the Old West who preceded them. (Keith Collier.)

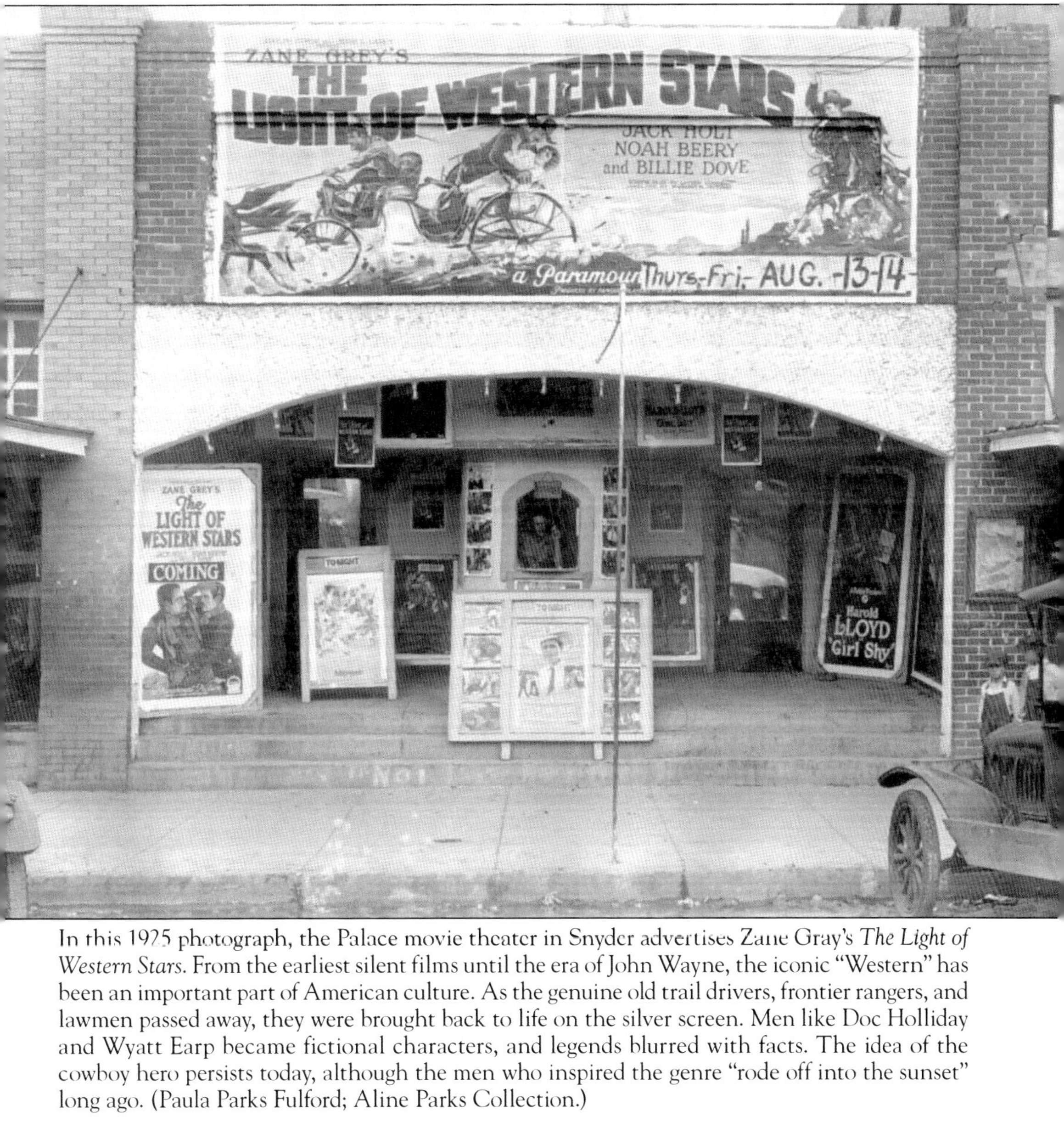

In this 1925 photograph, the Palace movie theater in Snyder advertises Zane Gray's *The Light of Western Stars*. From the earliest silent films until the era of John Wayne, the iconic "Western" has been an important part of American culture. As the genuine old trail drivers, frontier rangers, and lawmen passed away, they were brought back to life on the silver screen. Men like Doc Holliday and Wyatt Earp became fictional characters, and legends blurred with facts. The idea of the cowboy hero persists today, although the men who inspired the genre "rode off into the sunset" long ago. (Paula Parks Fulford; Aline Parks Collection.)